Printed in the United States
By Bookmasters

T0214318

Lecture Notes in Computer Science   11798

Founding Editors

Gerhard Goos
Karlsruhe Institute of Technology, Karlsruhe, Germany
Juris Hartmanis
Cornell University, Ithaca, NY, USA

Editorial Board Members

Elisa Bertino
Purdue University, West Lafayette, IN, USA
Wen Gao
Peking University, Beijing, China
Bernhard Steffen
TU Dortmund University, Dortmund, Germany
Gerhard Woeginger
RWTH Aachen, Aachen, Germany
Moti Yung
Columbia University, New York, NY, USA

More information about this series at http://www.springer.com/series/7412

Qian Wang · Alberto Gomez ·
Jana Hutter et al. (Eds.)

Smart Ultrasound Imaging and Perinatal, Preterm and Paediatric Image Analysis

First International Workshop, SUSI 2019
and 4th International Workshop, PIPPI 2019
Held in Conjunction with MICCAI 2019
Shenzhen, China, October 13 and 17, 2019
Proceedings

Springer

Editors
Qian Wang
Shanghai Jiao Tong University
Shanghai, China

Alberto Gomez 🄳
King's College London
London, UK

Jana Hutter 🄳
King's College London
London, UK

Additional Workshop Editors *see next page*

ISSN 0302-9743   ISSN 1611-3349   (electronic)
Lecture Notes in Computer Science
ISBN 978-3-030-32874-0   ISBN 978-3-030-32875-7   (eBook)
https://doi.org/10.1007/978-3-030-32875-7

LNCS Sublibrary: SL6 – Image Processing, Computer Vision, Pattern Recognition, and Graphics

© Springer Nature Switzerland AG 2019
This work is subject to copyright. All rights are reserved by the Publisher, whether the whole or part of the material is concerned, specifically the rights of translation, reprinting, reuse of illustrations, recitation, broadcasting, reproduction on microfilms or in any other physical way, and transmission or information storage and retrieval, electronic adaptation, computer software, or by similar or dissimilar methodology now known or hereafter developed.
The use of general descriptive names, registered names, trademarks, service marks, etc. in this publication does not imply, even in the absence of a specific statement, that such names are exempt from the relevant protective laws and regulations and therefore free for general use.
The publisher, the authors and the editors are safe to assume that the advice and information in this book are believed to be true and accurate at the date of publication. Neither the publisher nor the authors or the editors give a warranty, expressed or implied, with respect to the material contained herein or for any errors or omissions that may have been made. The publisher remains neutral with regard to jurisdictional claims in published maps and institutional affiliations.

This Springer imprint is published by the registered company Springer Nature Switzerland AG
The registered company address is: Gewerbestrasse 11, 6330 Cham, Switzerland

Additional Workshop Editors

Satellite Events Chair

Kenji Suzuki
Tokyo Institute of Technology
Yokohama, Japan

Workshop Chairs

Hongen Liao
Tsinghua University
Beijing, China

Hayit Greenspan
Tel Aviv University
Tel Aviv, Israel

Challenge Chairs

Qian Wang
Shanghai Jiaotong University
Shanghai, China

Bram van Ginneken
Radboud University
Nijmegen, The Netherlands

Tutorial Chair

Luping Zhou
University of Sydney
Sydney, Australia

SUSI and PIPPI Editors

SUSI 2019 Editors

Alberto Gomez
School of Imaging Sciences &
Biomedical Engineering, King's College
London, UK

Veronika Zimmer
School of Imaging Sciences &Biomedical
Engineering, King's College London, UK

Kristin McLeod
GE Vingmed Ultrasound, GE Healthcare,
Norway

Oliver Zettinig
ImFusion GmbH, Germany

PIPPI 2019 Editors

Jana Hutter
School of Imaging Sciences &
Biomedical Engineering, King's College
London, UK

Emma Robinson
School of Imaging Sciences &
Biomedical Engineering, King's College
London, UK

Esra Abaci Turk
Boston Children's Hospital, Boston, UK

Roxane Licandro
Computer Vision Lab, TU Vienna,
Austria

Daan Christiaens
School of Imaging Sciences &
Biomedical Engineering, King's College
London, UK

Andrew Melbourne
School of Imaging Sciences &
Biomedical Engineering, King's College
London, UK

Preface SUSI 2019

SUSI 2019 is the first workshop on Smart Ultrasound Imaging, organized as a half-day satellite event of the 22nd International Conference on Medical Image Computing and Computer Assisted Intervention (MICCAI 2019) in Shenzhen, China. This workshop aims at promoting ultrasound image computing, particularly focusing on smart computational methods applied on ultrasound images.

Ultrasound imaging is one of the most widespread imaging modalities, used in a large number of clinical applications. It is widely available, relatively inexpensive, and safe for all patients. It is the primary imaging modality in cardiac and maternity units, and safe to use on patients with implants of any kind. However, ultrasound imaging is generally difficult to acquire, interpret and analyze compared to other imaging modalities such as MRI, XRay, PET, and CT.

The MICCAI community has an established history of interest in ultrasound imaging, both in ultrasound image computing and ultrasound guided interventions. Ultrasound image analysis is one of the few topics that covers both the MIC and CAI aspects of this conference, and as such allows the possibility to unite researchers from each of these worlds in a common forum.

SUSI 2019 accepted 10 high-quality papers, all themed on computational methods applied to medical ultrasound imaging. The papers cover a wide range of medical applications of B-Mode ultrasound, including cardiac (echocardiography), abdominal (liver), fetal, musculoskeletal, and lung. The program has been organized into three oral sessions (six papers) and a poster session (four papers). The papers accepted for oral sessions have been grouped by methodology: guided ultrasound examinations, assisted image interpretation and biometrics, and image formation, reconstruction, and visualization. In addition to the peer-reviewed papers included in these proceedings, the workshop featured a keynote presentation by Professor Purang Abolmaesumi from the University of British Columbia, entitled "AI-driven ultrasound for diagnosis and intervention."

We wholeheartedly thank all authors for their submissions, as well as the Program Committee and the reviewers for their contribution to the workshop program. We also thank our sponsor, the PIC (Personalised In-silico Cardiology) Innovative Training Network.

August 2019

Alberto Gomez
Kristin McLeod
Veronika Zimmer
Oliver Zettinig

Organization

Organization Committee

Alberto Gomez	King's College London, UK
Kristin McLeod	General Electric Healthcare, Norway
Veronika Zimmer	King's College London, UK
Oliver Zettinig	ImFusion GmbH, Germany

Program Committee

Bishesh Khanal	NAAMII, Nepal
Lasse Løvstakken	Norwegian University of Science and Technology, Norway
Christian Baumgartner	ETH Zurich, Switzerland
Gemma Piella	Pompeu Fabra University, Spain
Ana I. Namburete	University of Oxford, UK
Kirsten Christensen-Jeffries	King's College London, UK
Bernhard Kainz	Imperial College London, UK
Mathieu De Craene	Philips Research Medisys, France
Jan D'Hooge	KU Leuven, Belgium
Stephen Aylward	Kitware, USA
Juan Cerrolaza	Accenture, Spain

Preface PIPPI 2019

The application of sophisticated analysis tools to fetal, neonatal, and paediatric imaging data has gained additional interest especially in recent years, with the successful large scale open data initiatives such as the developing Human Connectome Project, the Baby Connectome Project, and the NIH-funded Human Placenta Project. These projects enable researchers without access to perinatal scanning facilities to bring in their image analysis expertise and domain knowledge.

Advanced medical image analysis allows the detailed scientific study of conditions such as prematurity and the study of both normal singleton and twin development in addition to less common conditions unique to childhood. The PIPPI workshop complements the main MICCAI conference by providing a focused discussion of perinatal and paediatric image analysis. It provides a focused platform for the discussion and dissemination of advanced imaging techniques applied to young cohorts.

Emphasis is placed on novel methodological approaches to the study of, for instance, volumetric growth, myelination and cortical microstructure, placental structure and function. Methods will cover the full scope of medical image analysis: segmentation, registration, classification, reconstruction, atlas construction, tractography, population analysis, and advanced structural, functional, and longitudinal modeling with an application to younger cohorts or to the long term outcomes of perinatal conditions.

Challenges of image analysis techniques as applied to the preterm, perinatal, and paediatric setting are discussed and confounded by the interrelation between the normal developmental trajectory and the influence of pathology. These relationships can be quite diverse when compared to measurements taken in adult populations and exhibit highly dynamic changes affecting both image acquisition and processing requirements.

August 2019

Jana Hutter
Roxane Licandro
Emma Robinson
Daan Christiaens
Esra Abaci Turk
Andrew Melbourne

Organization

Organization Committee

Jana Hutter   King's College London, UK
Roxane Licandro   TU Vienna, Austria
Emma Robinson   King's College London, UK
Daan Christiaens   King's College London, UK
Esra Abaci Turk   Boston Children's Hospital, USA
Andrew Melbourne   King's College London, UK

Program Committee

Ana Ineyda Namburete   University of Oxford, UK
Veronika Zimmer   King's College London, UK
Cher Bass   King's College London, UK
John Onofrey   Yale University, USA
Ernst Schwartz   Medical University of Vienna, Austria
Jeffrey Stout   Boston Children's Hospital, USA
Michael Ebner   University College London, UK
Alena Uss   King's College London, UK

Contents

First Workshop on Smart UltraSound Imaging

Straight to the Point: Reinforcement Learning for User Guidance in Ultrasound

Fausto Milletari$^{(\boxtimes)}$, Vighnesh Birodkar, and Michal Sofka

4Catalyzer Inc., Santa Clara, USA
fausto.milletari@gmail.com

Abstract. Point of care ultrasound (POCUS) consists in the use of ultrasound imaging in critical or emergency situations to support clinical decisions by healthcare professionals and first responders. In this setting it is essential to be able to provide means to obtain diagnostic data to potentially inexperienced users who did not receive an extensive medical training. Interpretation and acquisition of ultrasound images is not trivial. First, the user needs to find a suitable sound window which can be used to get a clear image, and then he needs to correctly interpret it to perform a diagnosis. Although many recent approaches focus on developing smart ultrasound devices that add interpretation capabilities to existing systems, our goal in this paper is to present a reinforcement learning (RL) strategy which is capable to guide novice users to the correct sonic window and enable them to obtain clinically relevant pictures of the anatomy of interest. We apply our approach to cardiac images acquired from the parasternal long axis (PLAx) view of the left ventricle of the heart.

1 Introduction

Ultrasound (US) is a flexible, portable, safe and cost effective modality that finds several applications across multiple fields of medicine.

The characteristics of ultrasound make it extremely suitable for applications related with emergency medicine and point of care (POC) decision making. Recently, several ultra-portable and lightweight ultrasound devices have been announced and commercialized to enable these applications. These products have been envisioned to be extremely inexpensive, have a long battery life, a robust design and to be operated by inexperienced users who may have not received any formal training. In order to reach the latest goal, images need to be interpreted by a computer vision based system and accurate instruction for fine manipulation of the ultrasound probe need to be provided to the user in real time.

In this paper we show how to use deep learning and in particular deep reinforcement learning to create a system to guide inexperienced users towards the acquisition of clinically relevant images of the heart in ultrasound. We focus on acquisition through the parasternal long axis (PLAx) sonic window on the heart which is one of the most used views in emergency settings due to its accessibility.

© Springer Nature Switzerland AG 2019
Q. Wang et al. (Eds.): PIPPI 2019/SUSI 2019, LNCS 11798, pp. 3–10, 2019.
https://doi.org/10.1007/978-3-030-32875-7_1

In our acquisition assistance framework the user is asked to place the probe anywhere on the left side of the patient's chest and receives instructions on how to manipulate the probe in order to obtain a clinically acceptable parasternal long axis scans of the heart. Every time an image is produced by the ultrasound equipment, our deep reinforcement learning model predicts a motion instruction that is promptly displayed to the user. In this sense, we are learning a control policy that predicts actions (also called instructions) in correspondence of observations, which makes reinforcement learning a particularly suitable solution. This problem has several degrees of freedom. Apart from instructions regarding left-right and top-bottom motions, the user will also receive fine-grained manipulation indications regarding rotation and tilt of the probe.

Reinforcement learning has been recently employed to solve several computer vision related problems and specifically to achieve superhuman performances in playing ATARI games and 3D video-games such as "Doom" [3].

In [7,8] a convolutional deep neural network has been employed together with Q-learning to predict the expected cumulative reward $Q(s,a)$ associated with each action that the agent can perform in the game. In [5] a learning strategy that employs two identical networks, updated at different paces, is presented. In this paper, the target network is used for predictions and is updated smoothly at regular intervals, while the main network gets updated batch-wise through back-propagation. This is particularly useful in continuous control. In [13] the network architecture used to predict the Q-values is modified to comprise two different paths which predict, respectively, the value $V(s)$ of being in a certain state and the advantage of taking a certain action in correspondence to that state. This strategy has resulted in increased performances. In [12] target Q-values, which are learned during training, are computed differently than in [7]. Instead of having the network regress Q-values computed as the reward r_t plus $\gamma \arg\max_a Q^*(s_{t+1}, a)$, they use $r_t + \gamma Q^*(s_{t+1}, a_{t+1})$. The main difference is that, in the latter, the action a_{t+1} is the one that is selected by the network in correspondence of the state s_{t+1}, and not a which is the one yielding the maximum Q-value. This yields increased stability of the Q-values.

Reinforcement learning has been applied in medical domain for the first time in [10] to segment ultrasound images. In [9] a similar approach has been applied to heart model personalization on synthetic data. In [1] a DQN has been employed to solve a optimal view plane selection problem in MRI, through an agent trained to obtain a specific view of brain scans.

In this work we apply deep reinforcement learning (via a DQN) to a guidance problem whose goal is to provide instructions to users in order to enable them to scan the left ventricle of the heart using ultrasound through the parasternal long axis sonic window. We build our learning strategy to perform end-to-end optimization of the guidance performances and we train our agent using an simulated US acquisition environment. We compare the performances of our method with the ones obtained by training a classifier to learn a policy on the same data in a fully supervised manner.

2   Method

A RL problem is usually formulated as a Markov decision process (MDP) (Fig. 1 left). At each point in time, the agent observes a state S_t and interacts with the environment, using its policy $\pi \in \Pi$, through actions $a \in A$ obtaining a finite reward r_t together with a new state S_{t+1}. Π is the set of all possible policies while A is the set of all supported actions.

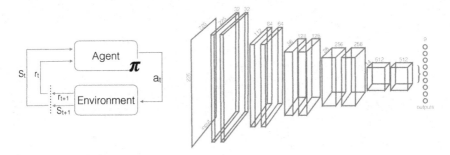

Fig. 1. Left: Schematic representation of the reinforcement learning framework. Right: Network architecture diagram.

The set of supported actions, in our system, contains 9 actions as shown in Table 1.

Table 1. Set of actions supported by the agent. These action are mapped to the corresponding effect in the simulated acquisition framework.

Action	Effect
NOP	Stops the virtual probe. Should be issued at correct view
Move Lateral	Translates the probe towards the patient's left
Move Medial	Translates the probe towards the patient's right
Move Superior	Translates the probe towards the patient's head
Move Inferior	Translates the probe towards the patient's feet
Tilt Supero-laterally	Tilts the probe towards the head of the patient
Tilt Infero-medially	Tilts the probe towards the feet of the patient
Rotate Clockwise	Rotates the probe clockwise
Rotate Counter-Clockwise	Rotates the probe counter-clockwise

In this section we present the details of our implementation.

2.1 Simulated Acquisition Environment

In order to learn from experience, our reinforcement learning agent needs to collect data according to its policy by physically moving the probe on the chest of the patient in order to obtain data and rewards. It is unfortunately impossible to implement real-time interaction due to the fact that acquiring the trajectories would take an enormous amount of time and a patient would need to be scanned for the whole duration of learning.

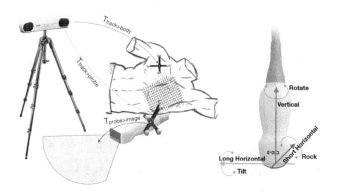

Fig. 2. Left: Schematic representation of our data acquisition system which comprises a probe and a tracking system in order to obtain tracked video frames from the patient. Right: Schematic representation of the degrees of freedom of the probe during acquisition.

We have resorted to acquiring, independently from our learning procedure, a large number of spatially tracked video frames from patients. By drawing spatial relationships between the frames, we are able to navigate the chest area offline and obtain simulated trajectories. We have defined, for each participant in the study, a work area covering a large portion of their chest. We have divided this area into 7 × 7 mm spatial bins. The bins from which it is possible to obtain a valid PLAx view by fine manipulation of the probe, are annotated as "correct" while all other bins remain unmarked. This annotation is necessary to implement the reward system.

Our system offers guidance for 4 out of the 5 degrees of freedom of probe motion (Fig. 2 right). We get data for the first two degrees of freedom, left-right and top-bottom translations, by moving the probe in a regular and dense grid pattern over the chest in order to "fill" each bin of the grid with at least 25 frames. In correspondence of the bins marked "correct", the sonographer is also asked to acquire 50 "correct" frames, showing the best view and 50 frames from each of the following scenarios: the probe is rotated by an excessive amount in the (i) clockwise or (ii) counterclockwise direction, or the probe is tilted by an excessive amount in the (iii) infero-medial or (iv) supero-lateral direction. In this way data for the last two degrees of freedom is obtained.

In order to build the environment we need to track both the body of the patient and the probe as data gets acquired. A schematic representation of our tracking system is shown in Fig. 2 (left). The tracking system, a NDI Polaris Vicra optical tracker, produces in real time a tracking stream consisting of two 4×4 transformation matrices $T_{track>probe}$ and $T_{track>body}$. The transform $T_{probe>image}$, which is necessary to obtain the true pose of each picture acquired through our system, is obtained by performing calibration with the open source software fCal, which is provided as part of the PLUS framework [4]. The video frames are acquired through an ultrasound probe and supplied to the data acquisition system through OpenIGTlink interface [11]. The tracking and video streams are handled and synchronized using the PLUS framework in order to obtain tracked frames.

During training/testing the agent interacts with the simulated environment by performing actions which result in state changes and rewards. The actions can have the effect of either stopping the virtual probe ("NOP" action), bringing it closer or further away from the nearest goal point.

At the beginning of each episode the environment is reset and a virtual "probe" is randomly placed in one of the bins. Actions bringing the agent further from the correct bin result in negative rewards of -0.1, motion towards the correct view result in a reward of 0.05, "NOPs" issued at the correct bin and for the correct view result in a 1.0 reward and "NOPs" issued in correspondence of an incorrect view result in a penalty of 0.25.

2.2   Deep Q-Network

In this work we implement the Q-learning paradigm already employed by [7,8]. This off-policy learning strategy leverages a convolutional neural network to regress Q-values which are the expected cumulative rewards associated with each action in correspondence of a state. As previously stated, the input of the model are ultrasound images, and its output is represented by nine Q-values, one for each action. Similarly to [5] we instantiate two copies of the same network. We have a target network which produces the values $Q_{\theta*}(s, a)$ and a main network which predicts $Q_\theta(s, a)$.

In order to train our agent we interact with the training environments. Each environment refers and represents to one patient. During an episode, we select an environment among those available for training and we reset the virtual probe to a random position. We then use the main network to collect experience by interacting with the environment. We implement exploration using an epsilon-greedy strategy which randomly hijacks and replaces the actions chosen through $\arg\max_a (Q_\theta(s, a))$ with random ones. In this way we are able to balance the needs for exploring the environment and the follow the learned policy. All agent's experiences are collected in an experience replay buffer of adequate size as previously done in [7]. Since all our data is pre-acquired it is possible to increase the memory efficiency of the experience replace buffer by storing in memory image paths on the file system instead of storing uncompressed images.

Once there is enough data in the experience replay buffer, we sample random training batches from it and we use them to update the parameters θ of the main network using back-propagation. The objective function that we minimize with respect to the parameters of the network, using ADAM as our optimizer, is

$$C(\theta, s_t, a_t) = \|Q_\theta(s_t, a_t) - T(s_t, a_t)\|_2^2$$
$$T(s_t, a_t) = r_t + \gamma \arg \max_a (Q_{\theta^*}(s_{t+1}, a))$$

The parameters θ^* of the target network are updated with the parameters of the main network once every 250 episodes.

A schematic representation of the network architecture is shown in Fig. 1 (right). This network makes use of global average pooling [6] applied after the output of the last convolutional layer. All the non-linearities employed throughout the network are exponential linear units (ELU) [2]. The network outputs a 9-dimensional vector representing Q values.

During testing, the target network interacts with the environment. All actions are chosen deterministically through $\arg\max_a(Q_{\theta^*}(s, a))$ which is, therefore, a stationary deterministic policy.

2.3   Supervised Policy Learning

In order to obtain means of comparison for our approach we have implemented a supervised policy learning approach which relies on classification and labeled data to learn the right action to perform in correspondence of each state. When we acquire data from patients we build environments where the parameters of the correct view in terms of translation, rotation and tilt are known. This enables us to label each image in each bin of the grid with one action, which would be the optimal action to perform in that state if we rely only on the Manhattan distance $abs(\mathbf{x} - \mathbf{x}_{goal})$ between the bin position $\mathbf{x}$ on the grid and the goal bin position $\mathbf{x}_{goal}$. In particular, for each bin of the grid, we choose the label for its images as the action that reduces the distance to the goal on the axis where the distance is currently the smallest.

We train a classifier with the same architecture shown in Fig. 1 (right), with the only exception that the last layer is followed by a soft-max activation function. We use all the data that is available to our reinforcement learning agent, shuffled and organized in batches of the same size of the ones used for our DQN.

During testing we use the same environments used by the reinforcement learning agent to test the supervised policy end-to-end on the guidance task. In this way we can compare on fair grounds the performances of the two strategies.

3   Results

We evaluate our method on the end-to-end guidance task described in the previous sections, using one environment for each patient. We train our approach on 22 different environments corresponding to circa 160000 ultrasound images, and we test our approach on 5 different environments which contain circa 40 thousand scans. During testing with start from each and every grid bin of each environment and we test the guidance performances of the approach.

As previously explained, we train both a RL-based approach and a supervised classification-based approach. Results are shown in Table 2.

We perform data augmentation for both the supervised and RL approaches. Each training sample is slightly rotated, shifted and re-scaled by a random quantity before being presented as input to the network. Also the gamma of the images is subject to augmentation. The episodes have a standard duration of 50 steps and "NOP" operations do not terminate the episode. Instead, a new, randomly selected, image from the same grid bin is returned to the agent. This is similar to what happens in practice when a user keeps the probe in the same location.

Table 2. Summary of performance of RL approach versus supervised approach on the test data-set.

Performances	Reinforcement learning	Supervised
Correct guidance	**86.1%**	77.8%
Incorrect guidance	**13.9%**	22.2%
Incorrect NOP percentage	**1.6%**	25.9%
Behaviour		
Avg. number negative rewards	**30.3%**	36.9%
Avg. number positive rewards	**69.6%**	63.1%

Our results are summarized in Table 2. The table is split in two parts: the first part summarizes the performances of the method on the end-to-end guidance task and inform us on the percentage of correct and incorrect guidance. That is, the percentage of episodes that have ended in a "correct" bin. Additionally we report the percentage of "NOPs" that have been issued at an incorrect location. Please note that "NOP" can be issued multiple times during a single episode. The agent may have briefly issued an "incorrect NOP" even during successful episodes. The evaluation reveals that the supervised approach is less successful than the RL approach on the guidance task. The second part of the table reveals information about the behaviour of the reward. Also these results demonstrate that our RL agent is performing more "correct" actions than its supervised counterpart.

4   Conclusion

Our approach employs reinforcement learning (RL) to guide inexperienced users during cardiac ultrasound image acquisition. The method achieves better results than a similar (non-RL) supervised approach trained on the same data and tested on the end-to-end guidance task. The intuition behind this is that RL is able to avoid and go around areas that are highly ambiguous as the agent learns to predicted rather low Q-Values in correspondence of actions leading to ambiguous states.

Although the results have shown to be promising there are still issues related with the data acquisition strategy of our approach and the long training time. In conclusion, we believe that this method is the one of the first step to converge towards a solution which aims to solve the guidance task end-to-end in a more reliable and effective manner.

References

1. Alansary, A., et al.: Automatic view planning with multi-scale deep reinforcement learning agents. In: Frangi, A.F., Schnabel, J.A., Davatzikos, C., Alberola-López, C., Fichtinger, G. (eds.) MICCAI 2018. LNCS, vol. 11070, pp. 277–285. Springer, Cham (2018). https://doi.org/10.1007/978-3-030-00928-1_32
2. Clevert, D.A., Unterthiner, T., Hochreiter, S.: Fast and accurate deep network learning by exponential linear units (ELUs). arXiv preprint arXiv:1511.07289 (2015)
3. Lample, G., Chaplot, D.S.: Playing FPS games with deep reinforcement learning. In: AAAI, pp. 2140–2146 (2017)
4. Lasso, A., Heffter, T., Rankin, A., Pinter, C., Ungi, T., Fichtinger, G.: PLUS: open-source toolkit for ultrasound-guided intervention systems. IEEE Trans. Biomed. Eng. **61**(10), 2527–2537 (2014)
5. Lillicrap, T.P., et al.: Continuous control with deep reinforcement learning. arXiv preprint arXiv:1509.02971 (2015)
6. Lin, M., Chen, Q., Yan, S.: Network in network. arXiv preprint arXiv:1312.4400 (2013)
7. Mnih, V., et al.: Playing atari with deep reinforcement learning. arXiv preprint arXiv:1312.5602 (2013)
8. Mnih, V., et al.: Human-level control through deep reinforcement learning. Nature **518**(7540), 529–533 (2015)
9. Neumann, D., et al.: A self-taught artificial agent for multi-physics computational model personalization. Med. Image Anal. **34**, 52–64 (2016)
10. Sahba, F., Tizhoosh, H.R., Salama, M.M.: A reinforcement agent for object segmentation in ultrasound images. Expert Syst. Appl. **35**(3), 772–780 (2008)
11. Tokuda, J., et al.: OpenIGTLink: an open network protocol for image-guided therapy environment. Int. J. Med. Robot. Comput. Assist. Surg. **5**(4), 423–434 (2009)
12. Van Hasselt, H., Guez, A., Silver, D.: Deep reinforcement learning with double q-learning. In: AAAI, pp. 2094–2100 (2016)
13. Wang, Z., Schaul, T., Hessel, M., Van Hasselt, H., Lanctot, M., De Freitas, N.: Dueling network architectures for deep reinforcement learning. arXiv preprint arXiv:1511.06581 (2015)

Registration of Untracked 2D Laparoscopic Ultrasound Liver Images to CT Using Content-Based Retrieval and Kinematic Priors

João Ramalhinho[1,2]([✉]), Henry Tregidgo[1,2], Moustafa Allam[3],
Nikolina Travlou[3], Kurinchi Gurusamy[3], Brian Davidson[3], David Hawkes[1,2],
Dean Barratt[1,2], and Matthew J. Clarkson[1,2]

[1] Wellcome/EPSRC Centre for Interventional and Surgical Sciences,
University College London, London, UK
joao.ramalhinho.15@ucl.ac.uk
[2] Centre for Medical Image Computing, University College London, London, UK
[3] Division of Surgery and Interventional Science, University College London,
London, UK

Abstract. Laparoscopic Ultrasound (LUS) can enhance the safety of laparoscopic liver resection by providing information on the location of major blood vessels and tumours. Since many tumours are not visible in ultrasound, registration to a pre-operative CT has been proposed as a guidance method. In addition to being multi-modal, this registration problem is greatly affected by the differences in field of view between CT and LUS, and thus requires an accurate initialisation. We propose a novel method of registering smaller field of view slices to a larger volume globally using a Content-based retrieval framework. This problem is under-constrained for a single slice registration, resulting in non-unique solutions. Therefore, we introduce kinematic priors in a Bayesian framework in order to jointly register groups of ultrasound images. Our method then produces an estimate of the most likely sequence of CT images to represent the ultrasound acquisition and does not require tracking information nor an accurate initialisation. We demonstrate the feasibility of this approach in multiple LUS acquisitions taken from three sets of clinical data.

Keywords: Laparoscopic Ultrasound · Multi-modal Registration · Bayesian models

1 Introduction

There are well known advantages of laparoscopic liver resection over open surgery. However, globally, only 5-30% of cases are deemed suitable for the

---

Electronic supplementary material The online version of this chapter (https://doi.org/10.1007/978-3-030-32875-7_2) contains supplementary material, which is available to authorized users.

© Springer Nature Switzerland AG 2019
Q. Wang et al. (Eds.): PIPPI 2019/SUSI 2019, LNCS 11798, pp. 11–19, 2019.
https://doi.org/10.1007/978-3-030-32875-7_2

laparoscopic approach, typically low risk cases in which tumours are small and far from major vessels [1]. Laparoscopic Ultrasound (LUS) can reduce this risk by imaging sub-surface structures of the liver. However, tumours are not always visible in these images. Therefore, registration of LUS to CT based on vessel information has been proposed as a guidance method.

Registering LUS images to CT is a very challenging problem in part due to the limited field of view of the LUS probe. The majority of US to CT registration methods rely on the acquisition of complete liver sections using transabdominal US [2,3]. However, LUS captures much smaller sections of the liver, providing less information to constrain the registration problem. Therefore, current methods either require manual point-picking of vessel bifurcations [4] or a fairly accurate initialisation [5]. During laparoscopic surgery, none of these options are desirable as they require a challenging and time consuming manual interaction with the intra-operative data. It has been demonstrated that a globally optimal registration can be obtained if enough LUS data is acquired [6]. However, tracking information is required to compose the LUS images in 3D space.

We propose a novel registration method that is globally optimal and uses a Content-Based Image Retrieval (CBIR) approach to register a group of untracked ultrasound slices. By simulating a finite number of ultrasound planes in the pre-operative model, we generate a discrete set of possible solutions for the alignment. For this to be feasible, we encode the vessel content of each image to a single feature vector [7]. A registration is then obtained by comparing the feature vector of a segmented ultrasound image with the pre-computed retrieval database. Due to differences between the pre-operative and intra-operative data, the simulated CT will not contain exact matches with the LUS input. Thus a set of possible matches must be considered. Assuming consecutive images are close in rotation and translation space, we employ a probabilistic model to estimate the most likely sequence of simulated images in CT space that represents the LUS acquisition. We formulate a discrete Hidden Markov Model (HMM) in which each state represents the probability of a CT match representing the original LUS and incorporate a kinematic prior as a boundary condition. The most likely combination of images is then estimated using the Viterbi algorithm. We hypothesise that this sequence estimation converges to a correct solution after enough LUS images hence states are combined in the algorithm.

Even though untracked ultrasound registration methods have been presented [8,9], the initialisation problem has not been solved. Our novel approach is the first to tackle the problem of initialisation and to work without a tracker. We perform tests in both synthetic and clinical LUS data from 3 different patients and show the feasibility of this method.

2   Methods

Given a set of N, 2D ultrasound images $\{I_1, ..., I_N\}$ and corresponding acquisition time stamps $\{t_1, ..., t_N\}$, we aim to recover the sequence of LUS slices, simulated from pre-operative CT slices $\{J_1, ..., J_N\}$ that most closely represent the LUS acquisition in terms of vascular content. In a first step we use CBIR to obtain a set of K possible slices $\{J_{1i}, ..., J_{Ki}\}$ as candidates for each image I_i. We then apply the Viterbi algorithm with kinematic prior information in order to find the optimal sequence.

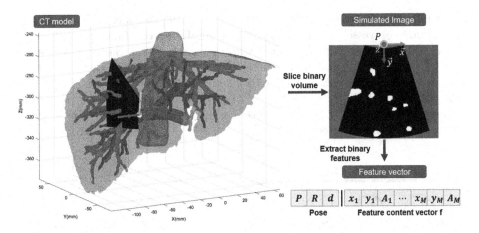

Fig. 1. CBIR database generation. For each position on the liver surface P determined by the surface mesh faces, each rotation $R = [\overrightarrow{x}, \overrightarrow{y}, \overrightarrow{z}]$, and each depth d along the surface normal, a binary image is simulated from the CT, capturing the vessels, which are encoded as a feature vector **f**.

2.1   Retrieval Based Candidate Selection

The pool of possible solutions J is generated by intersecting the CT segmented vascular model with 2D planes, bounded by an LUS field of view and parameterised by a set of evenly distributed points P_S along the segmented liver surface. At each of these points P_S, we create a virtual reference orientation of the LUS probe by placing it orthogonal to the liver surface normal and aligning its imaging plane with the sagittal plane. Several combinations of rotations R_x, R_y, and R_z are applied to this reference to generate rotated projections parameterised by $R = [\overrightarrow{x}, \overrightarrow{y}, \overrightarrow{z}]$. Additionally, we apply a translation d along the liver surface normal, simulating the case in which the probe compresses the liver tissue and images deeper structures. For each combination of P_S, R and d a binary image containing vessel sections is generated, as illustrated in Fig. 1. The 2D Centroid position and area are extracted from each of the M binary vessel sections and stored in a feature vector **f** as a single *feature triplet*, $\mathbf{f}_i$. Therefore, we establish a retrieval system in which **f** holds the content that encodes an image J and corresponding probe configuration $[P_S, R, d]$.

Image Retrieval: Assuming prior segmentation of LUS vessel lumens, we retrieve feasible candidate poses for an input LUS image, I, by comparing its feature vector $\mathbf{f}^I$ to all the generated pre-computed vectors **f**. Comparison between vectors is performed by calculating the weighted L^2 distance,

$$D(\mathbf{f}^S, M^S, \mathbf{f}^L, M^L) = \left(\frac{\sum_1^{M^L} A(\mathbf{f}_i^L)}{\sum_1^{M^S} A(m(\mathbf{f}_i^S, \mathbf{f}^L))} \right) \cdot \sum_{i=1}^{M^S} \| \mathbf{f}_i^S - m(\mathbf{f}_i^S, \mathbf{f}^L)) \|^2 \quad (1)$$

where $\mathbf{f}^S$ and are $\mathbf{f}^L$ are feature vectors with a smaller number M^S and larger number M^L of vessel sections respectively. In Eq. 1, the function $m(\mathbf{f}_i^S, \mathbf{f}^L)$ returns the feature triplet values in $\mathbf{f}^L$ with the closest lumen centroid to that of triplet $\mathbf{f}_i^S$, and the function $A(\cdot)$ returns the area value from a triplet. We introduce an area ratio to penalise the exclusion of triplets from the longer vector $\mathbf{f}^L$ - the total area of all vessels in $\mathbf{f}^L$ is divided by the sum of the ones that were included in the matching. The larger the excluded areas, the larger D becomes and the less similar the vectors.

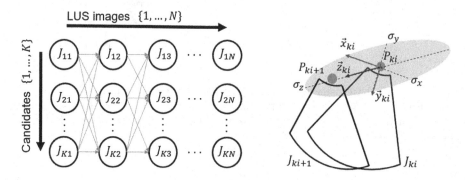

Fig. 2. HMM formulation of the problem. Left depicts the graphical model of the HMM that is optimised. Right is a visual representation of the translation probability density function of an image J_{ki} being followed by image J_{ki+1}.

To perform an efficient search over the database, we only search for vectors that have a number of sections similar to the input $\mathbf{f}^I$. For this reason, we group feature vectors in lookup tables F_M according to their size M. The search for the best candidates $\mathbf{f}^*$ is expressed in Eq. 2:

$$\mathbf{f}^* = \underset{\mathbf{f}^T \in F_T}{\arg\min} \frac{D(\mathbf{f}^I, M^I, \mathbf{f}^T, M^T)}{\min(M^I, M^T)} \quad , \quad F_T = \bigcup_{l=-r}^{r} F_{M_I + l} \quad (2)$$

Here, the distance D is computed between $\mathbf{f}^I$ and members of the lookup tables of size $M^I - r$ to $M^I + r$, where r is the allowable limit on feature vector length differences. The results are normalised by the minimum number of sections used in each comparison, and a set of lowest K candidate $\mathbf{f}^*$ vectors picked. Using the CBIR encoding, these vectors then become a set of CT images $\{J_{1i}, ..., J_{Ki}\}$ with corresponding probe poses.

2.2 Viterbi Algorithm Kinematic Constrained Optimisation

Once we obtain a pool of K possible matches $\{J_{1i}, ..., J_{Ki}\}$ for an image I_i we introduce kinematic prior information to select the optimal candidate. We hypothesise that, given enough LUS images and prior knowledge on the kinematics of the acquisition, we can pick the sequence of candidates $\{J_{k1}, ..., J_{kN}\}$ that best represents $\{I_1, ..., I_N\}$ in CT space. We formulate this problem as the optimisation of a discrete HMM as described in Fig. 2. In this model, nodes represent probabilities of images I_i matching a candidate J_{ki} and edges represent a probability associated with an input kinematic prior. We assume two main priors in the acquisition: firstly, there is smoothness in the acquisition; secondly, the probe follows a continuous path along the direction normal to the imaging plane without moving backwards. We then define the transition probability between 2 candidates with the following multivariate Gaussian:

$$P(J_{ki+1}|J_{ki}) = \frac{\exp(-\frac{1}{2}\delta_{ki+1,ki}^T \Sigma^{-1}\delta_{ki+1,ki})}{\sqrt{2\pi^4|\Sigma|}}, \quad \Sigma = (t_{i+1} - t_i)\begin{bmatrix} \Sigma_t & 0 \\ 0 & \sigma_\theta \end{bmatrix} \quad (3)$$

where $\delta_{ki+1,ki}$ is a vector containing the differences in rotation and translation between the 2 candidates. Specifically this is the 3D difference between probe contact points P_{ki+1} and P_{ki} projected along the orientation R_{ki} of J_{ki} and the angle between the imaging plane normals $\vec{z}_{ki+1}$ and $\vec{z}_{ki}$. The covariance matrix Σ is expressed in block matrix notation and holds a variance σ_θ and a diagonal translation covariance Σ_t with three terms σ_x, σ_y and σ_z. This equation models a Gaussian distribution centered at the pose of the previous image J_{ki} with variance proportional to the time difference. The lower the time difference, the lower the pose difference should be. Since we expect the probe to move along the imaging plane normal, we define the variance σ_z to be larger than σ_x and σ_y, favouring differences in that direction (see Fig. 2).

To find the optimal sequence of candidates we find the lowest cost path of this graphical model by applying the Viterbi algorithm. Since we are mainly interested in constraining the problem with kinematic information, we assume node probabilities $P(I_i|J_{ki})$ to be 1. During optimisation, we introduce a hard constraint in order to obtain trajectories that fulfil the forward movement prior. For every path in the graphical model, a sweep direction is defined as the difference between the two first probe contact positions. The probability $P(J_{ki+1}|J_{ki})$ is set to 0 if the angle between $P_{ki+1} - P_{ki}$ and that direction is above $90°$.

3 Experiments

We apply our method to data from 3 patients. Pre-operative models of the liver surface and vasculature are segmented[1] and respective databases generated using rotation angles in the intervals $R_x = R_z = [-40, 40°]$, $R_y = [-90, 90°]$ with steps of $10°$ and depth values in the interval $d = [0, 20\,\text{mm}]$ with steps of $5\,\text{mm}$.

---

[1] www.visiblepatient.com.

Initially, we test the validity of our model by registering synthetic sweeps generated from a CT model to itself. For each of the 3 patients we generate 3 smooth trajectories of 20 images with time stamps $t = [1, ..., 20\,s]$. Retrieval with search limit $r = 0$ is applied to find $K = 200$ candidates for each image and registrations are performed using model variances $\sigma_z = 1.5\,\text{mm}$, $\sigma_x = \sigma_y = 0.2\sigma_z$ and $\sigma_\theta = 2°$.

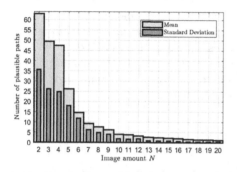
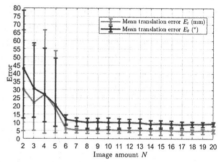

Fig. 3. Registration results for 9 synthetic sweeps. Left plot shows the number of plausible sequences found by the Viterbi algorithm. Right plot displays the translation and rotation error for each path's optimal registration. For visualisation purposes, the mean error for these nine optimal paths is displayed. Bars have been placed to show minimum achieved error and one standard deviation above the mean.

Mean results over the nine sweep registrations are summarised in Fig. 3. Since the Viterbi algorithm is recursive on the number of columns of the HMM, results are displayed as a function of the number of images used so far in the optimisation (from 2 to 20). The left hand graph shows the number of kinematically possible paths for N images. As expected, the number of plausible trajectories found by the algorithm converges to 1 if enough images are used ($N = 17$ in this case). The right hand graph shows the mean translation error E_t and mean rotation error E_θ across all N registered images for the lowest cost path. Here the convergence is observed in terms of error: at an average number of 7 images, these errors converge to 5 mm and 10°. Such values are expected since the rotation resolution of the database is 10° and the used liver surfaces have a spatial resolution in the range [3–4 mm].

To test the feasibility of the method on real data, we retrospectively register LUS acquired intra-operatively with a BK Medical 8666-RF[2] probe at a frame rate of 40 Hz. From each patient, we select 2 sequences of contiguous images that do not contain shadowing artefacts or large non-tubular vessel sections, and manually segment their vessels. To avoid redundancy, inside each dataset we pick evenly spaced images in time that differ in content. We apply the algorithm with a wider search of $r = 2$ to find $K = 1000$ candidates. We double the translation

---

[2] www.bkmedical.com.

Table 1. Results of registration of 6 sweeps of clinical LUS. N is the number of images in the sweep. N_C the number of images the Viterbi algorithm required to converge in error. E_t and E_θ are the mean translation and rotation error respectively. TRE represents the Root Mean Square (RMS) of the TRE of manually picked landmarks found in the sweep.

Dataset	Patient 1		Patient 2		Patient 3	
	Sweep 1	Sweep 2	Sweep 1	Sweep 2	Sweep 1	Sweep 2
N	42	12	25	11	23	19
N_C	6	8	16	6	19	16
E_t(mm)	14.7	18.7	11.2	10.3	19.1	15.3
E_θ (°)	14.8	33.3	17.2	13.9	44.1	32.3
TRE(mm)	18.8	3.7	14.2	11.4	25.3	21.9

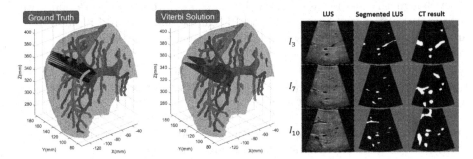

Fig. 4. Registration result of Sweep 2 of Patient 2. Left shows the 3D registration of the LUS planes using the Ground Truth (black planes with yellow dots) and the algorithm solution (red planes with red dots). Right shows LUS and segmented CT alignment results of 3 images in the sweep. (Color figure online)

variance values ($\sigma_z = 3$ mm) and keep the rotation the same. For each sweep, we manually register LUS images to CT and interpolate the result with a cubic polynomial to generate a ground truth trajectory. After obtaining a solution, we again measure the errors E_t and E_θ and assess the Target Registration Error (TRE) of a set of manually picked vessel bifurcations found in the path. Since these bifurcations may land in images in between the sequence that were not registered, we perform a cubic polynomial fit to predict their position given the algorithm solution.

Results on the six sweeps are summarised in Table 1. The best trajectory registration results are found in the sweeps of patient 2, with translation errors around 10 mm. A visual result with the registration of Sweep 2 is shown in Fig. 4. Lowest accuracies are obtained for patient 3, but these do not surpass 20 mm. This value is still usable as we are performing a globally optimised alignment. We also display the number of images N_C at which the errors converge as in the previous experiment. Since these vary greatly, we assume that this value depends on the uniqueness of the registered images that is specific to each dataset. TRE results are in the range of $[3.7 - 25.3\,mm]$ and are in reasonable agreement with the other errors.

4   Conclusions

Our results show that our framework can register smaller field of view images to a larger volume globally and without tracking information. While the proposed method does not perfectly register each LUS frame, the accuracy is sufficient to act as an initialisation for local registration methods such as [5]. We see this as a great step forward in this field. It poses both a reduction in manual interaction and less interruption to the clinical workflow as a tracking device is not required. Furthermore, our simulation was purely rigid: by increasing the realism of our database simulations with deformation, higher accuracies can be achieved.

Although the method used manually segmented vessels in ultrasound, we believe that automatic segmentation results can be obtained using state-of-the-art Deep Learning frameworks [10]. We did not include ultrasound images with large non-tubular sections in our validation. This is due to the fact that our retrieval based in position and area is not specific enough to identify such structures. We intend to tackle this problem by both refining our encoding and including modelling of physics in the simulation step.

It is worth noting that this framework can be translated to other registration problems. The only requirements are suitable priors on the acquisition and a robust image-to-feature encoding that describes the target anatomy.

Acknowledgements. JR was supported by the EPSRC CDT in Medical Imaging [EP/L016478/1] and EPSRC grant [EP/P034454/1]. MJC, DH and DB were supported by the Welcome/EPSRC [203145Z/16/Z]. BD was supported by the NIHR Biomedical Research Centre at University College London Hospitals NHS Foundations Trust and University College London. The imaging data used for this work was obtained with funding from the Health Innovation Challenge Fund (HICF-T4-317), a parallel funding partnership between the Wellcome Trust and the Department of Health. The views expressed in this publication are those of the author(s) and not necessarily those of the Wellcome Trust or the Department of Health.

References

1. Wakabayashi, G., Cherqui, D., Geller, D.A., Buell, J.F., Kaneko, H., et al.: Recommendations for laparoscopic liver resection: a report from the second international consensus conference held in Morioka. Ann. Surg. **261**(4), 619–629 (2015)
2. Wein, W., Brunke, S., Khamene, A., Callstrom, M.R., Navab, N.: Automatic CT-ultrasound registration for diagnostic imaging and image-guided intervention. Med. Image. Anal. **12**(5), 577–585 (2008). https://doi.org/10.1016/j.media.2008.06.006
3. Penney, G.P., Blackall, J.M., Hamady, M.S., Sabharwal, T., Adam, A., Hawkes, D.J.: Registration of freehand 3D ultrasound and magnetic resonance liver images. Med. Image. Anal. **8**(1), 81–91 (2004). https://doi.org/10.1016/j.media.2003.07.003

4. Song, Y., Totz, J., Thompson, S., Johnsen, S., Barratt, D., et al.: Locally rigid, vessel-based registration for laparoscopic liver surgery. IJCARS **10**, 1–11 (2015). https://doi.org/10.1007/s11548-015-1236-8
5. Ramalhinho, J., Robu, M., Thompson, S., Edwards, P., Schneider, C., et al.: Breathing motion compensated registration of laparoscopic liver ultrasound to CT. In: Proceedings of SPIE Medical Imaging (2017). https://doi.org/10.1117/12.2254488
6. Ramalhinho, J., Robu, M.R., Thompson, S., Gurusamy, K., Davidson, B., et al.: A pre-operative planning framework for global registration of laparoscopic ultrasound to CT images. IJCARS **13**(8), 1177–1186 (2018). https://doi.org/10.1007/s11548-018-1799-2
7. Petrakis, E.G.M., Faloutsos, A.: Similarity searching in medical image databases. IEEE Trans. Knowl. Data Eng. **9**(3), 435–447 (1997). https://doi.org/10.1109/69.599932
8. Cifor, A., Risser, L., Heinrich, M.P., Chung, D., Schnabel, J.A.: Rigid registration of untracked freehand 2D ultrasound sweeps to 3D CT of liver tumours. In: Yoshida, H., Warfield, S., Vannier, M.W. (eds.) ABD-MICCAI 2013. LNCS, vol. 8198, pp. 155–164. Springer, Heidelberg (2013). https://doi.org/10.1007/978-3-642-41083-3_18
9. Nir, G., Sahebjavaher, R.S., Kozlowski, P., Chang, S.D., Jones, E.C., et al.: Registration of whole-mount histology and volumetric imaging of the prostate using particle filtering. IEEE Trans. Med. Imaging **33**(8), 1601–1613 (2014). https://doi.org/10.1109/TMI.2014.2319231
10. Smistad, E., Løvstakken, L.: Vessel detection in ultrasound images using deep convolutional neural networks. In: Carneiro, G., et al. (eds.) LABELS/DLMIA -2016. LNCS, vol. 10008, pp. 30–38. Springer, Cham (2016). https://doi.org/10.1007/978-3-319-46976-8_4

Direct Detection and Measurement of Nuchal Translucency with Neural Networks from Ultrasound Images

Tianchi Liu[1]([✉]), Mengdi Xu[1], Ziyu Zhang[1], Changping Dai[2], Haiyu Wang[2], Rui Zhang[2], Lei Shi[3], and Shuang Wu[1]

[1] YITU Technology, Shanghai, China
tianchi.liu@yitu-inc.com
[2] Guangzhou Women and Children's Medical Center, Guangzhou Medical University, Guangzhou, China
[3] Hangzhou YITU Healthcare Technology, Hangzhou, China

Abstract. Nuchal Translucency (NT) in ultrasound images are commonly used to detect genetic disorder in fetuses. Due to lack of distinctive local features around NT region, existing NT detection methods first model some other prominent body parts, such as the fetal head. However, explicit detection of other body parts requires additional annotation, development and processing costs. It may also introduce cascading error in cases of unclear head location or non-standard head-NT relations. In this work, we design a convolutional neural network with fully connected layers to detect NT region directly. Furthermore, we apply U-Net with customized architecture and loss function to obtain precise NT segmentation. Finally, NT thickness measurement is calculated using principal component analysis. A dataset containing 770 ultrasound images were used for training and evaluation. Extensive experimental results show that our direct approach automatically detects and measures NT with promising performance.

1 Introduction

Nuchal Translucency (NT) is a fluid-filled region under the skin of posterior neck of fetus. In ultrasound images, NT is the bright-dark-bright region below head, as shown in Fig. 1. Abnormal thickness is related to cardiac defects and genetic abnormalities such as Down's Syndrome [14]. NT thickness measurement is commonly conducted by skilled operators in the first trimester of pregnancy via ultrasound scans. The manual approach to screening is laborious and prone to be inconsistent. Therefore, it is important and necessary to develop an accurate and automated NT measurement tool.

NT measurement is obtained by first detecting the region and then measuring the thickness. Automated region detection is a challenging task, as NT itself does not have highly distinctive local patterns and there can be more than one region with the bright-dark-bright pattern in the image. Both medical experts and

© Springer Nature Switzerland AG 2019
Q. Wang et al. (Eds.): PIPPI 2019/SUSI 2019, LNCS 11798, pp. 20–28, 2019.
https://doi.org/10.1007/978-3-030-32875-7_3

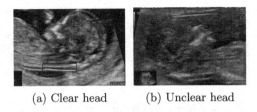

(a) Clear head   (b) Unclear head

Fig. 1. Ultrasound images of fetus with clear and unclear head. NT region is indicated by the blue bounding box. (Color figure online)

existing detection algorithms rely on the location of some other body parts with unique patterns to select the correct NT region. For example, Deng *et al.* [2] proposed a hierarchical structural model which explicitly locates the head and body of fetuses before detecting the NT region. Similarly, Park *et al.* [10] detected fetal head first then used this information to locate the NT region. The NT measurement methods proposed by Nie *et al.* [9] and Sciortino *et al.* [12] both require separate algorithms to provide prior knowledge of other body parts, such as fetal head, jaw bone, and choroid plexus. However, these two-stage approaches have two limitations. Firstly, it is costly to generate additional labels of the other body parts so as to develop their detection models; Secondly, it is error-prone for the NT detection model to rely on the output of the first stage, especially when the other body parts are unclear due to low resolution of ultrasound images as shown in Fig. 1(b) or when the fetuses have non-standard head-NT relations.

In this work, to alleviate the extra annotation cost and reduce the uncertainty associated with any additional detection models, we propose to detect NT region directly based on label information about only NT by using deep neural networks. Specifically, the contributions of this work are:

- For NT region detection, we design a convolutional neural network with fully connected layers to extract local patterns and model their relation;
- For precise NT segmentation, we customize U-Net architecture and use a loss function dedicated to handle the problem of imbalanced classes;
- We select the largest connected component as the final NT region and determine its orientation using principal component analysis (PCA) technique;
- Extensive experimental results show that the proposed subsystems are very effective in detecting and segmenting NT;
- We demonstrate that the system achieves promising NT measurement performance without any human annotation of other body parts.

2   Method

Figure 2 shows the pipeline of the proposed system. Given the ultrasound image, we first detect the center of NT using a neural network regression model. The region around the center point is cropped as NT region, and it is further segmented using a modified U-Net. NT thickness is calculated using PCA after size-based suppression.

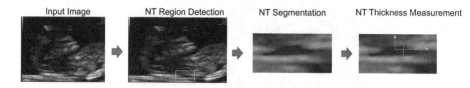

Fig. 2. Pipeline of the proposed system.

2.1 NT Region Detection

Instead of explicitly detecting head location and modeling the relation, we propose to use a simple yet effective convolutional neural network to make use of the head location implicitly so as to directly detect NT region without the need for annotating head locations. Building upon the classic VGG16 [13], we make several adjustments to cope with the small dataset in this task. We use less convolutional (Conv) layers in each convolutional block (CB) and use an additional CB to future reduce the size of feature maps before fully connected (FC) layer, so as to reduce the overall number of network parameters. Dropout layer is used to prevent overfitting, and batch normalization (BN) [6] layers are used to prevents model divergence and increase convergence speeds during training.

As shown in Table 1, the input to the network is a single-channel ultrasound image, and the outputs are normalized long-axial and short-axial coordinates of the center point. Each CB consists of one Conv layer, followed by BN, rectified linear unit (ReLU) layer, and max pooling (MaxPool) layer. The output of the last CB is flattened and connected to a FC layer. Finally, a FC layer with linear activation function gives the predicted center points. The region with pre-defined width and height around the center point is considered as NT region and the orientation of NT will be studied in the NT thickness measurement part. The model is trained using mean squared error loss.

Table 1. Network architecture of center point detection model. Here f denotes kernel size, s denotes stride length and n denotes number of filters.

Input ($526 \times 568 \times 1$)
Conv ($f = 3$, $s = 1$, $n = 24$) → BN → ReLU → MaxPool ($f = 2$, $s = 2$)
Conv ($f = 3$, $s = 1$, $n = 48$) → BN → ReLU → MaxPool ($f = 2$, $s = 2$)
Conv ($f = 3$, $s = 1$, $n = 96$) → BN → ReLU → MaxPool ($f = 2$, $s = 2$)
Conv ($f = 3$, $s = 1$, $n = 192$) → BN → ReLU → MaxPool ($f = 2$, $s = 2$)
Conv ($f = 3$, $s = 1$, $n = 192$) → BN → ReLU → MaxPool ($f = 2$, $s = 2$)
Conv ($f = 3$, $s = 1$, $n = 192$) → BN → ReLU → MaxPool ($f = 2$, $s = 2$)
FC (768) → BN → ReLU → Dropout
FC (2) → Linear
Output (2×1)

2.2   NT Segmentation

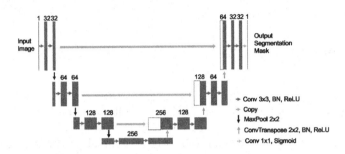

Fig. 3. Network architecture of segmentation model.

As a widely used network architecture for segmentation in medical applications, U-Net [11] consists of a encoder network, which takes a high resolution image as input and down-samples it to extract the abstract class information, and a decoder network, which up-samples the image and maps the abstract class information to high resolution segmentation mask. To tailor to our application of small dataset of only two classes, we reduce the depth of encoder and decoder network and reduce the number of filters in each layer. The network architecture is shown in Fig. 3. The segmented NT region can be only a small part of the input image, which leads to an imbalance between foreground and background classes, as shown in Fig. 2. To handle this, we use a loss function based on Dice-coefficient [8] to train the network. Instead of using fixed up-sampling filters (e.g., bilinear up-sampling), we apply transpose convolution (ConvTranspose) [7] followed by BN and ReLU in order to include both non-linearity and learnable weights.

2.3   NT Thickness Measurement

The segmentation mask produced by U-Net can consist of several disjoint regions, while it is known that there is only one NT per image. To remove false alarm regions, we propose to model the segmentation results as 8-way connected components and retain only the one with the largest area. It turns out the assumption that false alarm regions are of smaller size works well in this study. We name this process size-based suppression.

The final segmented NT region is always one connected component. We propose to approximate the region as an ellipse and use PCA to obtain its minor axes as the NT thickness. Specifically, given a set of pixels in the segmented region with coordinates (x_i, y_i), regarded as data points, the center point $(\bar{x}, \bar{y})$ is first obtained by averaging all data points within the region, and the mean-centered coordinates are computed as $(x'_i = x_i - \bar{x}, y'_i = y_i - \bar{y})$. We compute the two eigen values of the correlation matrix of data points and their corresponding eigenvectors. Finally, NT thickness is computed as the maximum distance between any pair of data points when projected along the direction of the second principal component[1].

3   Experiments

3.1   Dataset

The data used in this study were collected during ultrasound scanning in the first trimester of pregnancy. There are in total 770 ultrasound images from different subjects with clear NT and normal fetus orientation. NT thickness were labeled by medical doctors, and NT center as a point and NT as a polygon were labeled by trained experts. We randomly divided the dataset into three disjoint training, validation and test sets with 637, 66, and 67 samples, respectively. The images have pixel-level dimensions of 568×526 and have different pixel-to-mm ratios ranging from 5.61 to 25.61.

3.2   Experimental Setups

The proposed system was implemented using Keras with Tensorflow backend. For both NT center point detection and NT segmentation networks, training were done using SGD optimizer (weight decay $= 1e^{-6}$, momentum $= 0.9$), weights were initialized using the HE initializer [3], and the training mini-batch size was set to 32. The center point detection network was trained for 400 epochs with initial learning rate 0.001. For NT segmentation network, the training images were augmented 10 times by random cropping and horizontal flipping, and the network was first trained using initial learning rate of 0.01 and fine-tuned using learning rate of 0.001. All hyper-parameters and the best model were selected based on performance on the validation set. All experiments were conducted with 8 Nvidia GeForce GTX 1080Ti GPUs.

3.3   Results

For center point detection, we used average pixel-level L2 distance between ground-truth point and predicted center point as evaluation metric. A rectangular region centered at predicted center point with an aspect ratio of 4:3 was regarded as the NT region. We set the height to 128 pixels, which is around twice of the largest NT region height, to make sure the rectangle region encompasses NT. The predicted NT regions containing ground-truth center points are marked as true positive, otherwise as false positive. We also calculate recall rate to quantify how reliable center point detection is. We compared our proposed network with three state-of-the-art networks VGG16 [13] with two FC layers

---

[1] The second principal component is the eigenvector associated with the smaller eigen value and is the minor axis of the ellipse.

(768 nodes), and ResNet18 [4], ResNet34 [4] and DenseNet121 [5] with global average pooling. In addition, we implemented two variants of the proposed network, one without dropout layer and the other with two FC layers, to see effects of our design choices.

Table 2 shows center point detection results. VGG16 achieved much lower error than ResNet18, ResNet34 and DenseNet121. As an improvement of VGG, our proposed network achieved a detection error of 41.58 pixels on long-axis and 15.22 pixels on short-axis. In comparison, the network without dropout layer overfitted the training sets and performed poorly. The network with two FC layers achieved much larger errors in short-axis, which probably is also due to overfitting. The ground-truth center point is defined as the center of the thickest NT part; NT is an elongated region with similar thickness at many long-axial locations, which is possibly the reason why long-axis is prone to a larger error for all detection models. The proposed detection model achieved a detection recall of 97.01%, indicating that the proposed method is reliable for the subsequent segmentation task. Sciortino et $al.$ [12] reported a slightly higher detection recall of 99.95% using the two-stage method. It is worth noting that their method was test on a different dataset from only 12 patients and thus the two detection recall results can not be directly compared.

Table 2. Detection error (in pixel) of NT center point detection models. Here ϵ_l, ϵ_s, and ϵ_{2D} denote the average L2 distance on long-axis, short-axis and 2D space.

	VGG16	ResNet18	ResNet34	DenseNet121	Ours	w/2 FC	w/o dropout
ϵ_l	42.93	50.39	50.23	50.21	41.68	41.54	69.22
ϵ_s	24.91	21.38	26.71	39.49	15.22	19.89	65.63
ϵ_{2D}	49.63	54.74	56.89	63.88	44.37	46.06	95.39

We used intersection-over-union (IoU) as the metric to evaluate our NT segmentation network. We compared the proposed network with four state-of-the-art networks: U-Net, VGG16-based FCN32 [7], VGG16-based FCN8 [7], and SegNet [1] using their original cross entropy loss. We also implemented two variants of our proposed networks for comparison: one is trained using cross entropy (CE) loss, and the other is trained without data augmentation (DA).

As shown Table 3, both data augmentation and Dice-coefficient loss brought significant performance improvement. The proposed model achieved better segmentation performance than the state-of-the-art networks, indicating that it is highly suited for NT segmentation task. Figure 4 shows a visualization of the segmentation results. In Fig. 4(a), the ground-truth segmentation mask covers only a subset of NT, while the proposed segmentation model successfully identifies the entire NT. In Fig. 4(b), a region with similar pattern lies below the true NT region, the proposed size-based suppression successfully removed false alarm regions.

Table 3. IoU of NT segmentation models.

	U-Net	FCN8	FCN32	SegNet	Ours	w/o DA	w/CE
IoU	0.6991	0.6686	0.6359	0.6428	0.7199	0.6705	0.6249

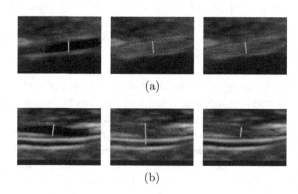

(a)

(b)

Fig. 4. Visualization of NT segmentation (blue/red mask) and NT thickness (green bar). Three columns contain ground truth, predictions before and after size-based suppression. (Color figure online)

The complete system performance is shown in Table 4. The mean error between the proposed system and manual labeling is 2.64 pixel and 0.21 mm. We also show a visualization of some typical cases in Fig. 5. Despite the low quality of the ultrasound images and unclear fetal head structures, the proposed system still achieved reliable detection results on most cases like Fig. 5(a) and (b). On 58.21% of the test set, thickness measurement error is less than 0.2 mm. Figure 5(c) and (d) are failure cases: Fig. 5(c) is due to inaccurate segmentation, and in Fig. 5(d), two disjoint regions were provided by the segmentation model but the wrong region was selected under the assumption that the smaller regions are false alarms. The current region selection strategy only considers the area of the region. In future work, other constraints on the shape and location can also be explored.

Table 4. The complete system performance. Mean and standard deviation of thickness measurement are shown.

Manual labeling		Proposed system		Error	
pixel	mm	pixel	mm	pixel	mm
17.38 ± 4.67	1.40 ± 0.41	16.94 ± 4.61	1.37 ± 0.40	2.64 ± 2.32	0.21 ± 0.19

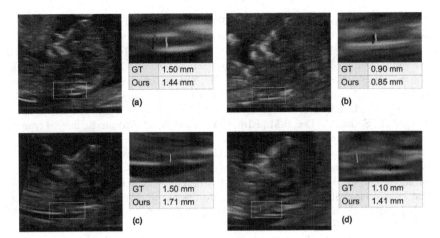

Fig. 5. Visualization of NT region detection, segmentation and measurement obtained by the complete system. Blue bar shows the ground truth NT thickness, and green bar shows the detection results. (Color figure online)

4   Conclusion

In this work, we proposed a deep neural network based NT detection and measurement system. Compared with existing two-stage NT detection methods, our system directly detects NT region and thus does not require the additional annotation or explicit modeling of other body parts. Qualitative and quantitative results show that the complete system produces accurate NT detection results and thickness measurements. It would be of interest to test our system on datasets including abnormal NT thickness, in order to assess its capability of Down's syndrome prediction based on NT measurement.

References

1. Badrinarayanan, V., Kendall, A., Cipolla, R.: SegNet: a deep convolutional encoder-decoder architecture for image segmentation. IEEE Trans. PAMI **39**(12), 2481–2495 (2017)
2. Deng, Y., Wang, Y., Chen, P.: Automated detection of fetal nuchal translucency based on hierarchical structural model. In: CBMS, pp. 78–84. IEEE (2010)
3. He, K., Zhang, X., Ren, S., Sun, J.: Delving deep into rectifiers: surpassing human-level performance on imageNet classification. In: ICCV, pp. 1026–1034 (2015)
4. He, K., Zhang, X., Ren, S., Sun, J.: Identity mappings in deep residual networks. In: Leibe, B., Matas, J., Sebe, N., Welling, M. (eds.) ECCV 2016. LNCS, vol. 9908, pp. 630–645. Springer, Cham (2016). https://doi.org/10.1007/978-3-319-46493-0_38
5. Huang, G., Liu, Z., Van Der Maaten, L., Weinberger, K.Q.: Densely connected convolutional networks. In: CVPR, pp. 4700–4708 (2017)
6. Ioffe, S., Szegedy, C.: Batch normalization: accelerating deep network training by reducing internal covariate shift. arXiv preprint arXiv:1502.03167 (2015)

7. Long, J., Shelhamer, E., Darrell, T.: Fully convolutional networks for semantic segmentation. In: CVPR, pp. 3431–3440 (2015)
8. Milletari, F., Navab, N., Ahmadi, S.A.: V-Net: fully convolutional neural networks for volumetric medical image segmentation. In: 3DV, pp. 565–571. IEEE (2016)
9. Nie, S., Yu, J., Chen, P., Wang, Y., Guo, Y., Zhang, J.Q.: Automatic measurement of fetal nuchal translucency from three-dimensional ultrasound data. In: EMBC, pp. 3417–3420. IEEE (2017)
10. Park, J.H., Sofka, M., Lee, S.M., Kim, D.Y., Zhou, S.K.: Automatic nuchal translucency measurement from ultrasonography. In: Mori, K., Sakuma, I., Sato, Y., Barillot, C., Navab, N. (eds.) MICCAI 2013. LNCS, vol. 8151, pp. 243–250. Springer, Heidelberg (2013). https://doi.org/10.1007/978-3-642-40760-4_31
11. Ronneberger, O., Fischer, P., Brox, T.: U-Net: convolutional networks for biomedical image segmentation. In: Navab, N., Hornegger, J., Wells, W.M., Frangi, A.F. (eds.) MICCAI 2015. LNCS, vol. 9351, pp. 234–241. Springer, Cham (2015). https://doi.org/10.1007/978-3-319-24574-4_28
12. Sciortino, G., Tegolo, D., Valenti, C.: Automatic detection and measurement of nuchal translucency. Comput. Biol. Med. **82**, 12–20 (2017)
13. Simonyan, K., Zisserman, A.: Very deep convolutional networks for large-scale image recognition. arXiv preprint arXiv:1409.1556 (2014)
14. Souka, A.P., Krampl, E., Bakalis, S., Heath, V., Nicolaides, K.H.: Outcome of pregnancy in chromosomally normal fetuses with increased nuchal translucency in the first trimester. Ultrasound Obstet. Gynecol. **18**(1), 9–17 (2001)

Automated Left Ventricle Dimension Measurement in 2D Cardiac Ultrasound via an Anatomically Meaningful CNN Approach

Andrew Gilbert[1,2(✉)], Marit Holden[3], Line Eikvil[3], Svein Arne Aase[1],
Eigil Samset[1,2], and Kristin McLeod[1]

[1] GE Vingmed Ultrasound, GE Healthcare, Oslo, Norway
andrew.gilbert@ge.com
[2] Department of Informatics, University of Oslo, Oslo, Norway
[3] Norwegian Computing Center, Oslo, Norway

Abstract. Two-dimensional echocardiography (2DE) measurements of left ventricle (LV) dimensions are highly significant markers of several cardiovascular diseases. These measurements are often used in clinical care despite suffering from large variability between observers. This variability is due to the challenging nature of accurately finding the correct temporal and spatial location of measurement endpoints in ultrasound images. These images often contain fuzzy boundaries and varying reflection patterns between frames. In this work, we present a convolutional neural network (CNN) based approach to automate 2DE LV measurements. Treating the problem as a landmark detection problem, we propose a modified U-Net CNN architecture to generate heatmaps of likely coordinate locations. To improve the network performance we use anatomically meaningful heatmaps as labels and train with a multi-component loss function. Our network achieves 13.4%, 6%, and 10.8% mean percent error on intraventricular septum (IVS), LV internal dimension (LVID), and LV posterior wall (LVPW) measurements respectively. The design outperforms other networks and matches or approaches intra-analyser expert error.

Keywords: Ultrasound · Echocardiography · Landmark detection · Deep learning · Convolutional neural networks

1 Introduction

Ultrasound imaging is the primary imaging modality used to assess cardiac morphology and function. Compared to other imaging modalities (e.g. MRI and CT), ultrasound imaging has a lower cost, is easier to perform, and, unlike CT, does not produce ionizing radiation. This makes it ideally suited for rapid diagnostic use for patients with cardiovascular disease. A diagnosis is made by acquiring

© Springer Nature Switzerland AG 2019
Q. Wang et al. (Eds.): PIPPI 2019/SUSI 2019, LNCS 11798, pp. 29–37, 2019.
https://doi.org/10.1007/978-3-030-32875-7_4

a set of images from different views of the heart and extracting measurements of heart function from those images. Some of the most frequent measurements in patient care settings are measurements of the left ventricle (LV) from the parasternal long-axis view. The typical set of measurements consists of the length of the intraventricular septum (IVS), left ventricular internal dimension (LVID), and left ventricular posterior wall (LVPW) at both the end-diastole (ED) and end-systole (ES) phases of the cardiac cycle. Several examples of these measurements are shown in Fig. 2. Because LV dimension measurements are performed frequently, automated measurement tools could provide tremendous time savings for clinical use.

Despite its widespread use, there is a high variability in LV dimension measurements due to variations in training and the difficulty of precisely detecting relevant structures. The 2010 HUNT study [11] measured inter-analyser (difference between experts reading the same exam) and intra-analyser (difference between the same expert reading the same exam several weeks apart) for several standard echocardiographic measurements. The intra-analyser mean percent error (MPE) for IVS, LVID, and LVPW measurements was 10%, 4%, and 10% respectively and inter-analyser results were similar. For IVS and LVPW measurements this corresponds to about half of the standard deviation of normal ranges [3] so a patient on the borderline could easily be put in a different diagnostic group. The high variability highlights the difficulty of the task at hand, but effective automation is one promising approach to reduce this variability and implement a more reproducible diagnostic pipeline.

Previous work on 2D ultrasound measurements has focused on individual measurements. Snare et al. used deformable models with Kalman filtering to outline the septum shape [9], achieving bias and standard deviation of 0.14 ± 1.36 mm for automated IVS measurements compared to manual measurements. Baracho et al. used perceptron style neural networks and filtering to generate a septum segmentation [1]. They achieved results of 0.5477 mm ± 0.5277 mm for IVS measurements but failed to validate directly against measurements from an expert cardiologist. Finally, Sofka et al. developed an automated method for detecting LVID measurements using convolutional neural networks (CNNs) [10]. Sofka et al. introduce a center of mass layer to regress keypoint locations and achieved a 50th percentile error of 4.9% and a 95th percentile error of 18.3%. We extend the work of Sofka et al. by targeting the IVS and LVPW measurements in addition to LVID. Including more measurements increases the difficulty of the task because the network should not only achieve high accuracy on all measurements but also find measurement vectors that have a logical relationship to each other (i.e. all measurement vectors should be parallel to follow clinical guidelines). Additionally, the upper IVS and lower LVPW endpoints do not fall at distinct gradient boundaries within the image making them more difficult to find, even for an expert.

As with Sofka et al., we frame the task as a landmark detection problem, where the goal is to identify 6 key points (the 2 endpoints of IVS, LVID, and LVPW measurements) from an input image. A landmark based approach was chosen to increase user-interpretability and allow editing of the found points by users in a clinical workflow. Many architecture variants have been applied in previous work on landmark detection problems, but the most common approach is to generate a heatmap of likely locations for each key point of interest [6,7,12]. The heatmap is directly compared to a reference heatmap generated from the key point's known location, or the coordinates of the key points are regressed from the heatmap and compared to known coordinates.

We propose several modifications to the general landmark detection strategy above because, in contrast to facial recognition, there is no defined local appearance of these landmarks. Instead, their location is determined from local appearance and global structural information. For example, while the septum typically extends through a large part of the image, ASE guidelines recommend measuring at the level of the mitral valve leaflets [4] which means an algorithm needs to be aware of structural information to find the correct IVS endpoints.

The novelty of our approach lies in it's ability to handle these challenges and achieve high accuracy. First, we generate anatomically meaningful ground truth heatmaps which follow the expected spatial distribution of the point. Second, we propose the integration of coordinate convolution layers [5] within feature detection networks for medical imaging. Third, we optimize network performance using a multi-component loss function which provides feedback to the network in multiple components including measurement endpoint coordinate locations, angle of measurement, and measurement distances. Including all these terms allows us to optimize for both measurement accuracy and a logical relationship between measurement vectors. Finally, we evaluate several different architectures within the constraints of our first two contributions to show the optimal architecture for the given task.

2 Methods

2.1 Network

The input to the proposed network is a single 2D frame. The accurate detection of ES and ED frames from a full cardiac loop is left for future work. The image is first passed through a CoordConv layer, which adds pixel-wise spatial location information to allow CNNs to more easily find objects [5]. The core of our approach is a U-Net [8]. A U-Net is a CNN with a sequence of down and up sampling paths with skip connections concatenating each down-sampling output to the corresponding up-sampling level. In each successive down-sampling layer, the number of filters doubles and the spatial resolution in each dimension is cut in half, while the reverse is true in up-sampling. We make several modifications in our implementation. The number of down-sampling levels and the number of filters are parameterized to tune the network. Padding is added on all layers to ensure output heatmap resolution matches the input. Batch normalization and spatial dropout layers are included between convolutional blocks for regularization, avoiding standard dropout since neighboring pixels are strongly correlated [12]. Each convolutional layer uses a kernel size of 3×3.

Our output is the same size as the original image but contains 6-channels, with each channel representing a heatmap corresponding to one landmark. Although the top and bottom endpoints of LVID typically match the bottom of IVS and top of LVPW respectively, they can be different for some pathologies which is the reason they are independent points in our framework. Each channel is normalized to be a probability map and passed through a differential spatial-numerical transform block [7] to calculate the center of mass in x and y: the endpoints of the three measurement vectors. From the coordinate endpoint locations, we calculate the final distance measurements. The network architecture is shown in Fig. 1.

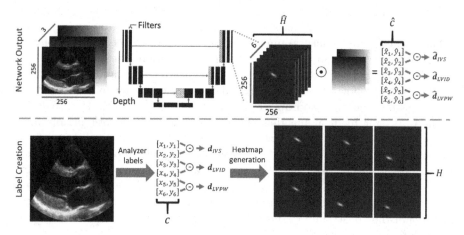

Fig. 1. Network architecture. The input image (256×256) is appended with x and y coordinate channels to create a 3 channel image and passed through a U-Net-based architecture. The output contains 6 heatmaps ($\hat{H}$), one for each detected landmark. The center of mass of each heatmap is extracted as the found coordinates ($\hat{c}$), and vectors for each measurement are obtained ($\hat{d}$). Label distances (d) and heatmaps (H) are generated from labeled endpoints (c) to compare to the network output.

2.2   Loss Function

Our labels are the coordinate locations of all caliper endpoints. We extrapolated these to match the network output including heatmaps of coordinate locations, and distances between coordinate pairs. For the label heatmaps, a 2D gaussian is centered at the location of the labeled coordinate. The gaussian is elongated in one dimension with a ratio of 20 to 1 between the variances of the long and short axes and rotated such that the long axis was orthogonal to the direction of measurement (see H in Fig. 1 for example). This both followed the expected spatial distribution of the points and gave the network feedback that a miss orthogonal to the direction of measurement was more acceptable than one parallel to the measurement, which would substantially affect measurement results. The variance of the gaussian in the long axis is 14 pixels (or 5% of the image size).

L2 loss is used for the six coordinate locations and three distance measurements, although the distance loss was divided by the relative actual distance (d) to equally weight each measurement. The heatmap loss is the root mean squared error (RMSE) between the generated and output heatmaps, following Newell et al. [6]. The heatmap loss helps the network converge to a reasonable result quickly, because feedback is provided to the network at every pixel in the output, rather than just a single metric fed back to all pixels such as with the distance or coordinate measures. The difference in the relative angles of the measurement vectors is also included in the loss function as the cosine similarity between the two vector sets. Including the angle loss is critical because even if the network can correctly find point delineations across the relevant structure (e.g. septum), if the measurement vector is not orthogonal to that structure then the measurement will be overestimated. The angle and coordinate loss also help promote a logical relationship between measurement vectors.

3   Experiments

3.1   Datasets and Pre-processing

LV intraventricular septum (IVS), internal diameter (LVID), and posterior wall (LVPW) dimensions were annotated in parasternal long axis 2DE scans. To avoid overfitting to a single acquisition protocol, exams were collected from four sites. All measurements were performed by a single cardiologist experienced in 2DE measurements. Diagnostic information was stripped from the images, but a mix of normal patients and varied pathologies is typical for the chosen sites. Exams were labeled at ED and ES except for where image quality in one phase prohibited accurate measurements. A total of 585 images were gathered from 309 unique patients. To generate a comparison with intra-analyser variability, 32 recordings (mixed ED and ES) were labeled multiple times by the same expert. These 64 images were set aside to be used as the test set for the network leaving 521 images for training and validation. The training, validation, and test sets were split such that images from the same patient would always remain in the same set. The coordinates and image data from the relevant frames were extracted from the stored files and converted to 256×256 one-channel images.

During training, random brightness, contrast, and gamma transformations were applied to each image. Additionally, we used mean normalization and applied random translations of 0 to 40 pixels in each direction, while ensuring coordinate locations were never within 16 pixels of the image boundaries.

3.2   Implementation Details

The network was implemented using PyTorch 0.4.1 with Python 3.6 on an Ubuntu 18.04 machine with an NVIDIA Titan X GPU. The batch size was 16 images for training and 4 images for validation. We trained for 120 epochs and reduced the learning rate by a factor of 10 every 50 epochs. Using 10% of the

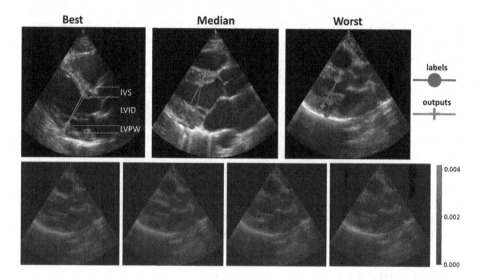

Fig. 2. Top row: Qualitative results on the best, median and worst images from the test set showing expert labels and network outputs for each measurement. Bottom row: Characteristic heatmaps showing how the network learns to prioritize a small distribution in the direction parallel to the measurement direction. Only four heatmaps are shown for simplicity since the top and bottom LVID endpoints overlap with the bottom of IVS and top of LVPW respectively and produce very similar heatmaps.

training set for validation of hyperparameters, we found 4 levels was the optimal network depth and 2^6 was the optimal number of filters in the first layer.

The primary metric important for clinical use is the accuracy of the distances for each of the three measurements. The coordinate locations of the endpoints and angle of the measurement vectors are secondary metrics that are important to create a tool that accurately follows clinical guidelines. For clinical use, it is not important that the generated heatmap matches the artificial heatmap. However, we found that keeping the relative weighting of the heatmap loss high compared to the other metrics helped improve network accuracy on all metrics.

3.3   Evaluation and Comparison

The primary metric for evaluation was the mean percent error between the network output and ground truth distance measurements on IVS, LVID, and LVPW. The test set was composed of the 32 images that had been labeled multiple times. The median of the two labels was set as ground truth although comparing to a randomly chosen label yielded very similar results.

While much of the strategy revolved around pre- and post-processing, we implemented several other networks in addition to U-Net for comparison. Results were compared to a stacked hourglass network [6], which currently obtains state of the art results on the FLIC and MPII human pose estimation metrics as well as ResNet18, ResNet34, and ResNet50 networks [2]. We tuned the number of stacks (4) and blocks (2) of the stacked hourglass network on the validation set.

We implemented the ResNet networks following the strategy proposed by Nibali et al. [7], reducing the stride in several layers to increase output heatmap resolution, while using dilated convolutions to maintain receptive field sizes. The output heatmap size for the ResNet and stacked hourglass networks was 64×64 and we appended up-sampling layers to achieve 256×256 resolution. A Coord-Conv layer was added to the beginning of all networks and the same coordinate regression method and loss function were used. For a fair comparison to the other networks, results with default values of an out-of-the-box implementation of U-Net is included (no batch normalization or dropout, depth and number of filters set to 5 and 2^6 respectively).

4   Results

The best, median, and worst examples (in terms of RMSE) from the test set are shown in Fig. 2. The network achieves intra-analyser accuracy on LVPW and LVID measurements, and slightly worse than intra-analyser on IVS measurements. The algorithm's worse performance on IVS measurements possibly occurs because the upper septum is often not defined as a clear gradient boundary because the septum blurs together with trabeculae in this region (see median image in Fig. 2, although the network correctly found the location in this case). Expert labelers typically rely on scrolling back and forth between several frames to accurately find these points. In general, intra-analyser error is high on this task since boundaries are often blurred and lost in the noise (see the upper LVPW boundary in the worst image in Fig. 2 for example). The network's ability to approach intra-analyser error using only a single frame indicates that it is accurately detecting the important structures despite the high noise level. Full results on the final test set are summarized in Table 1. The proposed network compares favorably to the other networks implemented on this task, achieving lower error on most metrics. We hypothesize that the performance of the other deeper networks would improve if the training dataset size were increased. However, our network has fewer parameters (which translates to a smaller memory size) and faster inference time. It is encouraging that close to expert level performance was achieved with a small network since efficient and fast implementations are important for clinical implementations.

5   Conclusion

In this work we present an effective landmark detection network for 2D measurements of the LV. We demonstrate the application of these techniques in determining LV dimensions. Implementation of this network could reduce high clinical inter-/intra-analyser variability in these measurements and lead to a more repeatable diagnostic pipeline. Additionally, it enables rapid historical analysis of patients to provide robust long-term analysis. We expect that many of the techniques presented here would be applicable to other landmark detection problems in 2D and 3D ultrasound. In the future we will increase the size of the

Table 1. Comparison of proposed network to implementations of state-of-the-art networks in landmark detection and intra-analyser results. Inference time is for a single image.

Model	Mean percent error (%)				Params	Time (ms)
	Total	IVS	LVID	LVPW		
ResNet18	12.8	12.7	11.7	14.2	1e7	21
ResNet34	13.0	**11.2**	12.1	15.8	2e7	38
ResNet50	11.6	13.7	8.8	12.3	2e7	43
Stacked Hourglass	11.3	12.1	7.4	14.4	3e7	79
U-Net	13.5	14.0	8.3	18.1	3e7	**10**
Modified U-Net	**10.0**	13.4	**6.0**	**10.8**	**7e6**	11
Intra-analyser	8.9	8.0	5.2	13.8	n/a	–

datasets, apply cross-validation, automate the detection of ED and ES frames from a full cardiac cycle, and add a confidence metric for detecting outlier results to provide a fully automated measurement tool for clinical use.

References

1. Baracho, S., Pinheiro, D., De Melo, V., Coelho, R.: A hybrid neural system for the automatic segmentation of the interventricular septum in echocardiographic images. In: Proceedings of International Joint Conference on Neural Networks, October, pp. 5072–5078 (2016)
2. He, K., Zhang, X., Ren, S., Sun, J.: Deep Residual Learning for Image Recognition. In: CVPR, pp. 770–778 (2016)
3. Kou, S., et al.: Echocardiographic reference ranges for normal cardiac chamber size: results from the NORRE study. Eur. Heart J. Cardiovasc. Imaging **15**(6), 680–690 (2014)
4. Lang, R.M., Badano, L.P., et al.: Recommendations for cardiac chamber quantification by echocardiography in adults: an update from the American society of echocardiography and the European association of cardiovascular imaging. Eur. Heart J. Cardiovasc. Imaging **16**(3), 233–271 (2015)
5. Liu, R., Lehman, J., et al.: An Intriguing Failing of Convolutional Neural Networks and the CoordConv Solution (2018)
6. Newell, A., Yang, K., Deng, J.: Stacked hourglass networks for human pose estimation. In: Leibe, B., Matas, J., Sebe, N., Welling, M. (eds.) ECCV 2016. LNCS, vol. 9912, pp. 483–499. Springer, Cham (2016). https://doi.org/10.1007/978-3-319-46484-8_29
7. Nibali, A., He, Z., Morgan, S., Prendergast, L.: Numerical coordinate regression with convolutional neural networks. CoRR abs/1801.07372 (2018)
8. Ronneberger, O., Fischer, P., Brox, T.: U-Net: convolutional networks for biomedical image segmentation. In: Navab, N., Hornegger, J., Wells, W.M., Frangi, A.F. (eds.) MICCAI 2015. LNCS, vol. 9351, pp. 234–241. Springer, Cham (2015). https://doi.org/10.1007/978-3-319-24574-4_28
9. Snare, S.R., Mjølstad, O.C., et al.: Automated septum thickness measurement-A Kalman filter approach. Comput. Methods Programs Biomed. **108**(2), 477–486 (2012)

10. Sofka, M., Milletari, F., Jia, J., Rothberg, A.: Fully convolutional regression network for accurate detection of measurement points. In: Cardoso, J.M., et al. (eds.) DLMIA/ML-CDS -2017. LNCS, vol. 10553, pp. 258–266. Springer, Cham (2017). https://doi.org/10.1007/978-3-319-67558-9_30

11. Thorstensen, A., Dalen, H., Amundsen, B.H., Aase, S.A., Stoylen, A.: Reproducibility in echocardiographic assessment of the left ventricular global and regional function, the HUNT study. Eur. J. Echocardiogr. **11**(2), 149–156 (2010)

12. Tompson, J., Goroshin, R., Jain, A., LeCun, Y., Bregler, C.: Efficient object localization using convolutional Networks. In: CVPR, 07–12 June, pp. 648–656 (2015)

SPRNet: Automatic Fetal Standard Plane Recognition Network for Ultrasound Images

Jiajun Liang[1], Rian Huang[1], Peiyao Kong[1], Shengli Li[2],
Tianfu Wang[1(✉)], and Baiying Lei[1(✉)]

[1] School of Biomedical Engineering, National-Regional Key Technology
Engineering Laboratory for Medical Ultrasound, Guangdong Key Laboratory
for Biomedical Measurements and Ultrasound Imaging, Shenzhen University,
Shenzhen, China
{tfwang,leiby}@szu.edu.cn
[2] Department of Ultrasound, Affiliated Shenzhen Maternal and Child Healthcare
Hospital of Nanfang Medical University, Shenzhen, China

Abstract. Fetal standard plane recognition is a crucial clinical part of prenatal diagnosis. However, it is also a sophisticated, subjective, and highly empirical process. Thus, there is a huge demand for proposing an effective and precise automatic method to help experienced as well as inexperienced doctors to complete this process, efficiently. In order to satisfy this clinical need, we propose an automatic fetal standard plane recognition network called SPRNet. Specifically, we adopt DenseNet as the basic network of SPRNet and implement data-based partial transfer learning on it by weight-sharing strategy. We then train our network with a task dataset (fetal ultrasound images) and a transferring dataset (placenta ultrasound images) so that our network can discover and learn the potential relationship between these two datasets to improve the performance and avoid overfitting. Finally, we achieve automatic fetal standard plane recognition by utilizing the feature extracted from SPRNet. The experimental results indicate that our network can attain an accuracy of 99.00% and perform better than conventional networks.

Keywords: Fetal standard plane recognition · Data-based partial transfer learning · Fetal ultrasound images · Placenta ultrasound images

1 Introduction

Prenatal diagnosis is an effective examination to assess the growth of fetuses and it is also helpful to reduce birth defect rate and neonatal mortality. Due to the advantages of the non-invasion, no radiation and low cost, ultrasonography plays an important role in prenatal diagnosis, nowadays. This ultrasonography method can be generally divided into five steps: ultrasound images scanning, standard planes recognition, structural observation, parameter measurement, and diagnosis. Among these steps, standard plane recognition is the key part of the process, as the standard planes are the foundation of parameter measurement and directly reveal the congenital anomaly of fetus [1].

© Springer Nature Switzerland AG 2019
Q. Wang et al. (Eds.): PIPPI 2019/SUSI 2019, LNCS 11798, pp. 38–46, 2019.
https://doi.org/10.1007/978-3-030-32875-7_5

Currently, the recognition of standard planes mainly depends on artificial examination. Slight differences exist between standard planes and non-standard planes and an example is shown in Fig. 1. This high similarity between the planes make it hard for sonographers to effectively distinguish the planes and increases likelihood for misdiagnosis, especially when they are working in a high-workload environment. In addition, underdeveloped areas are lacking of experienced prenatal diagnosis doctors. This is detrimental to decline the birth defect rate and neonatal mortality. Therefore, it is great significance to propose an effective and automatic method to help experienced as well as inexperienced sonographers to efficiently distinguish fetal standard planes from non-standard planes.

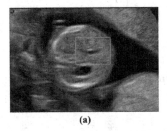 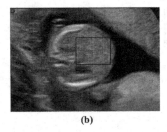

(a)   (b)

Fig. 1. Abdominal standard plane (a) and non-standard plane (b) appear in two adjacent frames of an ultrasound video. The green and red boxes show the nuanced difference between these two images. (Color figure online)

Recently, the-state-of-the-art deep learning based method, convolutional neural network (CNN) and it variants like VGG [2], ResNet [3] and SeNet [4], showed high performance in different image classification tasks. It can also provide a new insight for researchers to realize automatic fetal standard planes recognition. Accordingly, many works also have been devoted into this area [5, 6]. Although some of these works addressed the automatic recognition of certain fetal standard planes, their frameworks have limitations in the generalization ability and accuracy. Recently, Kong et al. [11] and Cai et al. [12] address these issues by higher performance network and multi-task learning respectively. Inspired by their works, we propose an automatic fetal standard plane recognition network called SPRNet. Specifically, the proposed SPRNet is based on DenseNet architecture [7], which could maximize the use of features and outperform other different deep neural network architectures. However, it still suffers from the problem of overfitting. Inspired by work in Wang et al. [8], we propose a transfer learning method called data-based partial transfer learning to alleviate overfitting and adopt a placenta ultrasound image dataset as the transferring dataset. After preprocessing, the features extracted from SPRNet are used to classify input images into corresponding categories by Softmax layer. The experimental results indicate that, with the transfer learning method we proposed, our network can utilize the potential relationships between two different datasets to improve classification performance, show higher generalization ability, and outperform other conventional networks.

2   Methodology

The overall architecture of the proposed SPRNet is shown in Fig. 2. The principles of the method used in this network are demonstrated as follow.

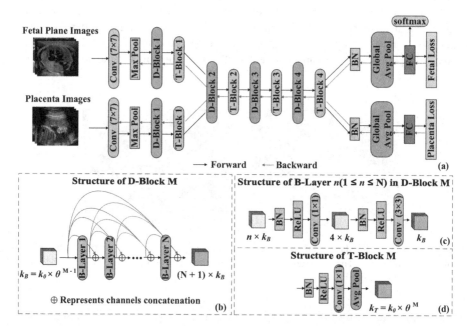

Fig. 2. Overall structure of the proposed method. (a) the architecture of SPRNet; (b), (c) and (d) represent the basic modules in our network. k_0 is the number of initial feature channels, k_B and k_T denote the number of feature channels, M represents the index of D-Block and T-Block, N is the amount of B-Layer in D-Block M, n ($1 \leq n \leq N$) refers to the index of B-Layer in D-Block M, and θ ($0 < \theta \leq 1$) denotes the channel decay coefficient.

2.1   Data Processing

The datasets used to train SPRNet is composed of a task dataset and a transferring dataset. The task dataset is constituted by fetal plane images in ultrasound and contains seven categories: 4 channel chamber (4CH), abdomen, brain, axial face (AF), coronal face (CF), sagittal face (SF) and others. Others are a collection of all non-standard planes, and the rest categories are collections of corresponding structures' standard planes. The transferring dataset is a collection of placenta ultrasound images, and it is divided into four grades: grade 0 to 3, according to Grannum standards [9].

The sizes of task and transferring datasets are summarized in Tables 1 and 2, respectively. Due to the limited number of cases and the difficulties of data annotation, the size of transferring dataset is significantly smaller than task dataset. This problem may impose an adverse effect on the performance of SPRNet. Therefore, we extend the training set of transferring dataset by cropping original images (700 × 500 pixels) into

448 × 448 pixels from top left corner to bottom right corner with different strides for different grades. The horizontal cropping strides for grade 0 to grade 3 are 126 pixels, 84 pixels, 63 pixels, and 21 pixels, respectively, and the longitudinal cropping stride for all images is 26 pixels. Eventually, we get more than 1,000 images in each category of transferring dataset and solve the problem of unbalanced data.

Table 1. The size of every category of training and testing in task dataset.

Fetal	4CH	Abdomen	Brain	AF	CF	SF	Others
Training set	1927	1349	1472	966	1542	1376	9208
Testing set	481	337	367	241	385	343	2301

Table 2. The size of every grade of original and extended training and testing in transferring dataset.

Placenta	Grade 0	Grade 1	Grade 2	Grade 3
Original training set	149	108	68	28
Extended training set	1341	1296	1020	1092
Testing set	37	26	16	7

2.2   Basic Modules

We adopt the B-Layer (Bottleneck Layer), D-Block (Dense Block) and T-Block (Transition Block) in DenseNet as the basic modules of our network.

D-Block is an intensive connection mechanism. It connects each layer to the previous layers in the same block and reuse the features extracted from previous layers by concatenation. The advantage of this connection strategy is that, it protects the information while reusing them and allows gradient to propagate from deep layers to shallow layers more easily. With this structure, D-Block performs better than the residual block in ResNet with less parameters and alleviates the problems of gradient vanishing and model degradation. B-Layer is the basic unit of D-Block, which is used for extracting information. T-Block, which is an interlayer between two D-Blocks, is mainly used for reducing the number of parameters.

In our SPRNet, there are 4 D-Block and 4 T-Block, and we set $k_0 = 32$ and $\theta = 0.5$. From D-Block 1 to 4, N is 6, 16, 24 and 24, respectively.

2.3   Data-Based Partial Transfer Learning

Transfer learning is used to utilize the knowledge learned from transferring dataset to improve the performance of CNN in task dataset and it was proved to be effective to augment the generalization ability of CNN by Yosinski et al. [10]. The conventional methods of transfer learning are based on transferring the weights of a pre-trained model to a new model as initial weights and then fine-tuning the new model. Although this method can boost the generation ability of network, it ignores the relationship between task dataset and transferring dataset during the fine-tuning process and still suffers from the problem of overfitting when dataset size is limited. Wang et al. proposed a novel transfer learning method called data-based transfer learning [8]. In this method, networks for different datasets are integrated into a general network by weight-sharing strategy, but they still possess their own fully connected layer and loss function to finish their own task. With this structure, the general network is able to extract and learn the potential relationship between task dataset and transferring dataset, prevent network from overfitting to any one dataset and perform better generalization ability than conventional transfer learning methods.

Conventional transfer learning method usually adopt natural images like ImageNet [13] as transferring data, but for transfer learning in medical area, there is huge difference between medical images and natural images, such as morphological difference and acquisition method, which may bring some adverse effects. So, in order to avoid these disadvantages, we also try to adopt the placenta ultrasound images as transferring data. Although there is still huge morphological difference between placenta ultrasound images and fetal plane ultrasound images, we believe that the different medical images which are collected by the same method have some common features which can be used for transfer learning.

When we apply data-based transfer learning into our network, we discover that the performance of our network declines. The reason is that, unlike the datasets used in Wang's et al. work [8], which are selected and closely related, there are huge morphological differences between our task dataset and transferring dataset, and these differences make it difficult for shallow layers, which are prone to extract morphological information like textures and corner point, to extract common features from task dataset and transferring dataset. To settle this problem, we do not apply weight-sharing strategy into shallow layers and only use deep layers to extract the common features hidden in the task and transferring datasets. Therefore, our network can avoid the performance decline while the task dataset and transferring dataset are not closely related to each other. We call this method as data-based partial transfer learning.

3 Experiments and Results

3.1 Experiment Design

We design a control experiment which uses three different networks (DenseNet-145, DenseNet-145-global-transfer and SPRNet) to finish two tasks (fetal standard plane recognition and placenta maturity grading), respectively, to demonstrate the improvement of SPRNet. DenseNet-145 is a densely connected convolutional networks with 145 convolutional layers. DenseNet-145-global-transfer is a network where weight-sharing strategy is applied on every convolutional layer. SPRNet is our proposed and it also includes 145 convolutional layers.

We randomly divide both datasets into 80% for training set and 20% as testing set, and data processing is applied to the training set.

The experiments are implemented using Python via Tensorflow and runs at a 32 GBs-RAM computer with a GeForce GTX 1080 Ti GPU. Accuracy (ACC), sensitivity (SEN), specificity (SPE), and F1-Score (F1) are adopted to evaluate the performance of the networks.

3.2 Results

As shown in Table 3, benefitting from data-based partial transfer learning, SPRNet outperforms other methods in fetal standard plane recognition as well as placenta maturity grading. However, for the DenseNet-145-global-transfer, there is a performance degradation in both tasks, if we regard DenseNet-145 as the benchmark. This degradation of performance mainly caused by the huge morphological differences between task dataset and transferring dataset. As shown in Fig. 3(b) and (c), the features extracted from the separated shallow layers in SPRNet mainly contain morphological information, such as corner point and texture, and there are huge differences between the features extracted from different datasets, which will result in an intense antagonism in shallow weight-sharing convolutional layers. For the data-based global transfer learning, this intense antagonism is too strong for it to find a proper point to learn common information from both datasets and yields performance degradation. On the contrary, data-based partial transfer learning, which cancels the weight-sharing on shallow layers, can effectively weaken this strong antagonism, ensuring the network will not be impaired. Furthermore, the improvement of SPRNet in placenta maturity grading task suggest that data-based partial transfer learning can effectively prevent the overfitting problem which is caused by limited data and improve the performance of network by extracting common features from task dataset and transferring dataset.

Table 3. The performance of the proposed SPRNet against other networks.

Task	Network	ACC %	SEN %	SPE %	F1 %
Fetal standard plane recognition	DenseNet-145	98.86	96.04	99.34	95.24
	DenseNet-145-global-transfer	98.03	93.11	98.85	92.25
	SPRNet	**99.00**	**96.51**	**99.41**	**95.58**
Placenta maturity grading	DenseNet-145	92.44	84.88	94.96	85.13
	DenseNet-145-global-transfer	91.27	82.55	94.18	83.02
	SPRNet	**94.76**	**89.53**	**96.51**	**90.85**

Table 4 shows the SPRNet's recognition results of different fetal planes, indicating that SPRNet achieves the best results in this task. The confusion matrix shown in Fig. 4 reveals the specific recognition result of SPRNet and prove the effectiveness of the proposed method.

To further explain the effectiveness of SPRNet, we implement feature visualization by t-SNE. Specifically, we reshape all the input test images and the feature extracted from SPRNet to a matrix, respectively, in which every row represents an images or features, and then demonstrate the distribution of these two matrixes by the t-SNE

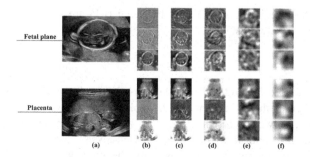

Fig. 3. Feature maps extracted from SPRNet. (a) is the original input image. (b) is the output of the first convolutional layer. (c)–(f) refer to the feature extracted from D-Block 1 to 4, respectively.

Table 4. Recognition results

Classes	ACC %	SEN %	SPE %	F1 %
4CH	99.51	97.54	99.75	97.74
Abdomen	99.00	95.60	99.27	93.54
Brain	99.17	98.92	99.20	95.21
AF	99.37	99.58	99.36	94.50
CF	99.42	93.81	99.97	96.67
SF	99.04	96.56	99.22	93.87
Others	97.48	96.16	98.89	97.53

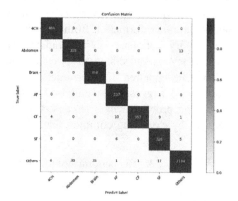

Fig. 4. Confusion matrix of SPRNet.

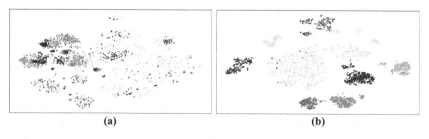

Fig. 5. Feature visualization via t-SNE. (a) the distribution of the input test images; (b) the distribution of the features extracted from SPRNet.

function provided in the sklearn. Different colors refer to different categories of fetal ultrasound planes. As shown in Fig. 5, the distribution of the input test images is unordered, showing that the distinction of standard fetal planes and non-standard planes is unobtrusive. On the contrary, after feature extraction of SPRNet, corresponding categories are grouped together, and the distribution of features becomes separable. This result further proves the effectiveness of the proposed network.

4 Conclusion

In this paper, we propose an effective fetal standard plane recognition network, which adopts D-Block and T-Block as the basic module and introduces data-based partial transfer learning. The experimental results demonstrate that SPRNet is accurate and effective, and the data-based partial transfer learning brings a considerable improvement to our network. In the future, we will expand our dataset to realize standard plane recognition on more fetal structures and try to apply automatic parameter measurement and structure localization to our method.

References

1. Li, J., Wang, Y., et al.: Automatic fetal head circumference measurement in ultrasound using random forest and fast ellipse fitting. IEEE J. Biomed. Health Inf. **22**, 215–223 (2018)
2. Simonyan, K., Zisserman, A.: Very deep convolutional networks for large-scale image recognition arXiv:1409.1556 (2014)
3. He, K., Zhang, X., Ren, S., Sun, J.: Deep residual learning for image recognition. In: Proceedings of the IEEE Conference on Computer Vision and Pattern Recognition, pp. 770–778 (2016)
4. Hu, J., Shen, L., Sun, G.: Squeeze-and-excitation networks. In: Proceedings of the IEEE Conference on Computer Vision and Pattern Recognition, pp. 7132–7141 (2018)
5. Cai, Y., Sharma, H., Chatelain, P., Noble, J.: SonoEyeNet: standardized fetal ultrasound plane detection informed by eye tracking. In: 2018 IEEE 15th International Symposium on Biomedical Imaging (ISBI 2018), pp. 1475–1478 (2018)
6. Baumgartner, C.F., Kamnitsas, K., Matthew, J., Fletcher, T.P., Smith, S., Koch, L.M.: SonoNet: real-time detection and localisation of fetal standard scan planes in freehand ultrasound. IEEE Trans. Med. Imaging **36**, 2204–2215 (2017)
7. Huang, G., Liu, Z., Van Der Maaten, L., et al.: Densely connected convolutional networks. In: Proceedings of the IEEE Conference on Computer Vision and Pattern Recognition, pp. 4700–4708 (2017)
8. Wang, L., Wang, Z., Qiao, Y., et al.: Transferring deep object and scene representations for event recognition in still images. Int. J. Comput. Vis. **126**(2–4), 390–409 (2018)
9. Grannum, P.A., Berkowitz, R.L., Hobbins, J.C.: The ultrasonic changes in the maturing placenta and their relation to fetal pulmonic maturity. Am. J. Obstet. Gynecol. **133**(8), 915 (1979)
10. Yosinski, J., Clune, J., Bengio, Y., Lipson, H.: How transferable are features in deep neural networks?. In: Advances in Neural Information Processing Systems, pp. 3320–3328 (2014)

11. Kong, P., Ni, D., Chen, S., Li, S., Wang, T., Lei, B.: Automatic and efficient standard plane recognition in fetal ultrasound images via multi-scale dense networks. In: Melbourne, A., et al. (eds.) PIPPI/DATRA -2018. LNCS, vol. 11076, pp. 160–168. Springer, Cham (2018). https://doi.org/10.1007/978-3-030-00807-9_16

12. Cai, Y., Sharma, H., Chatelain, P., Noble, J.A.: Multi-task SonoEyeNet: detection of fetal standardized planes assisted by generated sonographer attention maps. In: Frangi, Alejandro F., Schnabel, Julia A., Davatzikos, C., Alberola-López, C., Fichtinger, G. (eds.) MICCAI 2018. LNCS, vol. 11070, pp. 871–879. Springer, Cham (2018). https://doi.org/10.1007/978-3-030-00928-1_98

13. Deng, J., Dong, W., Socher, R., Li, L.J., Li, K., Fei-Fei, L.: Imagenet: a large-scale hierarchical image database. In: 2009 IEEE Conference on Computer Vision and Pattern Recognition, pp. 248–255 (2009)

Representation Disentanglement for Multi-task Learning with Application to Fetal Ultrasound

Qingjie Meng$^{(\boxtimes)}$, Nick Pawlowski, Daniel Rueckert, and Bernhard Kainz

Department of Computing, BioMedIA, Imperial College London, London, UK
q.meng16@imperial.ac.uk

Abstract. One of the biggest challenges for deep learning algorithms in medical image analysis is the indiscriminate mixing of image properties, *e.g.* artifacts and anatomy. These entangled image properties lead to a semantically redundant feature encoding for the relevant task and thus lead to poor generalization of deep learning algorithms. In this paper we propose a novel representation disentanglement method to extract semantically meaningful and generalizable features for different tasks within a multi-task learning framework. Deep neural networks are utilized to ensure that the encoded features are maximally informative with respect to relevant tasks, while an adversarial regularization encourages these features to be disentangled and minimally informative about irrelevant tasks. We aim to use the disentangled representations to generalize the applicability of deep neural networks. We demonstrate the advantages of the proposed method on synthetic data as well as fetal ultrasound images. Our experiments illustrate that our method is capable of learning disentangled internal representations. It outperforms baseline methods in multiple tasks, especially on images with new properties, *e.g.* previously unseen artifacts in fetal ultrasound.

1 Introduction

Image interpretation using convolutional neural networks (CNNs) has been widely and successfully applied to medical image analysis during recent years. However, in contrast to human observers, CNNs exhibit weaknesses of being generalized to tackle previously unseen entangled image properties (*e.g.* shape and texture) [6]. In Ultrasound (US), the image property entanglement can be observed when acquisition-related artifacts (*e.g.* shadows) obfuscate the underlying anatomy (see Fig. 1). A CNN simultaneously learns anatomical features and artifacts features for either anatomy classification or artifacts detection [15]. As a result, the model trained by images with certain entangled properties (*e.g.* images without acoustic shadows) can hardly handle images with new entangled properties which are unseen during training (*e.g.* images with shadows).

Approaches for representation disentanglement have been proposed in order to learn semantically disjoint internal representations for improving image interpretation [12]. These methods pave a way for improving the generalization of

© Springer Nature Switzerland AG 2019
Q. Wang et al. (Eds.): PIPPI 2019/SUSI 2019, LNCS 11798, pp. 47–55, 2019.
https://doi.org/10.1007/978-3-030-32875-7_6

Fig. 1. Examples of fetal US data. Green framed images are shadow-free and red framed images contain acoustic shadows. (Color figure online)

CNNs in a wide range of medical image analysis problems. Specifically for a practical application in this work, we want to disentangle anatomical features from shadow features so that to generalize anatomical standard plane analysis for a better detection of abnormality in early pregnancy.

Contribution: In this paper, we propose a novel, end-to-end trainable representation disentanglement model that can learn distinct and generalizable features through a multi-task architecture with adversarial training. The obtained disjoint features are able to improve the performance of multi-task networks, especially on data with previously unseen properties. We evaluate the proposed model on specific multi-task problems, including shape/background-color classification tasks on synthetic data and standard-plane/shadow-artifacts classification tasks on fetal US data. Our experiments show that our model is able to disentangle latent representations and, in a practical application, improves the performance for anatomy analysis in US imaging.

Related work: Representation disentanglement has been widely studied in the machine learning literature, ranging from traditional models such as Independent Component Analysis (ICA) [10] and bilinear models [18] to recent deep learning-based models such as InfoGAN [4] and β-VAE [3,9]. Disentangled representations can be utilized to interpret complex interactions of underlying factors within data [2,5] and enable deep learning models to manipulate relevant information for specific tasks [7,8,13]. Particularly related to our work is the work by Mathieu et al. [14], which proposed a conditional generative model with adversarial networks to disentangle specific and unspecific factors of variation in deep representations without strong supervision. Compared to [14], Hadad et al. [8] proposed a simpler two-step method with the same aim. Their network directly utilizes the encoded latent space without assuming the underlying distribution, which can be more efficient for learning various unspecified features. Different from their aim – disentangling one *specific* representation from *unspecific* factors – our work focuses on disentangling several *specific* factors. Further related to our research question is to learn only unspecific invariant features, for example, for domain adaptation [11]. However, unlike learning invariant features, which ignores task-irrelevant information [2], our method aims to preserve information for multiple tasks while enhancing feature generalizability.

In the medical image analysis community, few approaches have focused on disentangling internal factors of representations in discriminative tasks. Ben-Cohen et al. [1] proposed a method to disentangle lesion type from image appearance and use disentangled features to generate more training samples for data augmentation. Their work improves liver lesions classification. In contrast, our work aims to utilize disentangled features for generalization of deep neural networks in medical image analysis.

2   Method

Our goal is to disentangle latent representations Z of the data X into distinct feature sets (Z_A, Z_B) that separately contain relevant information for corresponding different tasks (T_A, T_B). The main motivation of the proposed method is to learn feature sets that are maximally informative about their corresponding task (e.g. $Z_A \rightarrow T_A$) but minimally representative for irrelevant tasks (e.g. $Z_A \rightarrow T_B$). While our approach scales to any number of classification tasks, in this work we focus on two tasks as a proof of concept. The proposed method consists of two classification tasks (T_A, T_B) with an adversarial regularization. The classification aims to map the encoded features to their relevant class identities, and is trained to maximize $I(Z_A, Y_A)$ and $I(Z_B, Y_B)$. The adversarial regularization penalizes the mutual information between the encoded features and their irrelevant class identities, in other words, minimizes $I(Z_A, Y_B)$ and $I(Z_B, Y_A)$. The training architecture of our method is shown in Fig. 2.

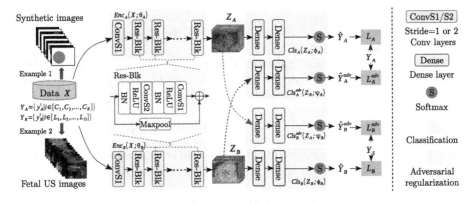

Fig. 2. Training framework for the proposed method. Res-Blk refers to residual-blocks. Example 1/2 are two data set examples used in Sect. 3. The classifications enables the encoded features Z_A, Z_B to be maximally informative about related tasks while the adversarial regularization encourages these features to be less informative about irrelevant tasks.

Classification is used to learn the encoded features that enable high prediction performance for the class identity of the relevant task. Each of the two classification networks is composed of an encoder and a classifier for a defined task. Given data $X = \{x_i \mid i \in [1, N]\}$, the matching labels are $Y_A = \{y_A^i \mid y_A^i \in \{C_1, C_2, ..., C_K\}, i \in [1, N]\}$ for T_A and $Y_B = \{y_B^i \mid y_B^i \in$

$\{L_1, L_2, ..., L_D\}, i \in [1, N]\}$ for T_B. N is the number of images and K, D are the number of class identities in each task. Two independent encoders map X to Z_A and Z_B with parameters θ_A and θ_B respectively, yielding $Z_A = Enc_A(X; \theta_A)$ and $Z_B = Enc_B(X; \theta_B)$. Two classifiers are used to predict class identity for the corresponding task, where $\hat{Y}_A = Cls_A(Z_A; \phi_A)$ and $\hat{Y}_B = Cls_B(Z_B; \phi_B)$. ϕ_A and ϕ_B are the parameters of the corresponding classifiers. We define the cost functions $\mathcal{L}_A$ and $\mathcal{L}_B$ as the softmax cross-entropy between Y_A and $\hat{Y}_A$ and between Y_B and $\hat{Y}_B$ respectively. The classification loss $\mathcal{L}_{cls} = \mathcal{L}_A + \mathcal{L}_B$ is minimized to train the two encoders and the two classifiers ($\min_{\{\theta_A, \theta_B, \phi_A, \phi_B\}} \mathcal{L}_{cls}$) for obtaining Z_A and Z_B that are maximally related to their relevant task.

Adversarial regularization is used to force the encoded features to be minimally informative about irrelevant tasks, which results in disentanglement of internal representations. The adversarial regularization is implemented by using an adversarial network for each task as shown in Fig. 2. These adversarial networks are utilized to map the encoded features to class identity of the irrelevant task, yielding $\hat{Y}_A^{adv} = Cls_A^{adv}(Z_B; \psi_A)$ and $\hat{Y}_B^{adv} = Cls_B^{adv}(Z_A; \psi_B)$. Here, ψ_A and ψ_B are the parameters of the corresponding adversarial networks. By referring to $\mathcal{L}_A^{adv}$ and $\mathcal{L}_B^{adv}$ as the softmax cross-entropy between Y_A and $\hat{Y}_A^{adv}$ and between Y_B and $\hat{Y}_B^{adv}$, the adversarial loss is defined as $\mathcal{L}_{adv} = \mathcal{L}_A^{adv} + \mathcal{L}_B^{adv}$. During training, the adversarial networks are trained to minimize $\mathcal{L}_{adv}$ while two encoders and two classifiers are trained to maximize $\mathcal{L}_{adv}$ ($\min_{\{\psi_A, \psi_B\}} \max_{\{\theta_A, \theta_B, \phi_A, \phi_B\}} \mathcal{L}_{adv}$). This competition between the encoders/classifiers and the adversarial networks encourages the encoded features to be invalid for irrelevant tasks.

By combining the two classifications with the adversarial regularization, the whole model is optimized iteratively during training. The training objective for optimizing the two encoders and the two classifiers can be written as

$$\min_{\{\theta_A, \theta_B, \phi_A, \phi_B\}} \{\mathcal{L}_A + \mathcal{L}_B - \lambda * (\mathcal{L}_A^{adv} + \mathcal{L}_B^{adv})\}, \ \lambda > 0. \tag{1}$$

Here, λ is the trade-off parameter of the adversarial regularization. The training objective for the optimization of the adversarial networks thus follows as

$$\min_{\{\psi_A, \psi_B\}} \{\mathcal{L}_A^{adv} + \mathcal{L}_B^{adv}\}. \tag{2}$$

Network Architectures: $Enc_A(X; \theta_A)$ and $Enc_B(X; \theta_B)$ both consist of six residual-blocks implemented as proposed in [17] to reduce the training error and to support easier network optimization. $Cls_A(Z_A; \phi_A)$ and $Cls_B(Z_B; \phi_B)$ both contain two dense layers with 256 hidden units. The adversarial networks $Cls_A^{adv}(Z_B; \psi_A)$ and $Cls_B^{adv}(Z_A; \psi_B)$ have the same architecture as $Cls_A(Z_A; \phi_A)$ and $Cls_B(Z_B; \phi_B)$ respectively.

Training: Our model is optimized for 400 epochs and λ is chosen heuristically and independently for each data set using validation data. For more stable optimization [8], in each iteration, we train the encoders and classifiers once, followed by five training steps of the adversarial networks. Similar to [8], we use the Adam optimizer (beta $= 0.9$, learning rate $= 10^{-5}$) to train the encoders and classifiers based on Eq. 1, and use Stochastic Gradient Descent (SGD) with momentum optimizer (momentum $= 0.9$, learning rate $= 10^{-5}$) to update the parameters of the adversarial networks in Eq. 2. We apply L2 regularization (scale $= 10^{-5}$) to all weights during training to prevent over-fitting. The batch size is 50 and the images in each batch have been randomly flipped as data augmentation. Our model is trained on a Nvidia Titan X GPU with 12 GB of memory.

3   Evaluation and Results

Evaluation on Synthetic Data: We use synthetic data as a proof of concept example to verify our model. This data set contains a randomly located gray circle or rectangle on a black or white background. We split the data into $1200/300/300$ images for train/validation/test and these images consist of circles on white background, rectangles on black background and rectangles on white background. To keep the balance between image properties in the training split, we use circle:rectangle $= 1{:}1$ and black:white $= 7{:}5$. In this case, T_A is a background color classification task and T_B is the a shape classification task. We implement our model as outlined in Sect. 2 and choose $\lambda = 0.01$. We evaluate our model on the test data. The experimentation illustrates that the encoded features successfully identify the class identities of the relevant task (e.g. $Z_A \to T_A$: $\text{OA}_{acc} = 100\%$, $Z_B \to T_B$: $\text{OA}_{acc} = 99.67\%$) but fail to handle irrelevant task (e.g. $Z_A \to T_B$: $\text{OA}_{acc} = 62\%$, $Z_B \to T_A$: $\text{OA}_{acc} = 59.67\%$). Here, OA_{acc} is the overall accuracy. To show the utility of the proposed method on images with previously unseen entangled properties, we additionally compare the shape classification performance of our model and a baseline (our model without the adversarial regularization) on images with a previously unseen entangled properties (circles on black background). The proposed model achieves $\text{OA}_{acc} = 99\%$ and outperforms the baseline which achieves $\text{OA}_{acc} = 10\%$. We use PCA to examine the learned embedding space at the penultimate dense layer of the classifiers. The top row of Fig. 3 illustrates that the extracted features is able to identify class identities for relevant tasks (see (a, c)) but unable to predict correct class identities for irrelevant tasks (see (b, d)).

Evaluation on Fetal US Data: We verify the applicability of our method on fetal US data. Here, we refer to an anatomical standard plane classification task as T_A and an acoustic shadow artifacts classification task as T_B. We want to learn the corresponding disentangled features Z_A for all anatomical information, separated from Z_B containing only information about shadow artifacts. Y_A is the label for different anatomical standard planes while $Y_B^i = 0$ and $Y_B^i = 1$ are the labels of the shadow-free class and the shadow-containing class respectively.

Data Set: The fetal US data set contains 8.4 k images sampled from 4120 2D US fetal anomaly screening examinations with gestational ages between $18-22$ weeks. These sequences consist of eight standard planes defined in the UK FASP handbook [16], including three vessel view (3VV), left ventricular outflow tract

Table 1. Data split. "Others" contains standard planes 4CH, femur, kidneys, lips and RVOT. Test_seen, LVOT(W_S) and Artifacts (OTHS) are used for testing.

		Train	Validation	Test_seen	LVOT(W_S)	Artifacts(OTHS)
3VV	W/O_S (W_S)	180 (320)	50 (50)	334 (41)	– (–)	– (–)
LVOT	W/O_S (W_S)	500 (–)	50 (–)	79 (–)	– (418)	– (–)
Abd	W/O_S (W_S)	125 (375)	50 (50)	190 (220)	– (–)	– (–)
Others	W/O_S (W_S)	– (–)	– (–)	– (–)	– (–)	3159 (2211)

(LVOT), abdominal (Abd.), four chamber view (4CH), femur, kidneys, lips and right ventricular outflow tract (RVOT), and are classified by expert observers as shadow-containing (W_S) or shadow-free (W/O_S) (Fig. 1). We split the data as shown in Table 1. Train, Validation and Test_seen are separate data sets. Test_seen contains the same entangled properties (but different images) as used for the training data set, while LVOT (W_S) and Artifacts (OTHS) contain new combinations of entangled properties.

Evaluation Approach: We refer to *Std plane only* as the networks for standard plane classification only (consists of Enc_A and Cls_A), and *Artifacts only* as the networks for shadow artifacts classification only (consists of Enc_B and Cls_B). *Proposed$_{w/o\_adv}$* refers to the proposed method without the adversarial regularization and *Proposed* is our method in Fig. 2.

The proposed method is implemented as outlined in Sect. 2 choosing $\lambda = 0.1$. $Cls_A(Z_A; \phi_A)$ contains three dense layers with 256/256/3 hidden units while $Cls_B(Z_B; \phi_B)$ contains two dense layers with 256/2 hidden units. We choose a bigger network capacity for $Cls_A(Z_A; \phi_A)$ by assuming that anatomies have more complex structures than shadows to be learned.

Table 2 shows that our method improves the performance of standard plane classification by 16.08% and 13.19% on Test_seen when compared with the *Std plane only* and the Proposed$_{w/o\_adv}$ method (see OA$_{acc}$ in Col. 5). It achieves minimal improvement (*Artifacts only*: +0.35% and Proposed$_{w/o\_adv}$: +0.31% classification accuracy) for shadow artifacts classification (see OA$_{acc}$ in Col. 8). We also demonstrate the utility of the proposed method on images with previously unseen entangled properties. Table 2 shows that the proposed method achieves 73.68% accuracy of standard plane classification on LVOT (W_S) ($\sim$36% higher than other comparison methods) while it performs similar to other methods on Artifacts (OTHS) for shadow artifacts classification.

We evaluate the performance of disentanglement by using the encoded features for the irrelevant task on Test_seen, *e.g.* $Z_A \rightarrow T_B$ and $Z_B \rightarrow T_A$. Here, Z_A and Z_B are encoded features of the proposed method. Proposed$_{irr\_task}$ in Table 2 indicates that Z_B contains much less anatomical information for standard plane classification (OA$_{acc}$ = 94.44% in proposed vs. OA$_{acc}$ = 64.35% in Proposed$_{irr\_task}$), while Z_A contains less shadow features information (OA$_{acc}$ = 79.05% in proposed vs. OA$_{acc}$ = 72.57% in Proposed$_{irr\_task}$). We additionally use PCA to show the embedded test data on the penultimate dense layer. The

Table 2. The classification accuracy (%) of different methods for the standard classification (T_A) and shadow artifacts classification (T_B) on Test_seen data set and data sets with unseen entangled properties (LVOT(W_S) and Artifacts(OTHS)). "Proposed" uses encoded features for relevant tasks, namely, $Z_A \rightarrow T_A$ and $Z_B \rightarrow T_B$. "Proposed$_{irr\_task}$" uses encoded features for irrelevant tasks, namely, $Z_A \rightarrow T_B$ and $Z_B \rightarrow T_A$. OA$_{acc}$ is the overall accuracy.

Col. 1	Col. 2	Col. 3	Col. 4	Col. 5	Col. 6	Col. 7	Col. 8	Col. 9	Col. 10
Methods	Test_seen							LVOT (W_S)	Artifacts (OTHS)
	3VV	LVOT	Abd.	OA$_{acc}$	W/O_S	W_S	OA$_{acc}$		
Std plane only	60.80	96.59	67.09	78.36	–	–	–	34.93	–
Artifacts only	–	–	–	–	77.94	80.46	78.70	–	69.26
Proposed$_{w/o\_adv}$	63.73	97.80	78.48	81.25	78.77	77.78	78.74	37.56	69.50
Proposed	**93.87**	97.56	81.01	**94.44**	87.89	58.62	**79.05**	**73.68**	68.49
Proposed$_{irr\_task}$	39.20	83.90	82.28	64.35	68.49	81.99	72.57	–	–

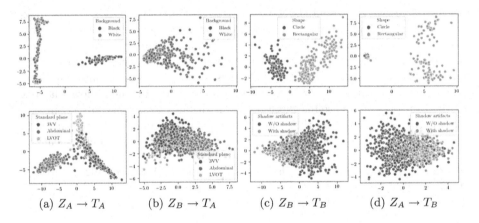

(a) $Z_A \rightarrow T_A$ (b) $Z_B \rightarrow T_A$ (c) $Z_B \rightarrow T_B$ (d) $Z_A \rightarrow T_B$

Fig. 3. Visualization of the embedded data on the penultimate dense layer. The top row shows embedded synthetic test data while the bottom row shows embedded fetal US Test_seen data. (a, c) are the results of using encoded features for relevant tasks, e.g. Z_A for T_A and Z_B for T_B; separated clusters are desirable here. (b, d) are the results of using encoded features for irrelevant tasks, namely, Z_A for T_B and Z_B for T_A; mixed clusters are desirable in this case.

bottom row in Fig. 3 shows that encoded features are more capable of classifying class identities in the relevant task than the irrelevant task (e.g. (a) vs. (d)).

Discussion: Acoustic shadows are caused by anatomies which block the propagation of sound waves or by destructive interference. With this dependency between anatomy and artifacts, separating shadow features from anatomical features may lead to decreased performance of artifacts classification (Table 2, Col. 7, Proposed). However, this separation enables feature generalization so that the model is less limited to certain image formation and able to tackle new combinations of entangled properties (Table 2, Col. 9, Proposed).

Generalization of supervised neural networks can also be achieved by extensive data collection across domains and in a limited way by artificial data augmentation. Here, we propose an alternative through feature disentanglement, which requires less data collection and training effort. Figure 3 shows PCA plots for the penultimate dense layer. Observing entanglement in earlier layers reveals that disentanglement occurs in this very last layer. This is due to the definition of our loss functions and is partly influenced by the dense layers interpreting the latent representation for classification. Finally, perfect representation disentanglement is likely infeasible because image features are rarely totally isolated in reality. In this paper we have shown that even imperfect disentanglement is able to provide great benefits for artifact-prone image classification in medical image analysis.

4   Conclusion

In this paper, we propose a novel disentanglement method to extract generalizable features within a multi-task framework. In the proposed method, classification tasks lead to encoded features that are maximally informative with respect to these tasks while the adversarial regularization forces these features to be minimally informative about irrelevant tasks, which disentangles internal representations. Experimental results on synthetic and fetal US data show that our method outperforms baseline methods for multiple tasks, especially on images with entangled properties that are unseen during training. Future work will explore the extension of this framework to multiple tasks beyond classification.

Acknowledgments. We thank the Wellcome Trust IEH Award [102431], Nvidia (GPU donations) and Intel.

References

1. Ben-Cohen, A., Mechrez, R., Yedidia, N., Greenspan, H.: Improving CNN training using disentanglement for liver lesion classification in CT. arXiv:1811.00501 (2018)
2. Bengio, Y., Courville, A., Vincent, P.: Representation learning: a review and new perspectives. IEEE Trans. Pattern Anal. Mach. Intell. **35**(8), 1798–1828 (2013)
3. Burgess, C.P., et al.: Understanding disentangling in β-VAE. arXiv:1804.03599 (2018)
4. Chen, X., Duan, Y., Houthooft, R., Schulman, J., Sutskever, I., Abbeel, P.: InfoGAN: interpretable representation learning by information maximizing generative adversarial nets. In: NeurIPS 2016, pp. 2180–2188. Curran Associates Inc., USA (2016)
5. Chen, X., et al.: Variational lossy autoencoder. In: ICLR 2017 (2017)
6. Geirhos, R., Rubisch, P., Michaelis, C., Bethge, M., Wichmann, F.A., Brendel, W.: ImageNet-trained CNNs are biased towards texture; increasing shape bias improves accuracy and robustness. arXiv:1811.12231 (2018)
7. Gonzalez-Garcia, A., van de Weijer, J., Bengio, Y.: Image-to-image translation for cross-domain disentanglement. In: NeurIPS 2018, pp. 1287–1298. Curran Associates, Inc. (2018)

8. Hadad, N., Wolf, L., Shahar, M.: A two-step disentanglement method. In: CVPR 2018 (2018)
9. Higgins, I., Matthey, L., Pal, A., Burgess, C., Glorot, X., Botvinick, M., Mohamed, S., Lerchner, A.: beta-VAE: learning basic visual concepts with a constrained variational framework. In: ICLR 2017 (2017)
10. Hyvärinen, A., Oja, E.: Independent component analysis: algorithms and applications. Neural Netw. **13**(4–5), 411–430 (2000)
11. Kamnitsas, K., et al.: Unsupervised domain adaptation in brain lesion segmentation with adversarial networks. In: Niethammer, M., et al. (eds.) IPMI 2017. LNCS, vol. 10265, pp. 597–609. Springer, Cham (2017). https://doi.org/10.1007/978-3-319-59050-9_47
12. Kim, H., Mnih, A.: Disentangling by factorising. CoRR arXiv/1802.05983 (2018)
13. Liu, A.H., Liu, Y.C., Yeh, Y.Y., Wang, Y.C.F.: A unified feature disentangler for multi-domain image translation and manipulation. In: NeurIPS, pp. 2590–2599. Curran Associates, Inc. (2018)
14. Mathieu, M.F., Zhao, J.J., Zhao, J., Ramesh, A., Sprechmann, P., LeCun, Y.: Disentangling factors of variation in deep representations using adversarial training. In: NeurIPS 2016, pp. 5040–5048 (2016)
15. Meng, Q., et al.: Weakly supervised estimation of shadow confidence maps in fetal ultrasound imaging. IEEE Trans. Med. Imaging (2019). https://ieeexplore.ieee.org/document/8698843
16. NHS: Fetal anomaly screening programme: programme handbook June 2015. Public Health England (2015)
17. Pawlowski, N., et al.: DLTK: state of the art reference implementations for deep learning on medical images. arXiv:1711.06853 (2017)
18. Tenenbaum, J.B., Freeman, W.T.: Separating style and content with bilinear models. Neural Comput. **12**(6), 1247–1283 (2000)

Adversarial Learning for Deformable Image Registration: Application to 3D Ultrasound Image Fusion

Zisheng Li$^{(\boxtimes)}$ and Masahiro Ogino

Research & Development Group, Hitachi, Ltd., Tokyo, Japan
zisheng.li.fj@hitachi.com

Abstract. We present an adversarial learning algorithm for deep-learning-based deformable image registration (DIR) and apply to 3D liver ultrasound image fusion. We consider DIR as a parametric optimization model that aims to find displacement field of deformation. We propose an adversarial learning framework inspired by generative adversarial network (GAN) to predict the displacement field without ground-truth spatial transformation. We use convolutional neural network (CNN) and a spatial transform layer as registration network to generate the registered image. Similarity metrics of image intensity and vessel masks are used as loss function for the training. We also optimize a discrimination network to measure the divergence between the registered image and the fixed image. Feedback from the discrimination network can guide the registration network for more accurate and realistic deformation. Moreover, we incorporate an autoencoder network to extract anatomical features from vessel masks as shape regularization. Our approach is end-to-end, only requires image pair as input in registration tasks. Experiments show that the proposed method outperforms state-of-the-art deep-learning-based methods.

Keywords: GAN · Deformable image registration · Deep learning

1 Introduction

Radiofrequency ablation (RFA) a low invasive therapy for liver cancer. In RFA, doctors often use ultrasound image fusion during or after the operation to assess the treatment effect. Deformable image registration (DIR) is significant technology for image fusion since it can deal with tissue deformation and body movement. In DIR, a dense, non-linear correspondence is estimated between a pair of 2D or 3D images. Most registration methods [1–5] solve an optimization problem that aligns voxels with similar appearance. However, it requires calculation of image similarity in every optimizing iteration. Therefore, it is computationally intensive and extremely slow in practice.

Several recent works proposed machine-learning-based methods to learn a transformation function to replace the iterative optimization in deformable registration. Most of these [6–9] rely on ground-truth or synthesized displacement fields which are difficult to be obtained in medical imaging applications. Recent works in [10, 11, 17, 18] presented weakly supervised or unsupervised methods based on a convolutional neural

© Springer Nature Switzerland AG 2019
Q. Wang et al. (Eds.): PIPPI 2019/SUSI 2019, LNCS 11798, pp. 56–64, 2019.
https://doi.org/10.1007/978-3-030-32875-7_7

network (CNN) and a spatial transformation network (STN) [12]. For better registration accuracy and robustness, generative adversarial network (GAN) [13, 14] was adopted in [19–21]. However, the work in [20] requires initial registration ground-truth, and the methods in [19, 21] only work on training data of 3D ROIs or 2D synthesized slices.

In this work, we propose a framework of adversarial learning for deformable image registration (AL-DIR). The AL-DIR model can run deformable registration in one pass and can be trained without ground-truth spatial transformation. AL-DIR consists of three networks: a CNN-based registration network (generator) using similarity metrics of image intensity and vessel masks as loss function; a discrimination network (discriminator) that distinguishes between the registered image and the fixed image; an autoencoder for measuring the anatomical shape difference before and after an iteration of registration. Main contributions of this work are as follow:

- We propose an end-to-end registration network to predict 3D displacement field of DIR without ground-truth spatial transformation. The single-pass prediction leverages information of image intensity and anatomical shape features (such as vessels and organs) and only requires image pair as input.
- We present an adversarial learning framework to train the registration network. The discrimination network can guide the registration for more accurate and realistic deformation. Unlike most of GAN-based supervised methods, our approach only requires vessel masks for training, so it is in weakly supervised manner.
- We incorporate the encoder part of an autoencoder to extract anatomical shape difference for better convergence of deformation.

2 Methodology

Image registration aims to find a spatial transformation between a moving image $M(x)$, and a fixed image $F(x)$. Here, x refers to coordination of image pixels. Image registration can be considered as an optimization problem for minimizing a cost function:

$$C(\mu) = -S(F(x), M(g(x; \mu))) + \lambda C_r(\mu), \tag{1}$$

where g is transformation function; μ is displacement field; S is similarity measure between $F(x)$ and $M(g(x; \mu))$; C_r is a regularization term for smooth deformation; λ is a weighting factor.

In this work, we present an adversarial learning framework to predict the displacement field. As shown in Fig. 1, the proposed framework consists of three networks: a registration network, a discrimination network and an autoencoder network. After training, the registration network only requires image pair as input, as shown in Fig. 2.

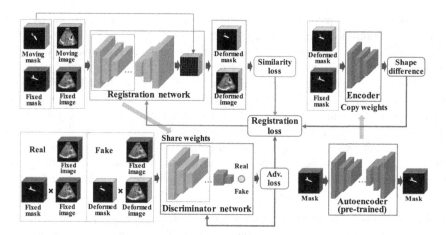

Fig. 1. The proposed adversarial learning framework of DIR.

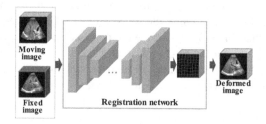

Fig. 2. Registration procedure.

2.1 Registration Network

In registration network, we adopt a CNN architecture that is similar to U-Net [15]. In training, a pair of training images to align, $F(x)$ and $M(x)$, are concatenated and input to the CNN. Displacement of each voxel in $M(x)$, i.e. the displacement field μ, is output as prediction. Since it is difficult to obtain the ground-truth of μ, we use similarity metrics of image intensity and vessel region as loss function of the registration network: image similarity metric that penalizes appearance difference between $F(x)$ and $M(g(x;\mu))$, and anatomical region (vessel region in our work) correspondence that guarantees deformation accuracy on important tissues and areas. We adopt local cross-correlation (CC) of $F(x)$ and $M(g(x;\mu))$ as image similarity metric:

$$\text{CC}(F(x), M(g(x;\mu))) = \sum_{x}\left[\frac{\left(\sum_{y\in N(x)}\hat{F}(y)\hat{M}(g(y;\mu))\right)^2}{\left(\sum_{y\in N(x)}\hat{F}(y)^2\right)\left(\sum_{y\in N(x)}\hat{M}(g(y;\mu))^2\right)+\epsilon}\right], \quad (2)$$

where $\hat{F}(y)$ and $\hat{M}(g(y;\mu))$ denote images with local mean intensities subtracted out. The local mean is calculated over a $N(x)$ local volume around each voxel y. ϵ is a small constant to avoid numerical issues. Size of the local volume $N(x)$ is set as $11 \times 11 \times 11$ experimentally.

We also calculate the similarity of anatomical region correspondence to guarantee accuracy on clinically important regions. In this work, we measure $l1$ distance between liver vessel masks $F(x)_m$ and $M(g(x;\mu))_m$. We also adopt gradient of displacement field as the regularization term $C_r(\mu)$. Therefore, the training of the registration network requires correspond vessel regions and is in weakly supervised manner. The registration network loss is calculated as follows:

$$\mathcal{L}_{reg} = -\mathrm{CC}(F(x), M(g(x;\mu))) + \lambda_m \left\| F(x)_m - M(g(x;\mu))_m \right\|_{l1} + \lambda_r C_r(\mu). \quad (3)$$

The network consists of an encoder-decoder with skip connections that is responsible for estimating μ given $F(x)$ and $M(x)$. Figure 3 shows the network architecture. The input of the network is formed by concatenating the $F(x)$ and $M(x)$ into a two-channel 3D image of size $N_1 \times N_2 \times N_3 \times 2$. We apply 3D convolution layers followed by layers of ReLU activation, batch normalization and dropout. The convolution kernel size is fixed to $3 \times 3 \times 3$. The network output μ is of size of $N_1 \times N_2 \times N_3 \times 3$. The last 3 channels of the output represent voxel displacement of a coordination x in $M(x)$.

2.2 Discrimination Network

On the purpose of better guidance for the training of registration network, we propose a discrimination network and train it simultaneously with the registration network. As shown in Fig. 1, the discrimination network also has a two-channel 3D image as input. The first channel is the fixed image $F(x)$ in both of the real case and the fake case. The second channel is the vessel segmented region $F(x)_{ves} = F(x) \cdot F(x)_m$ in the "real" case and the corresponding region of the deformed image $M(g(x;\mu))_{ves} = M(g(x;\mu)) \cdot M(g(x;\mu))_m$ in the "fake" case. The loss of discrimination network is defined as a binary cross-entropy metric as follows:

$$\mathcal{L}_{adv} = E\big(-\log\big(D\big(F(x), F(x)_{ves}\big)\big)\big) + E\big(-log\big(1 - D\big(F(x), M(g(x;\mu))_{ves}\big)\big)\big). \quad (4)$$

The discrimination network is optimized by maximizing the perfect registration (by minimizing $-\log\big(D\big(F(x), F(x)_{ves}\big)\big)$) and by minimizing the registration without high accuracy (by minimizing $-log\big(1 - D\big(F(x), M(g(x;\mu))_{ves}\big)\big)$). In this way, the training of the discrimination network does not require any ground-truth of spatial transformation, which makes our approach be easier to be utilized in practical medical imaging applications.

The architecture of the discrimination network is shown in Fig. 4(a). In order to achieve faster and better training convergence, the first half of discrimination network adopts the same configuration of the encoder part (without skip connections) of the registration network and shares the network weights during training. The resting part of the discrimination network consists of 3D convolution layers and fully connected layers. The convolution kernel size is fixed to $3 \times 3 \times 3$. The output is the classification result of "real" or "fake". The loss $\mathcal{L}_{adv}$ is not only used to fit the discrimination network but also used to feedback to the registration network.

2.3   Autoencoder of Anatomical Shape

Deformation of image fusion tasks is required to be smooth and realistic, especially on important tissues and regions for medical imaging applications. We incorporate a loss term by training an autoencoder network on liver vessel masks of fixed images $F(x)_{\mathrm{m}}$. The encoder part reduces the vessel mask to low resolution features $Enc(F(x)_{\mathrm{m}})$ in non-liner manner [16], and the decoder part generates the original vessel mask $F(x)_{\mathrm{m}}$ from $Enc(F(x)_{\mathrm{m}})$. In this work, the autoencoder network is pre-trained, and the encoder part is leveraged to extract anatomical shape features of $F(x)_{\mathrm{m}}$ and $M(g(x;\mu))_{\mathrm{m}}$ in each iteration of registration training. The architecture of the autoencoder network is shown in Fig. 4(b). The loss retrieved from the encoder network is defined as the $l2$ distance between features of $F(x)_{\mathrm{m}}$ and $M(g(x;\mu))_{\mathrm{m}}$:

$$\mathcal{L}_{\mathrm{enc}} = \left\| Enc(F(x)_{\mathrm{m}}) - Enc(M(g(x;\mu))_{\mathrm{m}}) \right\|_{l2}. \tag{5}$$

2.4   Adversarial Learning

In this work, the networks of registration, discrimination and the pre-trained encoder are combined to an adversarial learning framework. The registration network and discrimination network are trained simultaneously. The loss in the combined training procedure of the proposed AL-DIR is defined as follows:

$$\mathcal{L}_{\mathrm{AL-DIR}} = \mathcal{L}_{\mathrm{reg}} + \lambda_{\mathrm{adv}} \cdot \mathcal{L}_{\mathrm{adv}} + \lambda_{\mathrm{enc}} \cdot \mathcal{L}_{\mathrm{enc}}, \tag{6}$$

where $\lambda_{\mathrm{adv}} = 1.0$ and $\lambda_{\mathrm{enc}} = 0.25$ are set experimentally. By minimizing $\mathcal{L}_{\mathrm{AL-DIR}}$, accurate, smooth and realistic deformation of $M(x)$ can be obtained.

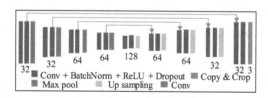

Fig. 3. Architecture of registration network.

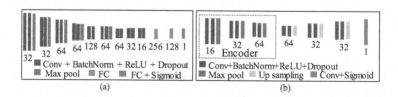

Fig. 4. Architectures of discrimination network and autoencoder network.

3   Experiments and Results

3.1   Materials and Training/Evaluation Details

We use clinical image data acquired in liver RFA surgery to evaluate the proposed method. In total, 510 image pairs from 98 patients are used, and 3-fold cross-validation is performed in the experiments. All images are resampled to size of $128 \times 112 \times 96$ with resolution of $1.0 \times 1.0 \times 1.0$ mm^3. Corresponding masks of liver vessels are annotated for training. The study was approved by the ethics committee of Hitachi group headquarters.

The proposed method is implemented in Keras with Tensorflow^{TM} backend. All the experiments are run on an 11 GB NVIDIA GTX^{TM} 1080 Ti GPU. In the training stage, we use an Adam optimizer with a learning rate of 10^{-4}. We set batch size as 1 for reducing GPU memory usage. First, we train the autoencoder network with the vessel masks of fixed images for 20,000 iterations. Then we train the registration network and discrimination network with the resulted encoder for 40,000 iterations.

As pre-registration, a rigid registration is firstly performed on each image pair by using the vessel masks in the evaluation experiment. After that, the proposed AL-DIR model is trained, and evaluation of deformable registration is run. Distance between corresponding landmarks of portal vein branches on $F(x)$ and $M(g(x; \mu))$ are used to measure the registration error. Moreover, Dice coefficient between vessel regions on the fixed images and the deformed images are calculated:

$$\text{Dice} = \frac{2 \left(F(x)_{\mathrm{m}} \cap M(g(x; \mu))_{\mathrm{m}} \right)}{\left(F(x)_{\mathrm{m}} \cup M(g(x; \mu))_{\mathrm{m}} \right)}. \tag{7}$$

We compare the proposed AL-DIR with two deep-learning-based methods: VoxelMorph-2 [17] and LabelReg [18]. We apply the same pre-registration results to both models and follow the implementation details and training parameters in [17, 18]. VoxelMorph is trained on image pairs without vessel masks, and LabelReg is trained by using both image pairs and vessel masks.

In order to evaluate the effect of the proposed discrimination network and autoencoder network, we also evaluate the following combinations of registration networks: (1) registration network only (referred as "Reg"), (2) registration network with discrimination network (referred as "Reg + GAN") and (3) registration network with autoencoder network (referred as "Reg + Enc").

3.2   Evaluation Results

Target registration errors (TREs) on portal vein branches and Dice coefficients of vessel regions are measured and listed in Table 1. As mentioned before, all the evaluated methods start deformable registration after the rigid registration (TRE = 10.6 mm, Dice = 0.33). We can see that VoxelMorph is able to achieve relatively good accuracy of TREs but is gives the worst performance of vessel region Dice, because it only uses information of image intensity to train the registration model. On the other hand, LabelReg achieves good performance of vessel region Dice since it is trained based on the loss of vessel region Dice directly. However, the loss of LabelReg does not adopt any image similarity metrics, so it gives a worse TRE than VoxelMorph. Compared to this methods, the registration network (Reg) in this work utilizes similarity metrics of both image and vessel masks, so better performance of both TRE and Dice can be achieved. Moreover, the discrimination network and autoencoder network contribute on better training guidance for the registration networks. As a result, the combination of the three networks, i.e., the proposed AL-DIR, gives the best performance of both TRE and Dice. The running time of AL-DIR is 0.3 s on the GPU.

Table 1. Evaluation results.

Methods	TRE	Dice
Before registration	26.5 mm	0.18
Rigid registration	10.6 mm	0.33
VoxelMorph-2 [17]	5.1 mm	0.48
LabelReg [18]	5.3 mm	0.56
Reg	4.7 mm	0.61
Reg + GAN	4.4 mm	0.63
Reg + Enc	4.5 mm	0.64
AL-DIR	**4.2 mm**	**0.66**

Some examples of registration results of AL-DIR are shown in Fig. 5. The registration is run on 3D images, and 2D axial slices are given here. Vessel masks before and after registration are highlighted by circles. We can see that AL-DIR can handle large changes in shapes and provide accurate deformation on important anatomical regions (liver vessels in this work) defined by user.

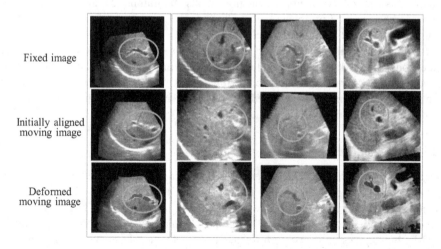

Fig. 5. Examples of deformable registration results.

4   Conclusion

We propose an adversarial learning framework for deep-learning-based deformable image registration. The end-to-end registration network can be trained to predict displacement field of deformable registration without ground-truth spatial transformation. The single-pass prediction leverages information of image intensity and anatomical shape features and only requires image pair as input. The discrimination network can guide the registration for more accurate and realistic deformation. Moreover, the autoencoder network can extract anatomical shape difference for better convergence. We apply our method to image fusion of 3D liver ultrasound images, and experimental results show that our method achieve better performance than the state-of-the-art deep-learning-based methods.

References

1. Roche, A., Pennec, X., Malandain, G., Ayache, N.: Rigid registration of 3-D ultrasound with MR images: a new approach combining intensity and gradient information. IEEE Trans. Med. Images **20**(10), 1038–1049 (2001)
2. Penney, G.P., Blackall, J.M., Hamady, M.S., Sabharwal, T.: Registration of freehand 3D ultrasound and magnetic resonance liver images. Med. Image Anal. **8**, 81–91 (2004)
3. Wein, W., Brunke, S., et al.: Automatic CT-ultrasound registration for diagnostic imaging and image-guided intervention. Med. Image Anal. **12**, 577–585 (2008)
4. Wein, W., Ladikos, A., Fuerst, B., Shah, A., Sharma, K., Navab, N.: Global registration of ultrasound to MRI using the LC^2 metric for enabling neurosurgical guidance. In: Mori, K., Sakuma, I., Sato, Y., Barillot, C., Navab, N. (eds.) MICCAI 2013. LNCS, vol. 8149, pp. 34–41. Springer, Heidelberg (2013). https://doi.org/10.1007/978-3-642-40811-3_5
5. Lange, T., Papenberg, N., et al.: 3D ultrasound-CT registration of the liver using combined landmark-intensity information. Int. J. CARS **4**, 79–88 (2009)
6. Krebs, J., et al.: Robust non-rigid registration through agent-based action learning. In: Descoteaux, M., Maier-Hein, L., Franz, A., Jannin, P., Collins, D.Louis, Duchesne, S. (eds.) MICCAI 2017. LNCS, vol. 10433, pp. 344–352. Springer, Cham (2017). https://doi.org/10.1007/978-3-319-66182-7_40
7. Rohé, M.-M., Datar, M., Heimann, T., Sermesant, M., Pennec, X.: SVF-Net: learning deformable image registration using shape matching. In: Descoteaux, M., Maier-Hein, L., Franz, A., Jannin, P., Collins, D.L., Duchesne, S. (eds.) MICCAI 2017. LNCS, vol. 10433, pp. 266–274. Springer, Cham (2017). https://doi.org/10.1007/978-3-319-66182-7_31
8. Sokooti, H., de Vos, B., Berendsen, F., Lelieveldt, B.P.F., Išgum, I., Staring, M.: Nonrigid image registration using multi-scale 3D convolutional neural networks. In: Descoteaux, M., Maier-Hein, L., Franz, A., Jannin, P., Collins, D.L., Duchesne, S. (eds.) MICCAI 2017. LNCS, vol. 10433, pp. 232–239. Springer, Cham (2017). https://doi.org/10.1007/978-3-319-66182-7_27
9. Yang, X., Kwitt, R., Styner, M., Niethammer, M.: Quicksilver: fast predictive image registration–a deep learning approach. NeuroImage **158**, 378–396 (2017)
10. de Vos, B.D., Berendsen, F., Viergever, M.A.: End-to-end unsupervised deformable image registration with a convolutional neural network. In: Deep Learning in Medical Image Analysis and Multimodal Learning for Clinical Decision Support, pp. 204–212 (2017)

11. Li, H., Fan, Y.: Non-rigid image registration using fully convolutional networks with deep self-supervision. arXiv preprint arXiv:1709.00799 (2017)
12. Jaderberg, M., Simonyan, K., Zisserman, A.: Spatial transformer networks. In: NIPS 2015, pp. 2017–2025 (2015)
13. Goodfellow, I., et al.: Generative adversarial nets. In: NIPS 2014, pp. 2672–2680 (2014)
14. Zhu, J.Y., Park, T., Isola, P., Efros, A.A.: Unpaired image-to-image translation using cycle-consistent adversarial networks. In: ICCV 2017, pp. 2223–2232 (2017)
15. Ronneberger, O., Fischer, P., Brox, T.: U-Net: convolutional networks for biomedical image segmentation. In: Navab, N., Hornegger, J., Wells, W.M., Frangi, A.F. (eds.) MICCAI 2015. LNCS, vol. 9351, pp. 234–241. Springer, Cham (2015). https://doi.org/10.1007/978-3-319-24574-4_28
16. Oktay, O., Ferrante, E., Kamnitsas, K.: Anatomically constrained neural networks (ACNNs): application to cardiac image enhancement and segmentation. IEEE Trans. Med. Imaging **37** (2), 384–395 (2018)
17. Balakrishnan, G., Zhao, A., Sabuncu, M.R.: An unsupervised learning model for deformable medical image registration. In: CVPR 2018, pp. 9252–9260 (2018)
18. Hu, Y., Modat, M., Gibson, E., Ghavami, N.: Label-driven weakly-supervised learning for multimodal deformable image registration. In: ISBI 2018, pp. 1070–1074. IEEE (2018)
19. Fan, J., Cao, X., Xue, Z., Yap, P.-T., Shen, D.: Adversarial similarity network for evaluating image alignment in deep learning based registration. In: Frangi, A.F., Schnabel, J.A., Davatzikos, C., Alberola-López, C., Fichtinger, G. (eds.) MICCAI 2018. LNCS, vol. 11070, pp. 739–746. Springer, Cham (2018). https://doi.org/10.1007/978-3-030-00928-1_83
20. Hu, Y., et al.: Adversarial deformation regularization for training image registration neural networks. In: Frangi, A.F., Schnabel, J.A., Davatzikos, C., Alberola-López, C., Fichtinger, G. (eds.) MICCAI 2018. LNCS, vol. 11070, pp. 774–782. Springer, Cham (2018). https://doi.org/10.1007/978-3-030-00928-1_87
21. Mahapatra, D., Antony, B., Sedai, S.: Deformable medical image registration using generative adversarial networks. In: ISBI 2018, pp. 1449–1453. IEEE (2018)

Monitoring Achilles Tendon Healing Progress in Ultrasound Imaging with Convolutional Neural Networks

Piotr Woznicki[1,2(✉)], Przemyslaw Przybyszewski[2,3], Norbert Kapinski[2], Jakub Zielinski[2], Beata Ciszkowska-Lyson[4], Bartosz Borucki[2], Tomasz Trzcinski[5,6], and Krzysztof Nowinski[2]

[1] Medical University of Warsaw, Warsaw, Poland
piotrekwoznicki@gmail.com
[2] Interdisciplinary Centre for Mathematical and Computer Modelling, Warsaw, Poland
[3] SGH Warsaw School of Economics, Warsaw, Poland
[4] Carolina Medical Center, Warsaw, Poland
[5] Warsaw University of Technology, Warsaw, Poland
[6] Tooploox, Wrocław, Poland

Abstract. Achilles tendon rupture is a debilitating injury, which is typically treated with surgical repair and long-term rehabilitation. The recovery, however, is protracted and often incomplete. Diagnosis, as well as healing progress assessment, are largely based on ultrasound and magnetic resonance imaging. In this paper, we propose an automatic method based on deep learning for analysis of Achilles tendon condition and estimation of its healing progress on ultrasound images. We develop custom convolutional neural networks for classification and regression on healing score and feature extraction. Our models are trained and validated on an acquired dataset of over 250.000 sagittal and over 450.000 axial ultrasound slices. The obtained estimates show high correlation with the assessment of expert radiologists, with respect to all key parameters describing healing progress. We also observe that parameters associated with i.a. intratendinous healing processes are better modeled with sagittal slices. We prove that ultrasound imaging is quantitatively useful for clinical assessment of Achilles tendon healing process and should be viewed as complementary to magnetic resonance imaging.

Keywords: Achilles tendon rupture · Deep learning · Ultrasound

1 Introduction

The Achilles tendon is the largest and strongest tendon in the human body. However, it is one of the most frequently injured tendons, especially among middle-aged people who participate in recreational sports. The incidence of Achilles tendon ruptures has been increasing over the last years [1]. Usually, the diagnosis of an acute rupture is based on detailed musculoskeletal examinations and

© Springer Nature Switzerland AG 2019
Q. Wang et al. (Eds.): PIPPI 2019/SUSI 2019, LNCS 11798, pp. 65–73, 2019.
https://doi.org/10.1007/978-3-030-32875-7_8

comprehensive medical history. Ultrasonography (US) and Magnetic Resonance Imaging (MRI) are routinely used for confirming the clinical diagnosis.

The surgical treatment of acute Achilles tendon rupture has been shown to reduce the risk of re-rupture, but it might also lead to a higher complication rate [1]. Furthermore, recent studies show that early functional rehabilitation could also stimulate tendon healing. For the above reasons, regular evaluation of the early tendon healing process is needed to establish patient prognosis and plan further treatment. The US findings correlate with several healing parameters, including cross-sectional area, tendon length or intratendinous morphology and are considered a safe and convenient method of assessing the healing progress [2]. However, some studies have found only a moderate correlation of US findings with clinical assessment of Achilles tendinopathy and clinical outcomes [3].

Quantitative methods based on deep learning are well-suited for modelling the complex relationships between medical images and their interpretation. Recently, approaches using convolutional neural networks (CNNs) have outperformed traditional image analysis methods and proved their usefulness in the analysis of the Achilles tendon MRI scans [4].

In this study, we present a method for the automatic evaluation of the healing process of reconstructed Achilles tendon based on CNNs. We extend the approach proposed in [4] to US images in the axial and the sagittal plane and develop a novel method for healing phase estimation. To our knowledge, there are no other approaches in the literature to quantitatively asses the process of tendon healing through automated analyses of MRI and US imaging. Within this paper we also show that the method applied to MRI cannot by directly transferred to US data, which might result from problematic interpretation of the US images.

More precisely, we first train and evaluate neural networks for the task of binary classification of a single ultrasound slice as healthy or injured. We then present our approaches to modelling the healing progress with respect to 6 key healing parameters. We analyse the applicability of the method using outputs of a pre-trained network with a linear classifier on the PCA-reduced space of the features to assess the progress with the US data. We find that this method fails to learn the accurate representation of the healing phase, therefore we propose an end-to-end CNN performing regression on healing parameters as a new, alternative approach. We further discuss the meaningfulness of the results for US and compare them with MRI results, to finally determine the clinical usefulness of used modalities and applicability of automatic methods for healing assessment.

2   Methods

In this section we describe our method based on the Convolutional Neural Networks. CNNs are discriminative deep architectures, able to extract high-level spatial and configuration information from an image, thus making them suitable for classification of 2D US imaging.

We use models with weights pretrained on ImageNet and train them to explicitly model radiologist assessments. To this end, we modify the architecture of the top dense layer of the CNN in such a way that the output layer performs linear regression on the high-level features from the penultimate layer. For initial tests we use three models of various complexity to eventually select Inception-v3 [5] architecture as a base for our final solution. These experiments are described as the supervised approach. We then exploit the latent representation and reduce the dimensionality, which makes it possible to obtain a single-number summary of the tendon condition on one US examination. We refer to it as semi-supervised approach. In general, our approach leverages the ability of neural networks to approximate non-linear mappings directly and implicitly accounts for the intermediate feature representations. It maps the images to the tendon healing scores for the different protocols and clinical parameters. We train separate models for both US planes and for all of the ground-truth parameters described in the next subsection.

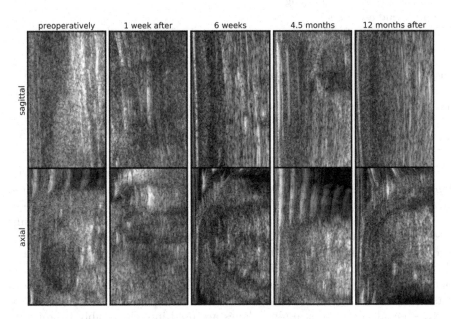

Fig. 1. Achilles healing process for a chosen patient on US imaging. On the sagittal images one can observe the gradual recovery of the fibrillary pattern of tendon fibres with hyperechoic bands. In the axial plane the typical change is the widening of the Achilles tendon and the loss of the hypoechoic fluid collection surrounding the tendon. The images also exemplify certain artifacts typical for ultrasound, including reverberation, refraction and acoustic shadowing.

2.1   Healing Progress Scoring

Our ground-truth is a survey that has been devised by expert radiologists, in order to quantitatively characterize their subjective assessment of Achilles tendon healing progress based on MRI and US. The survey evaluates the anatomy,

Table 1. Five-fold cross-validation results for the balanced dataset of 2D US scans.

Architecture	Sagittal			Axial		
	Accuracy	Precision	Recall	Accuracy	Precision	Recall
AlexNet	0.846 ± 00.087	0.92 ± 00.08	0.78 ± 00.11	0.843 ± 00.075	0.93 ± 00.06	0.73 ± 00.11
Inception-v3	**0.916** ± 00.049	0.97 ± 00.04	0.90 ± 00.06	0.901 ± 00.052	0.95 ± 00.3	0.87 ± 00.07
ResNet50	0.907 ± 00.039	0.96 ± 00.05	0.89 ± 00.08	**0.912** ± 00.046	0.95 ± 00.04	0.88 ± 00.06

metabolic activity and general functionality of the tendon. The following 6 parameters describing the tendon healing process were proposed [4]:

1. Structural changes within the tendon (SCT)
2. Tendon thickening (TT)
3. Sharpness of the tendon edges (STE)
4. Tendon edema (TE)
5. Tendon uniformity (TU)
6. Tissue edema (TisE)

Each parameter is evaluated on a 7-point scale, where 1 corresponds to healthy and 7 to severely injured tendon. We use the scores as ground-truth labels in the training process. Our image dataset is presented in the next subsection.

2.2   Dataset

The original ultrasound dataset includes 49 patients with acute Achilles tendon rupture, all of whom underwent repair surgery and were closely monitored thereafter. The age of patients ranged from 18 to 50 years with a mean age of 36 years. The ultrasound examination was performed at 10 respective intervals: preoperatively, 1 week, 3, 6, 9, 12 weeks after, 4.5, 6, 9 and 12 months after the reconstruction. Additionally, 18 healthy volunteers have been scanned once. For all the examinations a GE 3D high-resolution Voluson E8 Expert ultrasound machine has been used with linear probes 5–18 MHz. The total dataset consists of 565 3D US exams but in this work, we focus on 2D scans only. Clinically, sagittal and axial scanning planes are used interchangeably by rotating the transducer, so we conduct the experiments separately for both. Considering the 2D slices, the final dataset includes 253,639 sagittal scans, 245,366 from patients with ruptured tendon and 8,273 from healthy patients. Alternatively, it consists of 467,548 axial scans, 450,816 injured and 16,732 healthy. The healing progression for an exemplary patient is shown in Fig. 1.

Though a detailed analysis can be done only by a trained medical professional, one can observe that the filamentous structures are more visible on the sagittal cross-sections while axial slices present in more details the tissue surrounding, edema and internal tendon pattern.

3   Experiments

3.1   Binary Classification

We train three network architectures: AlexNet [6], Inception-v3 and ResNet50 [7] independently on sagittal and axial slices for the task of binary classification of the tendon on a 2D US scan as healthy or injured. The injured class is represented by all the exams of ruptured Achilles tendon performed preoperatively or 1 week after surgery. In order to balance the two classes we use mirroring on the healthy slices and we subsample injured patients for every training epoch.

The accuracy is assessed in 5-fold cross-validation (Table 1). ROC and Precision-Recall Curves of the best performing model in terms of highest accuracy (Inception-v3 on sagittal slices) are presented in Fig. 2. For both Inception-v3 and ResNet50 we obtained an accuracy of over 90% on both sagittal and axial scans, which proves that a CNN can be successfully trained on ultrasound data to differentiate between healthy and injured state.

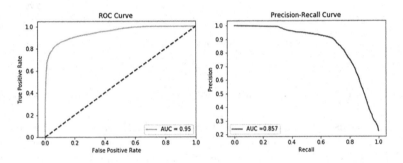

Fig. 2. ROC and Precision-Recall curves for the Inception-v3 on sagittal US images.

We also experiment with the region of interest (ROI) segmentation as a preprocessing step for sagittal scans, applying *Active Contours Without Edges* [8], which is widely used in the medical field. We hypothesize that focusing exclusively on the tendon region might reduce the noise and artifacts inherently present in US imaging. However, the experiments show lower accuracy with ROI segmentation cropping as compared to non-cropped images, which suggests that the tissues surrounding the Achilles tendon contribute relevant information to the classification.

3.2   Healing Progress Estimation

Semi-supervised Approach. The neural networks trained for binary classification are used as feature extractors for the task of computing the healing progress score. Principal Component Analysis (PCA) is applied on the feature space to reduce its dimensionality and the first principal component is considered as a representative score for the 2D US scan. For every examination, the

Table 2. 5CV results for the tendon healing progress using end-to-end approach

Network		Sagittal					
		SCT	TT	STE	TE	TU	TisE
AlexNet	**MAE**	0.96 ± 0.41	0.80 ± 0.27	0.82 ± 0.29	0.95 ± 0.41	0.87 ± 0.39	1.08 ± 0.47
	MAX-AE	1.75	1.32	1.87	1.35	1.61	2.03
	Corr	0.53 ± 0.47	0.69 ± 0.38	0.11 ± 0.32	0.68 ± 0.44	0.31 ± 0.51	0.22 ± 0.53
Inception-v3	**MAE**	**0.88 ± 0.35**	**0.67 ± 0.23**	**0.80 ± 0.31**	**0.82 ± 0.23**	**0.84 ± 0.32**	**0.93 ± 0.29**
	MAX-AE	1.69	1.32	1.69	1.31	1.58	1.64
	Corr	0.83 ± 0.44	0.71 ± 0.40	0.19 ± 0.34	0.64 ± 0.47	0.56 ± 0.40	0.71 ± 0.40
ResNet50	**MAE**	**0.89 ± 0.12**	**0.74 ± 0.15**	**0.83 ± 0.22**	0.81 ± 0.31	**0.92 ± 0.31**	**0.99 ± 0.32**
	MAX-AE	1.53	1.22	1.64	1.43	1.67	1.71
	Corr	0.62 ± 0.31	0.38 ± 0.51	0.23 ± 0.41	0.62 ± 0.51	0.12 ± 0.43	0.43 ± 0.50
		Axial					
		SCT	TT	STE	TE	TU	TisE
AlexNet	**MAE**	0.98 ± 0.39	0.83 ± 0.33	0.82 ± 0.35	0.94 ± 0.52	0.95 ± 0.50	0.86 ± 0.28
	MAX-AE	1.79	1.36	1.86	1.41	1.61	1.59
	Corr	0.45 ± 0.33	0.62 ± 0.39	0.20 ± 0.45	0.60 ± 0.47	0.03 ± 0.42	0.59 ± 0.40
Inception-v3	**MAE**	**1.03 ± 0.46**	**0.70 ± 0.24**	**0.76 ± 0.26**	**0.86 ± 0.19**	**0.87 ± 0.32**	**0.85 ± 0.25**
	MAX-AE	2.52	1.45	1.45	1.24	1.67	1.56
	Corr	0.77 ± 0.47	0.69 ± 0.40	0.22 ± 0.37	0.65 ± 0.41	0.55 ± 0.44	0.72 ± 0.41
ResNet50	**MAE**	**1.05 ± 0.31**	**0.78 ± 0.33**	**0.80 ± 0.24**	**1.02 ± 0.25**	**0.87 ± 0.15**	**0.91 ± 0.28**
	MAX-AE	1.98	1.51	1.59	1.63	1.45	1.57
	Corr	0.52 ± 0.41	0.47 ± 0.44	0.22 ± 0.35	0.65 ± 0.55	0.18 ± 0.54	0.57 ± 0.39

aggregate score is calculated as a truncated mean of all 2D scan scores within a single study.

Although this method was proven to work for MRI scans [4], for ultrasound we observed a very weak correlation with actual healing parameters, which should be attributed to lower variance preserved by the first principal components and higher variance between scans from one examination. Therefore we do not present the results here. We believe that speckle noise, a random granular pattern produced mainly by multiplicative disturbances, as well as frequent artifacts are the main reasons for the weak performance of the tested method.

Supervised Approach. Healing scores are evaluated in 5-fold cross-validation using mean absolute error (MAE), maximal absolute error for a single exam (MAX-AE) and mean correlation, computed with the use of Fisher Z-Transformation (Table 2).

We observe a good correspondence between the estimated healing scores and the experts' assessment, with MAE ranging from 0.67 to 1.08, on a 7 point scale. For all the networks we notice a positive mean correlation of our method's output and healing parameters. Although the results are consistent between different networks, Inception-v3 usually achieves the best fit and the simplest network architecture, AlexNet, performs noticeably worse. Two healing parameters, SCT and TT are more accurately estimated on sagittal rather than axial US images and one parameter, TisE, vice versa.

The final evaluation of the regression task has been done on a separate test set, consisting of 4 injured patients who underwent a full rehabilitation process, i.e. 40 studies in total (Table 3). For the best performing Inception-v3, we report MAE ranging from 0.53 to 0.87 and correlations in the range of 0.31 to 0.80. The resulting healing progress for a selected parameter is compared with radiologist evaluation in Fig. 3. In general, axial and sagittal models give similar results, which tend to correlate well with ground-truth labels.

4 Discussion

We show that a neural network learns to extract features from the US images which strongly correlate with the healing progress score assigned by expert radiologists. Out of the three healing parameters: tendon uniformity (TU), structural changes (SCT) and tendon thickening (TT), which correspond to morphological changes within the Achilles tendon and are typically evaluated in the longitudinal axis, SCT and TT are better modeled by the sagittal ultrasound, while TU still retains MAE of <1 point. On the other hand, sharpness of the tendon edges (STE), tendon edema (TE) and tissue edema (TisE) are typically evaluated on axial slices and for STE and TisE, all our networks achieve lower MAE and higher mean correlation when trained in the axial plane.

In comparison with the results from [4], we notice that a convolutional neural network is able to achieve a better accuracy of binary classification on MRI data rather than US data (99.83% vs. 91.6% for the best respective models). Furthermore, a high correlation of automated method output with the ground truth in terms of three parameters: TE, TisE and STE has been reported for MRI scans. MR-acquired stacks of axial images of the Achilles tendon have a major limitation in the form of lower spatial resolution along the longitudinal

Table 3. Results for the tendon healing progress using end-to-end approach on the test dataset

Network		Sagittal					
		SCT	TT	STE	TE	TU	TisE
AlexNet	MAE	0.90 ± 0.31	0.63 ± 0.12	0.69 ± 0.31	0.81 ± 0.11	0.89 ± 0.20	1.01 ± 0.35
	Corr	0.55 ± 0.15	0.70 ± 0.24	0.22 ± 0.49	0.61 ± 0.28	0.12 ± 0.43	0.28 ± 0.27
Inception-v3	MAE	**0.81 ± 0.38**	**0.63 ± 0.06**	**0.56 ± 0.18**	**0.85 ± 0.20**	**0.54 ± 0.04**	**0.87 ± 0.29**
	Corr	0.80 ± 0.39	0.77 ± 0.28	0.31 ± 0.33	0.52 ± 0.36	0.69 ± 0.34	0.62 ± 0.52
ResNet50	MAE	**0.88 ± 0.33**	**0.65 ± 0.15**	**0.66 ± 0.09**	**0.83 ± 0.25**	**0.75 ± 0.12**	**0.93 ± 0.22**
	Corr	0.60 ± 0.32	0.55 ± 0.38	0.25 ± 0.27	0.55 ± 0.41	0.34 ± 0.29	0.56 ± 0.38
		Axial					
		SCT	TT	STE	TE	TU	TisE
AlexNet	MAE	1.12 ± 0.36	0.81 ± 0.29	0.58 ± 0.12	0.87 ± 0.19	0.70 ± 0.24	0.85 ± 0.25
	Corr	0.46 ± 0.50	0.54 ± 0.32	0.26 ± 0.41	0.38 ± 0.38	0.12 ± 0.34	0.70 ± 0.31
Inception-v3	MAE	**0.84 ± 0.54**	**0.75 ± 1.45**	**0.58 ± 0.10**	**0.83 ± 0.10**	**0.53 ± 0.16**	**0.83 ± 0.30**
	Corr	0.69 ± 0.49	0.68 ± 0.41	0.45 ± 0.15	0.51 ± 0.42	0.66 ± 0.16	0.68 ± 0.39
ResNet50	MAE	**0.92 ± 0.37**	**0.76 ± 0.32**	**0.68 ± 0.08**	**0.81 ± 0.17**	**0.65 ± 0.20**	**0.94 ± 0.11**
	Corr	0.55 ± 0.41	0.57 ± 0.38	0.35 ± 0.31	0.44 ± 0.39	0.39 ± 0.35	0.61 ± 0.33

axis, which is determined by the slice selection pulse. Because of this spatial anisotropy, they are not suitable for assessing healing parameters, which rely on the intratendinous processes or the alignment of fibrous bands.

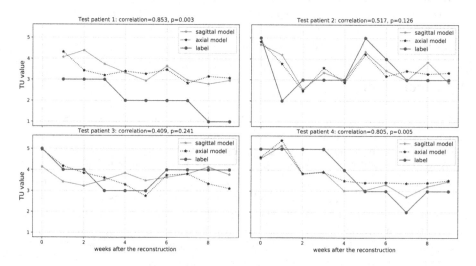

Fig. 3. Inception-v3 results for the TU parameter on test dataset (correlations refer to sagittal scans).

The results suggest that features extracted by deep learning models from MR and US imaging focus on different qualities of the rehabilitation process. This indicates that ultrasound should be viewed as an imaging method that complements MRI rather than one that competes with MRI in the evaluation of musculoskeletal abnormalities. It should be noted, however, that the previous work on MRI was validated on a smaller dataset and did not apply the supervised end-to-end approach, which limits us to an indirect qualitative comparison.

5   Conclusions

In this paper, we proposed deep learning models that achieve high performance in clinical classification and healing phase estimation of ruptured Achilles tendon. We have compared two approaches to modelling tendon rehabilitation progress and shown that the supervised method is superior to the semi-supervised method. Currently, monitoring the healing process requires a radiologist to analyze US and MRI data and subjectively evaluate the condition of the tendon.

As suggested in [2], tendon morphology may be the more robust measure to gauge patient healing progress over time compared to mechanical properties of the tendon. Therefore, we believe that a model which accurately estimates healing parameters from standardized images may be useful in clinical practice.

Future studies are needed to improve the generalizability of deep learning models for medical imaging in musculoskeletal disorders and to determine the effect of model assistance in the clinical setting.

References

1. Zhou, K., Song, L., Zhang, P., Wang, C., Wang, W.: Surgical versus non-surgical methods for acute achilles tendon rupture: a meta-analysis of randomized controlled trials. J. Foot Ankle Surg. **57**(6), 1191–1199 (2018)
2. Hiramatsu, K., Tsujii, A., Nakamura, N., Mitsuoka, T.: Ultrasonographic evaluation of the early healing process after achilles tendon repair. Orthop. J. Sports Med. **6**, 2325967118789883 (2018)
3. Khan, K.M., et al.: Are ultrasound and magnetic resonance imaging of value in assessment of achilles tendon disorders? A two year prospective study. Br. J. Sports Med. **37**(2), 149–153 (2003)
4. Kapinski, N., Zielinski, J., Borucki, B.A., Trzcinski, T., Ciszkowska-Lyson, B., Nowinski, K.S.: Estimating achilles tendon healing progress with convolutional neural networks. In: Frangi, A.F., Schnabel, J.A., Davatzikos, C., Alberola-López, C., Fichtinger, G. (eds.) MICCAI 2018. LNCS, vol. 11071, pp. 949–957. Springer, Cham (2018). https://doi.org/10.1007/978-3-030-00934-2_105
5. Szegedy, C., Vanhoucke, V., Ioffe, S., Shlens, J., Wojna, Z.: Rethinking the inception architecture for computer vision. CoRR, vol. abs/1512.00567 (2015)
6. Krizhevsky, A., Sutskever, I., Hinton, G.E.: ImageNet classification with deep convolutional neural networks. In: Pereira, F., Burges, C.J.C., Bottou, L., Weinberger, K.Q. (eds.) Advances in Neural Information Processing Systems, vol. 25, pp. 1097–1105. Curran Associates Inc. (2012)
7. He, K., Zhang, X., Ren, S., Sun, J.: Deep residual learning for image recognition. CoRR, vol. abs/1512.03385 (2015)
8. Chan, T.F., Vese, L.A.: Active contours without edges. Trans. Image Process. **10**, 266–277 (2001)

Deep Learning-Based Pneumothorax Detection in Ultrasound Videos

Courosh Mehanian[1,2(✉)], Sourabh Kulhare[1,2], Rachel Millin[1,2],
Xinliang Zheng[1,2], Cynthia Gregory[3], Meihua Zhu[3], Hua Xie[3],
James Jones[3], Jack Lazar[3], Amber Halse[3], Todd Graham[3],
Mike Stone[3,4], Kenton Gregory[1], and Ben Wilson[1,2]

[1] Inventive Government Solutions, LLC, Bellevue, WA 98005, USA
cmehanian@intven.com
[2] Intellectual Ventures Laboratory, Bellevue, WA 98007, USA
[3] Oregon Health Sciences University, Portland, OR 97239, USA
[4] Legacy Emanuel Hospital, Portland, OR 97227, USA

Abstract. Pneumothorax (PTX) is a medical and surgical emergency that can lead to hemodynamic instability and life-threatening collapse of the lung. PTX is usually detected using chest X-ray but can be detected using lung ultrasound, which requires interpretation by an expert radiologist. We are developing an AI based algorithm for the automated interpretation of lung ultrasound video to enable fast diagnosis of pneumothorax at the point of care by health care providers without extensive training in ultrasound. In this work, we developed and compared several deep learning methods for identifying pneumothoraces in 3-s ultrasound videos collected with a handheld ultrasound system. The first group of methods were based on convolutional neural networks (CNNs) paired with time-mapping preprocessing algorithms, including reconstructed M-mode and the proposed simplified optical flow transform (SOFT). These preprocessing methods were either used alone or in combination in a single "fusion" CNN. The second class of algorithm used a Deep Learning architecture that combines a CNN for processing spatial information (Inception V3) with a recurrent network (long-short-term-memory, or LSTM) for temporal analysis, enabling raw video to be fed directly into the neural network without preprocessing. We used data from a swine pneumothorax model to train and test the proposed algorithms, comparing their performance. Despite limited data, all algorithms achieved an AUC for pneumothorax detection greater than 0.83.

Keywords: Deep Learning · Pneumothorax · Lung ultrasound

1 Introduction

Pneumothorax, or collapsed lung, is a problem seen in trauma patients, as well as those with acute and chronic medical conditions. Undetected, pneumothorax can have disastrous consequences for high-risk patients. Chest X-ray (CXR) is the primary imaging modality used to screen for pneumothorax. Despite high specificity, CXR sensitivity for detection of pneumothorax is estimated at only 28–75% for blunt trauma [1]. Computed tomography (CT) is the current gold standard for diagnosis, but it has major

© Springer Nature Switzerland AG 2019
Q. Wang et al. (Eds.): PIPPI 2019/SUSI 2019, LNCS 11798, pp. 74–82, 2019.
https://doi.org/10.1007/978-3-030-32875-7_9

drawbacks including delay due to limited availability, high radiation dose, and high cost. Lung ultrasound (LUS) is an alternative imaging modality for the detection of pneumothorax, with a reported sensitivity of 95–100% and specificity of 91–100% depending on patient population and LUS features considered [1, 2]. One sonographic feature that can be used to detect pneumothorax is lack of lung sliding. In B-mode, lack of lung sliding appears as the absence of relative motion between the parietal and visceral pleura, which is normally visible in a healthy lung during respiration. In M-mode, a single 'barcode' pattern can be observed when there is lack of lung sliding [3], as shown in Fig. 1 below. The difficulty of image interpretation limits the adoption of LUS for point-of-care pneumothorax diagnosis.

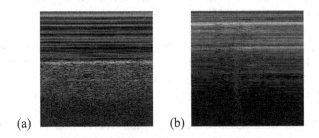

(a)   (b)

Fig. 1. Example M-mode images of (a) normal sliding and (b) absence of lung sliding.

In situations where trained radiologists are unavailable, automated ultrasound interpretation is an appealing alternative. Machine learning, part of the broad field of artificial intelligence, has made substantial progress in automated medical ultrasound imaging. Applications include classification, regression, and tissue segmentation on organs such as breast, heart, thyroid, liver, and fetus [4, 5]. However, there have been very few studies applying machine learning to pulmonary ultrasound, especially pneumothorax. One group has used deep learning for detecting pneumothorax based on B-mode image frames and M-mode images [6] and reports 99.8% and 98.3% accuracy respectively. We believe both of these results to be spurious for two reasons. First, the authors fail to enforce strict separation at the patient level between training and testing groups. Second, they elide the question of how individual B-mode frames were used to detect pneumothorax, a quintessentially temporal phenomenon.

To show the effectiveness of deep learning-based computer vision algorithms for the detection of pneumothorax, the current work leverages a swine model and ultrasound videos acquired with a handheld ultrasound system. We use video-based methods to extract the temporal information in B-mode videos to detect pneumothorax. Using a strict separation of animals into training or testing groups, we also compare performance between several deep learning architectures.

The main contribution of this work is the introduction of a novel, fast method of computing optical flow (SOFT), which is a useful pre-processing step for the detection of pneumothorax in B-mode ultrasound video. We have demonstrated this application using several deep learning methods, permitting near real-time diagnosis of pneumothorax with a low-cost, hand-held, radiation-safe, and user-friendly ultrasound device.

2   Approach

2.1   Animal Model, Data Collection and Annotation

All animal studies and ultrasound data were collected at Oregon Health & Sciences University, following approval by its Institutional Animal Care and Use Committee (IACUC) and the US Army Medical Research and Development Command's Animal Care Use Review Office. A swine model was developed to generate desired lung pathologies and ultrasound lung features were captured for both normal and abnormal lung. For pneumothorax, a total of four swine were used. A percutaneous thoracic puncture was performed on one side of the chest with a 6 Fr sheath insertion under ultrasound guidance. A total of 100 to 750 cc of air was injected in 100 to 150 cc increments to induce different degrees of pneumothorax. The lung was then vented using a one-way valve to expel the air at a rate of 250 ml each time to resolve the pneumothorax.

Ultrasound data were acquired using a Lumify curvilinear (C5-2, Philips, WA, USA) handheld system, with its default lung preset. According to the guideline of point-of-care LUS [7], the swine chest area was divided into 4 zones on each side, including upper anterior, lower anterior, upper lateral and basal lateral chest areas. The parasternal, anterior axillary, and posterior axillary lines were used as anatomical landmarks. For each zone, at least two 3-s B-mode videos were collected at a frame rate of 20 per second. Ultrasound videos were collected from each animal before insertion and following the injection of each increment of air, and the aspiration of the pneumothorax, for a total of 10 collection sessions per animal. Each video clip was then reviewed by a LUS expert and marked as either exhibiting lung sliding or absence of lung sliding, the latter being considered a positive pneumothorax diagnosis.

2.2   Algorithm Architectures

Reconstructed M-mode. Lung sliding was detected in each video using reconstructed M-mode images—the trace of an azimuthal line in the video over time (with dimensions of radial depth by frame count)—as described in [8]. (Direct M-mode from the device is not used here because our goal is to detect pneumothorax purely from B-mode video without the need for an additional data collection step.) Prior to M-mode image reconstruction, a single shot detector (SSD) [9] was used to determine a bounding box for the pleural line (PL), if present, in each intercostal space [8]. For each detected PL, the vertical location of the PL was identified as the position where the horizontal sum within the bounding box was maximum. The region of each video frame from 5 pixels above to 95 pixels below the PL was cropped and transformed from polar to cartesian coordinates. Azimuthal traces were extracted from the resulting cropped videos to obtain reconstructed M-mode images (Fig. 2a). M-mode images were reconstructed from 11 evenly-spaced columns centered about the middle of the PL bounding box in videos used for algorithm training. To minimize computation, only 5 such images are reconstructed for each intercostal space during inference. A custom convolutional neural network (CNN), depicted in Fig. 2c, top row, was trained on the reconstructed M-mode images. The trained system was then used for prediction: reconstructed M-mode images in the test set were classified as "sliding" or "no sliding". An intercostal space is designated as "no sliding" if at least 3 out of 5 M-lines are classified as "no sliding"; a video is classified as "no sliding" if any intercostal space is classified as "no sliding", and "sliding" otherwise.

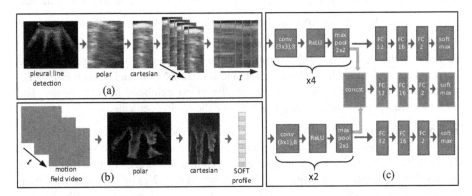

Fig. 2. (a) Preprocessing for reconstructed M-mode from B-mode video. (b) Preprocessing for SOFT from the same B-mode video. (c) Deep learning architectures for M-mode (top row) and SOFT (bottom row), and fusion architecture (middle row, green data path). (Color figure online)

Simplified Optical Flow Transform (SOFT). Notwithstanding the common use of M-mode to diagnose pneumothorax, many clinicians discern lung sliding, or lack thereof, directly from B-mode video, where lung sliding appears as shimmering of, and periodic lateral motion below, the pleural line. The use of optical flow to detect motion in video is commonplace [10]. Optical flow algorithms compute image gradients in x, y, t and solve the motion equation:

$$dI/dt = \nabla_t I + \nabla_x I (dx/dt) + \nabla_y I (dy/dt) = 0 \qquad (1)$$

for the underlying motion images, dx/dt and dy/dt. Here, I is ultrasound intensity. The solution must be obtained iteratively as no closed form general solutions are possible [10]. This renders the computation too slow for a real-time diagnostic device. The equation of motion can be simplified, however, by noting that movement induced by lung sliding is primarily lateral, *i.e.*, along x. With the assumption that $dy/dt = 0$ the motion equation admits a closed form solution:

$$dx/dt = -\nabla_t I / \nabla_x I \qquad (2)$$

We use this equation to compute dx/dt between every pair of consecutive frames; dx/dt is an x-motion field video that has one fewer frame than the original video.

The x-motion field video indicates the x-velocity of the lung motion as a function of position and time. Because of the periodic nature of lung sliding, it will have both positive and negative values. A measure of the amount of the lateral movement in the video is the absolute value of the x-motion field, which would indicate the speed of the lung motion vs. position and time. The absolute value of the x-motion field video may be summed across frames to obtain the time-integrated motion image: $\overleftrightarrow{\Delta x} = \sum |dx/dt|$, where the sum is taken over frames. The appearance of the time-integrated motion image $\overleftrightarrow{\Delta x}$ depends on video content, but it may be summed horizontally to compute a vertical x-motion profile, $v_x(y) = \sum \overleftrightarrow{\Delta x}$, where the sum is taken over image columns. We refer to the vertical x-motion profile as the SOFT profile. SOFT profiles were computed for each video in the training set, and a small CNN model, shown in Fig. 2c, bottom row, was trained based on whether the video exhibited sliding or not. The resulting model was tested on SOFT profiles of the testing set videos.

Fusion Architecture. We previously described a method that uses reconstructed M-mode images to detect lack of lung sliding, as well as a method involving the use of SOFT profiles. The two methods may be combined in a fusion architecture that has two separate input streams and a single output as shown in Fig. 2(c) by the green data path. The top stream ingests a reconstructed M-mode image and computes CNN features (using the convolutional layers of the top row of Fig. 2c), and the bottom stream receives the SOFT profile from the corresponding video and computes CNN features (using the convolutional layers of the bottom row of Fig. 2c). The two streams are concatenated and processed by two fully connected layers before being classified by the fully connected + softmax layer at the output (middle row). This network may be trained end-to-end using back propagation and stochastic gradient descent.

Long-Short-Term-Memory (LSTM). We utilized LSTM [11]—a type of recurrent neural network (RNN) that looks for temporal patterns in sequential data—to detect lateral movement around the pleural line. Unlike feed-forward neural networks, RNNs accept past variable states as temporal feedback—allowing information to flow in time—thus making them capable of learning long-term dependencies [12].

In this work, we first extracted Inception V3 [13] features from each frame and fed the feature vectors to the LSTM layers sequentially. We chose to use spatial feature extraction followed by LSTM rather than spatiotemporal convolutions (3D CNN) because the latter typically requires more data for end-to-end training. We used two LSTM layers with 2048 units/layer. After processing all the video frames, the last LSTM layer generated a 2048-dimensional spatiotemporal LSTM feature vector. The LSTM feature vector was further processed through two fully connected layers before applying the softmax activation function. The architectural diagram is shown in Fig. 3. Since we had a limited training dataset, we held the Inception weights fixed (at their ImageNet trained values) and learned only the LSTM weights and the subsequent fully connected layer weights. Video frames were resized to 300×300. The length of the input sequence was fixed to 60 frames in order to include a significant portion of a breath cycle. We used dropout (rate = 0.7), data augmentation (described in Sect. 2.3 below) and narrow dense layers to control overfitting on limited training data. The number of LSTM units had the most influence on overall performance, achieving optimal results with 2048 units.

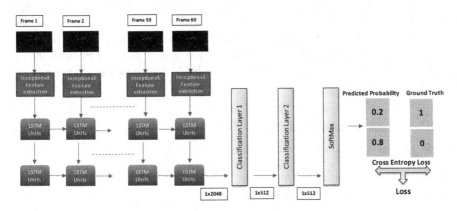

Fig. 3. LSTM architecture.

2.3   Training and Hyperparameters

For all methods, training and testing were performed in a cross-validated fashion over 4 folds, each with training data from 3 animals and the 4th reserved for testing. Approximately 20% of training data was assigned to a validation set to determine hyperparameters and assess model generalization. Prior to further processing, the following types of data augmentation were performed: horizontal and vertical shift, temporal scale, contrast increase/decrease, Gaussian blur, and random pixel value decrement.

For the LSTM, categorical cross entropy loss was minimized using the Adam optimizer [9], with batch size of 3 videos/iteration. For the remaining methods, cross-entropy loss was minimized over 2000 epochs using gradient descent with a batch size of 64, learning rate of 0.0004 and momentum 0.9. Batch normalization was employed prior to each non-linearity to accelerate training, and dropout was used to control overfitting. This process required 3–4 h on a NVIDIA DGX system. Weights at the iteration corresponding to minimum validation loss were selected for the final model.

3   Results

We compare the performance of four methods for identifying absence of lung sliding in swine pulmonary ultrasound videos: reconstructed M-mode, SOFT, fusion, and LSTM, which are described in Sect. 2. M-mode and fusion algorithms are only applied when a pleural line is detected; the M-mode detection algorithm achieves 95% sensitivity on pleural line detection using the method described in [8]. The results for all methods are reported only for videos with detectable pleural lines to simplify the comparison between the methods. The absence of intercostal space in a video was treated as a pleural line negative sample. The performance of each algorithm was assessed using 4-fold cross-validation, with data from 3 of the 4 animals used for training and validation, and videos from the remaining animal used for testing in each fold. This resulted in testing a total of 130 positive videos with absence of lung sliding caused by pneumothorax and 122 negative videos with normal lung sliding. Table 1 shows the final test results, averaged over cross-validation folds, for all 4 methods. We also compared the test performance of the 4 approaches via ROC curves, which are shown in Fig. 4. The inference time is also reported in Table 1. Models were run on a PC with Intel i7 6600U quad-core processor @ 2.6 GHz, 16 GB RAM with no GPU processor.

Table 1. Testing results.

Method	Sensitivity^	Specificity^	Mean AUC	Inference time (ms)
M-mode	78 ± 12%	85 ± 2%	0.837	230*
SOFT	83 ± 2%	82 ± 8%	0.863	1200
Fusion	82 ± 6%	87 ± 9%	0.872	1400*
LSTM	84 ± 4%	82 ± 9%	0.876	5300

^ mean ±standard deviation over 4 folds, using operating point that maximizes harmonic mean of sensitivity and specificity for each method and fold

*does not include time for pleural line detection

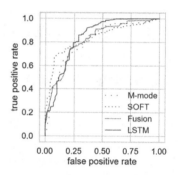

Fig. 4. ROC for test data

To partly compensate for the small number of animals, we used leave-one-animal-out cross-validation, so that data from all 4 animals could be used to assess performance. Furthermore, the dataset contains diversity because videos collected from the same animal have variation due to (1) differences in anatomy between zones, (2) small shifts in acquisition location within a zone, and (3) differences between collection sessions (air was injected in the same animal at multiple times to induce pneumothorax). Despite the small dataset, all models learned informative representations of the data, all achieving AUCs greater than 0.83 on unseen data. While all models performed similarly with the data available, this result may be impacted by data scarcity; models with a larger number of parameters (Fusion and LSTM) might especially benefit from increased training data.

4 Conclusions and Future Work

LUS is a promising diagnosis modality for pneumothorax because of its portability and use of non-ionizing sound waves. Widespread adoption of LUS is limited, however, by the difficulty of interpreting LUS images (due to lack of anatomical clues), shortage of personnel with adequate training, and inter- and intra- operator variability. We have shown that machine learning, and particularly deep learning, can be used to automate detection of absence of lung sliding from ultrasound B-mode video. Computer-assisted LUS video analysis, as demonstrated here, when coupled with a hand-held ultrasound device, can bring improved diagnosis capability to remote and resource-limited healthcare settings. In the future, we plan to address how pneumothorax can be differentiated from other causes of the absence of lung sliding algorithmically [17]. We will also use clinical patient data to train, assess, and improve the algorithms described here. This will help validate the efficacy of these methods in humans while providing sufficient patient diversity and data quantity to assess patient-level diagnostic accuracy.

Acknowledgments. The project is supported by Agreement # HR0011-17-3-001 between the Defense Advanced Research Project Agency and Inventive Government Solutions, LLC (IGS). Use, duplication, or disclosure is subject to the restrictions of the agreement. This project does not necessarily reflect the position or policy of the government. No official endorsement should be inferred. This work was also supported by the Global Good Fund I, LLC through IGS.

Conflict of Interest. Drs. Kenton Gregory and Cynthia Gregory have a Significant Financial Interest in Intellectual Ventures Laboratory, a company that may have commercial interest in the results of this research and technology. This potential conflict of interest has been reviewed and managed by OHSU.

References

1. Wilkerson, R.G., Stone, M.B.: Sensitivity of bedside ultrasound and supine anteroposterior chest radiographs for the identification of pneumothorax after blunt trauma. Acad. Emerg. Med. **17**(1), 11–17 (2010)
2. Lichtenstein, D.A.: Lung ultrasound in the critically ill. Ann. Intensive Care **4**(1), 1–12 (2014)
3. Stone, M.B.: Ultrasound diagnosis of traumatic pneumothorax. Pictorial CME **1**(1), 19–20 (2008)
4. Brattain, L., Telfer, B., Dhyani, M., Grajo, J., Samir, A.: Machine learning for medical ultrasound: status, methods, and future opportunities. Abdom. Radiol. **43**(4), 786–799 (2018)
5. Liu, S.F., et al.: Deep learning in medical ultrasound analysis: a review. Engineering **5**(2), 261–275 (2019)
6. Lindsey, T., Lee, R., Grisell, R., Vega, S., Veazey, S.: Automated pneumothorax diagnosis using deep neural networks. In: Vera-Rodriguez, R., Fierrez, J., Morales, A. (eds.) CIARP 2018. LNCS, vol. 11401, pp. 723–731. Springer, Cham (2019). https://doi.org/10.1007/978-3-030-13469-3_84
7. Volpicelli, G., Elbarbary, M., Blaivas, M., Lichtenstein, D., et al.: International evidence-based recommendations for point-of-care lung ultrasound. Intensive Care Med. **38**(4), 577–591 (2012)
8. Kulhare, S., et al.: Ultrasound-based detection of lung abnormalities using single shot detection convolutional neural networks. In: Stoyanov, D., et al. (eds.) POCUS/BIVPCS/CuRIOUS/CPM 2018. LNCS, vol. 11042, pp. 65–73. Springer, Cham (2018). https://doi.org/10.1007/978-3-030-01045-4_8

9. Liu, W., et al.: SSD: Single Shot MultiBox Detector. In: Leibe, B., Matas, J., Sebe, N., Welling, M. (eds.) ECCV 2016. LNCS, vol. 9905, pp. 21–37. Springer, Cham (2016). https://doi.org/10.1007/978-3-319-46448-0_2

10. Horn, B., Schunk, B.G.: Determining optical flow. Artif. Intell. **17**, 185–203 (1981)

11. Hochreiter, S., Schmidhuber, J.: Long short-term memory. Neural Comput. **9**(8), 1735–1780 (1997)

12. Bengio, Y., Simard, P., Frasconi, P.: Learning long-term dependencies with gradient descent is difficult. IEEE Trans. Neural Networks **5**(2), 157–166 (1994)

13. Szegedy, C., Vanhoucke, V., Ioffe, S., Shlens, J., Wojna, Z.: Rethinking the inception architecture for computer vision. In: IEEE Conference on Computer Vision and Pattern Recognition (CVPR) 2016, Las Vegas, pp. 2818–2826. IEEE (2016)

14. Jabbar, S., Day, C., Heinz, N., Chadwick, E.: Using Convolutional Neural Network for edge detection in musculoskeletal ultrasound images. In: International Joint Conference on Neural Networks (IJCNN) 2016, Vancouver, pp. 4619–4626. IEEE (2016)

15. Shin, J.Y., Tajbakhsh, N., Hurst, R.T., Kendall, C.B., Liang, J.M.: Automating carotid intima-media thickness video interpretation with convolutional neural networks. In: Conference on Computer Vision and Pattern Recognition (CVPR) 2016, Las Vegas, pp. 2526–2535. IEEE (2016)

16. Chen, H., et al.: Standard plane localization in fetal ultrasound via domain transferred deep neural networks. IEEE J. Biomed. Health Inform. **19**(5), 1627–1636 (2015)

17. Lichtenstein, D.A., Menu, Y.: A bedside ultrasound sign ruling out pneumothorax in the critically ill. Lung sliding. Chest **108**(5), 1345–1348 (1995)

Deep Learning Based Minimum Variance Beamforming for Ultrasound Imaging

Renxin Zhuang and Junying Chen[✉]

School of Software Engineering, South China University of Technology,
Guangzhou 510006, Guangdong, China
jychense@scut.edu.cn

Abstract. Deep learning has been applied to ultrasound imaging recently, and it needs to be further studied to improve ultrasound beamforming methods. According to the latest research, deep neural network was able to suppress off-axis scattering signals in ultrasound channel data, which enhanced the performance of beamforming and improved the contrast of the output ultrasound images. Minimum variance beamforming was capable to present high lateral resolution, but lacked of high image contrast of ultrasound images. In order to effectively improve the contrast of minimum variance beamforming, this work investigated the combination of deep neural network and minimum variance beamforming. In the experiments, the simulated point target and cyst scenarios were adopted to evaluate the performance of the proposed methods. The results demonstrated that combining deep neural network and minimum variance beamforming can effectively reduce the side lobe level and thus can improve the contrast of the ultrasound images while maintaining the lateral resolution performance.

Keywords: Minimum variance beamforming · Deep learning · High image contrast · Ultrasound imaging

1 Introduction

Beamforming is the critical procedure in ultrasound imaging. The most widely used beamforming method nowadays is delay-and-sum (DAS) beamforming [4]. It consists of two steps, of which the first step is applying phase delays to the channel data and the second step is summing the delayed channel data to get the pixel value. Minimum variance (MV) beamforming [11] is a kind of adaptive beamforming methods. The main difference between MV and DAS is that MV computes the adaptive channel apodization weights using the delayed channel data while DAS uses fixed channel weights. The ultrasound images produced by MV are of higher quality, especially higher lateral resolution. However, MV cannot effectively improve the contrast of ultrasound images, meanwhile the robustness of MV is not guaranteed. Hence, spatial averaging and diagonal loading techniques were utilized to enhance the robustness of MV. Moreover,

© Springer Nature Switzerland AG 2019
Q. Wang et al. (Eds.): PIPPI 2019/SUSI 2019, LNCS 11798, pp. 83–91, 2019.
https://doi.org/10.1007/978-3-030-32875-7_10

Asl *et al.* proposed forward-backward MV beamforming to improve MV's performance on both contrast and robustness [2] and they proposed eigenspace based MV (ESBMV) beamforming to improve image resolution and image contrast of ultrasound images [1]. Liu *et al.* combined ESBMV with sign coherence factor [8], which improved the image quality of ultrasound images as well as the robustness of MV.

In recent years, deep learning has been widely used in many applications such as natural language processing and computer vision. There have been two ways of combining deep learning and ultrasound imaging. One is the high quality reconstruction of poor quality ultrasound images, and the other is using deep learning techniques to enhance ultrasound beamforming performance. Our work focuses on the deep learning enhanced beamforming method. In 2012, Zaharis *et al.* proposed a novel neural network based adaptive beamforming method [12]. The method used mutation Boolean particle swarm optimization to compute the apodization weights which served as groundtruth during network training. The neural network consisted of an input layer, a hidden layer and an output layer. Such method effectively suppressed side lobes and enhanced main lobe. In 2016, an improved neural network architecture was designed to deal with MV's uncertainty about interference coherence [13]. The proposed network contained two hidden layers. The first hidden layer was divided into sublayers, and the number of sublayers was equal to the dimension of inputs. The neurons in each sublayer only connected their corresponding input. This method alleviated the performance degradation caused by the uncertainty about interference coherence. In 2018, Simson *et al.* proposed a fully convolutional neural network based beamformer, producing smooth images on sub-sampled raw data [10]. Luchies and Byram ensembled deep neural network (DNN) into a DAS beamformer [9], in which DNN was responsible for suppressing the off-axis scattering signals. The method effectively improved the contrast of the produced ultrasound images. Inspired by the previous work, we proposed a method combining DNN and MV beamforming, aiming to improve the contrast of MV beamforming.

The rest of the paper is organized as follows. Section 2 will illustrate two ways of combining DNN and MV beamforming and the detailed construction of the deep learning based high-contrast MV beamforming method. Experimental results will be presented in Sect. 3 and the conclusion will be drawn in Sect. 4.

2   Combining DNN and MV Beamforming

The core operation of MV is apodization weight calculation which is conducted on the delayed channel data. DNN is used to process the delayed channel data in order to suppress off-axis scattering signals. There are two ways to calculate apodization weights. The first one is to calculate the weights using delayed channel data before DNN processing (DNNMV_before), and the second one is to calculate the weights using delayed channel data after DNN processing (DNNMV_after). Figure 1 shows these two different ways. DNN acts as an optimization operator in the MV beamforming framework as shown in Fig. 1.

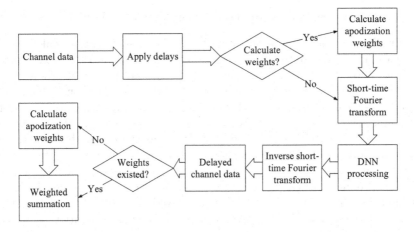

Fig. 1. The flow chart of DNN based MV beamforming with two different apodization weight calculation ways.

2.1 MV Beamforming with Spatial Averaging and Diagonal Loading

Assuming the number of receiving channels is M and the length of subaperture is L, then there are totally $(M - L + 1)$ subapertures. The subaperture signal vector $x_i, i = 1, 2, ..., M - L + 1$ contains delayed data from ith channel to $(i + L - 1)$th channel. The spatial covariance matrix R_{cov} of each subaperture is then calculated and averaged, as illustrated in (1):

$$R_{cov} = \frac{1}{M - L + 1} \sum_{i=1}^{M-L+1} x_i \cdot x_i^H. \tag{1}$$

Subsequently, diagonal loading is applied to R_{cov} by adding a certain proportion of Gaussian white noise, which is expressed as:

$$R_{cov} = R_{cov} + \sigma \cdot trace(R_{cov} \cdot I), \tag{2}$$

where σ is the diagonal loading factor which is often set as $1/(100L)$, and I is a unit matrix. The apodization weight vector w is calculated as:

$$w = \frac{R_{cov}^{-1} \cdot a}{a^H \cdot R_{cov}^{-1} \cdot a}, \tag{3}$$

where a is a steering vector of all ones. w is then combined with x_i to obtain the beamformed pixel amplitude value v.

$$v = \frac{1}{M - L + 1} \sum_{i=1}^{M-L+1} w^H \cdot x_i. \tag{4}$$

2.2   Suppressing Off-Axis Scattering Signals with DNN

To train DNN for the purpose of suppressing off-axis scattering signals, specific training data is needed so that DNN can learn how to distinguish off-axis scattering signals and then suppress them. Field II [6] is used to simulate the training data. The configuration of the simulated transducer is listed in Table 1. The inputs of DNN consist of individual responses from scatters which are randomly placed along the annular sector shown in Fig. 2. For scatters in the acceptance region, the outputs of DNN are exactly the same as the inputs, but for scatters in the rejection region, the outputs are all zeros which means the signals are totally suppressed.

After applying delays to the received channel data, short-time Fourier transform (STFT) is performed to convert the delayed channel data into frequency domain representation. STFT is indeed a series of discrete Fourier transforms (DFTs) operating on the segmented channel data. In the proposed method, a rectangle window function whose window length is 16 is used, and the stride is 1. Because the signal values are real numbers, the outcome of a DFT is conjugate symmetrical. Therefore, only 9 complex amplitudes of 9 Fourier frequencies are needed to record. After Fourier transforms, the real component and the imaginary component of complex amplitudes are separated. As a result, for each scanline with P imaging pixels, after performing STFT, a data matrix whose size is $(2 \times N_{elements}) \times 9 \times (P - 16 + 1)$ can be obtained, where $N_{elements}$ represents the number of receiving channel elements that is 128 in our setting.

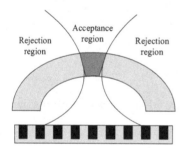

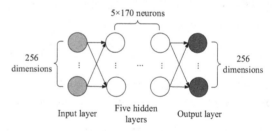

Fig. 2. Scatter placement, acceptance and rejection regions.

Fig. 3. Topology of the deep learning neural network.

Totally 9 neural networks are trained, each for one frequency. The first trained network is the network for the transmit center frequency, and transfer learning strategy is then adopted for the other 8 networks, which means that the trained network for the center frequency is used as the starting point of training of networks for the other 8 frequencies. The topology of the adopted neural network is shown in Fig. 3. The input and the output of the network are both of 256 dimensions. There are five hidden layers, and each network layer except the output layer is fully connected to its next layer. The training data set consists of responses from 10,000 scatters. Half of them are in the acceptance region and the other half of them are in the rejection region. The validation data set and the test data set both consist of responses from 2,500 scatters. Also half of them are in the acceptance region and the other half of them are in the rejection region. To better train the neural networks, Adam optimizer [7] which is a variant of gradient descent optimizers, is adopted with the learning rate of 1.1×10^{-3}. The learning rate decay is 4.1×10^{-8}. The weight initialization strategy is employed to initialize the weights of networks [5]. The activation function chosen for the neurons in hidden layers is ReLU function [3] and that chosen for the output layer is linear activation function.

Table 1. The simulated scenario configuration

Parameter	Value
Active elements	64
Transmit center frequency	5.208 MHz
Pitch	209 μm
Width	48 μm
Sampling frequency	20.832 MHz
Sound speed	1540 m/s
Transmit focal depth	70 mm

Table 2. Cyst image contrast and signal-to-noise ratio comparison

Metric	MV	DNNMV_after	DNNMV_before
CR	0.3568	0.3808	0.3900
SNR	1.708	1.4388	1.5156

3   Experiments and Results

3.1   Experimental Setup

For single scatter simulation, only one scatter was placed in the transmit focal depth. For cyst simulation, a spherical cyst was placed with its center in the focal depth. The imaging volume was filled with scatters with the density of 25 scatters per square micrometers and the phantom amplitudes of scatters within the cyst were set to zeros. The evaluation metrics of cyst simulation were image contrast (CR) and speckle signal-to-noise ratio (SNR). As shown in Fig. 4, two round regions with the same area as the cyst region were drawn in the left side and the right side of the cyst, respectively. The mean values of pixel amplitudes within these two regions were denoted as S_{out1} and S_{out2}, the mean value of them was denoted as S_{out}, and the mean value of pixel amplitudes within the cyst region was denoted as S_{in}. Hence, CR was calculated as:

$$CR = \frac{S_{out} - S_{in}}{S_{out}}, \tag{5}$$

where CR value was between 0 and 1. Moreover, SNR was calculated as:

$$SNR = \frac{\mu_{background}}{\sigma_{background}}, \tag{6}$$

where $\mu_{background}$ referred to the mean value of the uncompressed envelop signals and $\sigma_{background}$ referred to the standard deviation of the uncompressed envelop signals in the background speckle region.

3.2 Experimental Results and Discussions

As mentioned in Sect. 2, two different apodization weight calculation ways were examined. Figure 6 presented single scatter images of traditional MV and the proposed MV with two different apodization weight calculation ways. It was observed that after DNN processing, the tail of the scatter was greatly suppressed and the imaging results of two different calculation ways were comparable. As seen from the point target spread function comparison in Fig. 5, the proposed DNNMV_before and DNNMV_after methods suppressed the side lobe levels by approximately 60 dB, and not affecting the main lobe width, which means that the lateral resolution performance of MV was preserved.

For cyst simulation, Fig. 7 demonstrated the cyst images of traditional MV and the proposed MV with two different apodization weight calculation ways. With DNN processing, there were more dark regions within the cyst, meaning that off-axis scattering signals were indeed suppressed. Table 2 showed the image CR and SNR comparisons of cyst images, and higher CR value represented better contrast. It was observed from Table 2 that image contrasts of images using the proposed DNNMV_before and DNNMV_after methods were both higher than that of traditional MV, which was consistent with the demonstration in Fig. 7. But for speckle SNR, traditional MV performed better. This was because that signals within the cyst which consisted of responses from scatters in the rejection region were the signals which DNN learned to suppress, while signals in

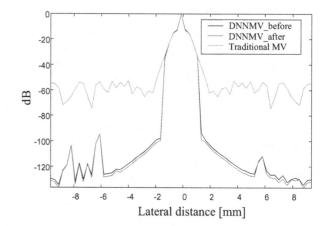

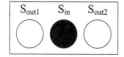

Fig. 4. Contrast calculation of a cyst image.

Fig. 5. Point target spread function comparison of traditional MV and the proposed MV with two different apodization weight calculation ways.

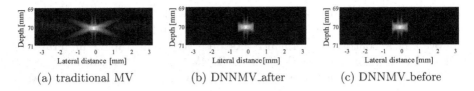

Fig. 6. Single scatter images of traditional MV and the proposed MV with two different apodization weight calculation ways.

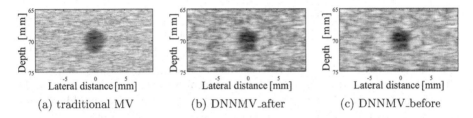

Fig. 7. Cyst images of traditional MV and the proposed MV with two different apodization weight calculation ways.

the background speckle which consisted of responses from scatters in the acceptance region were the signals which DNN learned to reconstruct. The SNR result demonstrated that reconstructing signals was harder to learn than suppressing signals, resulting the SNR performance not good enough to outperform that of traditional MV. This indicated that in future work, experiments with larger training data set with more random scatters in the acceptance region should be conducted for further improvements of speckle SNR as well as contrast.

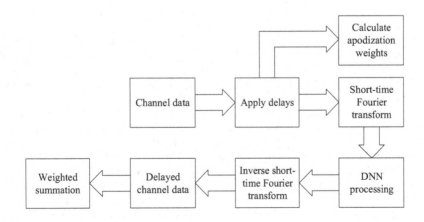

Fig. 8. The final determined model combining DNN and MV beamforming.

Reducing the level of side lobes can improve the contrast of ultrasound images, so it was beneficial to combine DNN and MV beamforming to improve MV's contrast performance. As observed from Table 2 in terms of both image contrast and speckle SNR, DNNMV_before performed better than DNNMV_after. Therefore, the final determined model of our method was DNNMV_before, as shown in Fig. 8.

4   Conclusion

In this work, we explored the combination of DNN and MV, and proposed a deep learning based MV beamforming method in which deep neural network acted as an optimization operator of the MV beamformer. The experimental results of simulated single scatter and cyst scenarios demonstrated that our method reduced the level of side lobes effectively and improved the image contrast while maintaining the resolution performance of MV. Future studies should be conducted to improve DNNMV's performance on speckle SNR with more scatters in the acceptance region. Moreover, more deep neural network structures for MV beamforming is worth exploring.

Acknowledgements. This work is supported by "National Natural Science Foundation of China" (No. 61802130), "Guangdong Natural Science Foundation" (No. 2018 A030310355), and "Guangzhou Science and Technology Program" (No. 201707010223).

References

1. Asl, B.M., Mahloojifar, A.: Eigenspace-based minimum variance beamforming applied to medical ultrasound imaging. IEEE Trans. Ultrason. Ferroelectr. Freq. Control **57**(11), 2381–2390 (2010)
2. Asl, B.M., Mahloojifar, A.: Contrast enhancement and robustness improvement of adaptive ultrasound imaging using forward-backward minimum variance beamforming. IEEE Trans. Ultrason. Ferroelectr. Freq. Control **58**(4), 858–867 (2011)
3. Goodfellow, I., Bengio, Y., Courville, A., Bengio, Y.: Deep Learning. MIT Press, Cambridge (2016)
4. Havlice, J.F., Taenzer, J.C.: Medical ultrasonic imaging: an overview of principles and instrumentation. Proc. IEEE **67**(4), 620–641 (1979)
5. He, K., Zhang, X., Ren, S., Sun, J.: Delving deep into rectifiers: surpassing human-level performance on imagenet classification. In: Proceedings of IEEE International Conference on Computer Vision, pp. 1026–1034 (2015)
6. Jensen, J.A.: Field: a program for simulating ultrasound systems. In: Proceedings of Nordic-Balttc Conference on Biomedical Imaging, pp. 351–353 (1996)
7. Kingma, D.P., Ba, J.: Adam: a method for stochastic optimization. In: Proceedings of International Conference for Learning Representations, pp. 1–15 (2015)
8. Liu, T., Zhao, H., Zheng, Y.: Eigenspace-based minimum variance beamforming combined with sign coherence factor for ultrasound beamforming. Acta Acustica **40**(6), 855–862 (2015). (in Chinese)
9. Luchies, A.C., Byram, B.C.: Deep neural networks for ultrasound beamforming. IEEE Trans. Med. Imaging **37**(9), 2010–2021 (2018)

10. Simson, W., Paschali, M., Navab, N., Zahnd, G.: Deep learning beamforming for sub-sampled ultrasound data. In: Proceedings of IEEE International Ultrasonics Symposium, pp. 1–4 (2018)
11. Synnevåg, J.F., Austeng, A., Holm, S.: Adaptive beamforming applied to medical ultrasound imaging. IEEE Trans. Ultrason. Ferroelectr. Freq. Control **54**(8), 1606–1613 (2007)
12. Zaharis, Z.D., Gotsisa, K.A., Sahalos, J.N.: Adaptive beamforming with low side lobe level using neural networks trained by mutated boolean PSO. Prog. Electromagnet. Res. **127**, 139–154 (2012)
13. Zaharis, Z.D., et al.: Implementation of antenna array beamforming by using a novel neural network structure. In: Proceedings of International Conference on Telecommunications and Multimedia, pp. 25–27 (2016)

4th Workshop on Perinatal, Preterm and Paediatric Image Analysis

Estimation of Preterm Birth Markers with U-Net Segmentation Network

Tomasz Włodarczyk[1](✉), Szymon Płotka[1,5], Tomasz Trzciński[1,4],
Przemysław Rokita[1], Nicole Sochacki-Wójcicka[2,3], Michał Lipa[2],
and Jakub Wójcicki[2,3]

[1] Warsaw University of Technology, Warsaw, Poland
wlodarczyk.tomasz@gmail.com
[2] Warsaw Medical University, Warsaw, Poland
[3] Ernest Wójcicki Prenatal Medicine Foundation, Wrocław, Poland
[4] Tooploox, Wrocław, Poland
[5] MedApp S.A., Bochnia, Poland

Abstract. Preterm birth is the most common cause of neonatal death.
Current diagnostic methods that assess the risk of preterm birth involve
the collection of maternal characteristics and transvaginal ultrasound
imaging conducted in the first and second trimester of pregnancy. Analysis of the ultrasound data is based on visual inspection of images by
gynaecologist, sometimes supported by hand-designed image features
such as cervical length. Due to the complexity of this process and its
subjective component, approximately 30% of spontaneous preterm deliveries are not correctly predicted. Moreover, 10% of the predicted preterm
deliveries are false-positives [1]. In this paper, we address the problem
of predicting spontaneous preterm delivery using machine learning. To
achieve this goal, we propose to first use a deep neural network architecture for segmenting prenatal ultrasound images and then automatically
extract two biophysical ultrasound markers, cervical length (CL) and
anterior cervical angle (ACA), from the resulting images. Our method
allows to estimate ultrasound markers without human oversight. Furthermore, we show that CL and ACA markers, when combined, allow
us to decrease false-negative ratio from 30% to 18%. Finally, contrary to
the current approaches to diagnostics methods that rely only on gynaecologist's expertise, our method introduce objectively obtained results.

Keywords: Preterm birth · Segmentation · Deep learning

1 Introduction

Preterm birth (PTB) affects 5–18% of pregnancies worldwide, which is equivalent
to 15 million preterm neonates each year [1]. Despite major advances in perinatal
care, preterm birth still accounts for 75% of neonatal deaths and over 50% of

© Springer Nature Switzerland AG 2019
Q. Wang et al. (Eds.): PIPPI 2019/SUSI 2019, LNCS 11798, pp. 95–103, 2019.
https://doi.org/10.1007/978-3-030-32875-7_11

neurological handicap in children [2]. Preterm birth is defined as birth before 37 weeks of gestation, however high mortality and morbidity mainly affects neonates delivered before 34 weeks, often referred to as early preterm (1–3% of all pregnancies) [3]. Prediction and early detection of women at high risk of PTB are crucial as it allows timely intervention. Despite potentially effective treatments like cervical cerclage, vaginal progesterone or pessaries, accurate, early diagnosis still remains a major challenge [4–9]. Current screening methods combine maternal characteristics, obstetric history and cervical length measured at 20–24 weeks [3]. A major disadvantage of this approach lies in failing to identify women with cervical incompetence before the second trimester and therefore missing the opportunity for successful intervention. Attempts have been made at validating the same screening markers in the first trimester with variable results, the best yielding a detection rate of 54.8% at a false-positive rate of 10% [10].

In this paper, we address the problem of spontaneous preterm birth prediction. We present a novel method for estimating two biophysical ultrasound markers: cervical length (CL) and anterior cervical angle (ACA). Cervical length marker refers to the length of the lower end of uterus. Anterior cervical angle is defined by angle between the uterine wall and the cervical canal. We introduce additional feature - ACA marker - for preterm birth prediction as suggested by the results published in [12]. Extending [12], we computed ACA automatically and combined the results with the CL marker, what significantly improved the overall prediction quality. To achieve that goal, we use a deep neural network architecture trained for segmenting prenatal ultrasound images. To overcome the fact that our ultrasound dataset, after balancing procedure, is very small and it could be a vital reason for poor performance, we decide to use a different dataset to perform prediction, to what is described in Sect. 3.3. Finally, we present that in comparison to regular analysis of ultrasound data, our method performs better and can be used to obtain different biophysical markers as well.

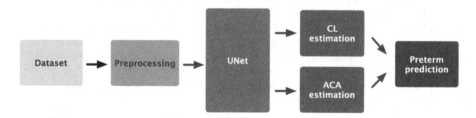

Fig. 1. The proposed workflow of estimation preterm birth markers. Our method after data preprocessing uses the U-Net network for segmentation of the cervix, and then allows the estimation of CL and ACA markers.

2   Method

In this section we present our method of estimation of CL and ACA markers that relies on cervix extraction with U-Net segmentation, as depicted in Fig. 1. The U-Net [11] architecture is an encoder-decoder neural network implementation used for semantic segmentation, mainly designed for biomedical image processing. This architecture is illustrated in Fig. 2

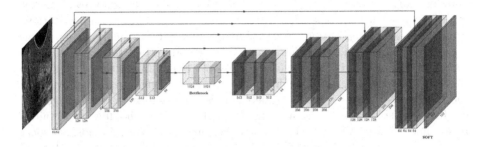

Fig. 2. The U-Net architecture [11]. Each box represents feature maps. The number of channels is signed under each feature map.

We start training a U-Net model for the segmentation task of extracting a cervical shape from ultrasound images. Once trained, we use our neural network to obtain binary masks of the cervix. Finally, we use them to estimate CL and ACA markers and then for binary classification task (preterm vs. control). To perform cervical length estimation we apply the centerline algorithm [13] to the binary masks. Such algorithm relies on a generation of a Voronoi diagram for given cervix shape to get the polygon skeleton where the skeleton centerline is selected and smoothed. We use the same extracted masks for ACA estimation with different approach based on a recurential split on centroid location for a given shape.

3 Experiments

In this section, we present results obtained with the proposed method. We first describe the dataset used in our experiments and show the results obtained using the segmentation algorithm. We then verify if the estimated CL and ACA metrics correspond to the ground truth one. In the second part we evaluate whether CL and ACA combined, perform better than current methods and present results of the classification task (preterm vs control).

The first stage in our workflow is cervical segmentation using the U-Net neural network. The segmentation results are used to estimate CL and ACA described in the second stage.

3.1 U-Net Segmentation

Dataset and Preprocessing: The data collection was collected at King's College London and Warsaw Medical University and it contains data from 359 pregnant women with 316 control pregnancies and 43 preterm deliveries, which is defined as birth before 37 weeks of gestation. The data was registered and

labeled using standard infrastructure for ultrasound imagery operated by spe-
cialized physicians. Since our dataset contains images (and not the raw data),
the annotations are embedded in the graphical layer and hence cannot be filtered
automatically out of the data. To overcome this shortcoming and prevent U-Net
from focusing only on annotated markers we decide to remove all annotations
from images using inpainting method. Inpainting methods using machine learning did not give satisfactory results on our ultrasound images, so we use standard
computer vision algorithms. At first we convert our dataset from the RGB to
the HSV colour space. Next, we define the range of colours of all annotations in
the HSV space, what allows us to detect these ones which we want to get rid
of. The next step is to create a mask. Then through thresholding we obtain a
binary image based on defined color range. We then use dilation (a morphological
operation on the image) to expand our mask to completely remove annotations
around the extracted pixels in the first step. The inpainting method was used
in order to prevent the U-Net network from focusing on coloured markers in
the images. The diagram of the method described above is presented in Figs. 3
and 4.

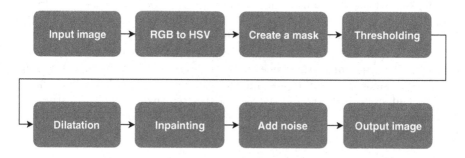

Fig. 3. Data preprocessing flow.

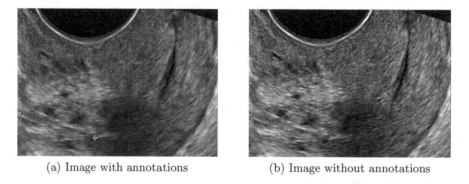

(a) Image with annotations   (b) Image without annotations

Fig. 4. Example of using our inpainting method. On the left, we presented the original
image, and on the right after applying our inpainting algorithm. Our method was used
in order to prevent the U-Net network from focusing on coloured markers in the images.

The dataset contains around 20% preterms which reflects the statistical occurrence of this phenomenon in reality. To mitigate this shortcoming we balanced the dataset by applying data augmentation to achieve a 50:50 ratio, to avoid heavily focusing on the majority class by classification algorithm. We augmented the dataset to 6359 images (359 original and 6000 augmented) by random rotations in the range of -10 to $10°$, random contrast and brightness adjustments. We divide it into training and validation subsets maintaining a ratio of 70:30.

Experimental Settings: We use our augmented dataset to train a network on a machine with AMD FX-8320 @ 3.5 Ghz CPU and NVIDIA TITAN X 12 GB GPU. We implement our models using the PyTorch library with CUDA support. We train U-Net for 650 epochs with a batch size of 4, Adam optimizer with a learning rate of 10^{-4} and weight decay of 10^{-4}. We use BCEWithLogits as a loss function. We use the 256 px $\times$ 256 px images as input while initializing weights with Xavier uniform method (also known as Glorot initialization) with $\sqrt{2}$ gain.

Binary Segmentation Mask: We evaluate the U-Net neural network on the task of cervix segmentation of the dataset. We use *Jaccard Index*, also known as *Intersection over Union (IoU)* as the evaluation metric during training. For two sets A and B, the Jaccard index is defined as the following:

$$J(A, B) = \frac{|A \cap B|}{|A \cup B|} \tag{1}$$

For cervix segmentation task we obtain average Jaccard Index of 0.91 (min - 0.89, max - 0.92, SD - 0.1). Several results are presented in Fig. 5. In the optimisation of the neural network, we controlled for both Dice and Jaccard index, but more consistent results were obtained with the Jaccard index.

3.2   CL and ACA Estimation

Cervical Length Estimation: For this task we use obtained cervix segmentation masks and perform centerline algorithm [13] on that image set. Then we evaluate whether the cervical length can be estimated by centerline length by conducting linear regression between estimated and ground truth lengths of cervix. We obtain a RMSE of 110.88 and a correlation coefficient of 0.94 what show that these two sets are almost linearly dependent with constant offset. The results are presented in Fig. 6a.

Anterior Cervical Angle Estimation: For this task we develop an algorithm which we apply to binary segmentation mask in order to obtain an estimation of Anterior Cervical Angle. Such algorithm is a recursion where on each step we split obtained cervical mask in two parts, based on its centroid location. We perform three iterations of that algorithm on every binary mask. Figure 7 presents results of each iteration. Then we evaluate whether our approach can be used to estimate anterior cervical angle by conducting linear regression between estimated and ground truth dataset. We obtain a RMSE of 16.22 and a correlation coefficient of 0.693. The results are presented in Fig. 6b.

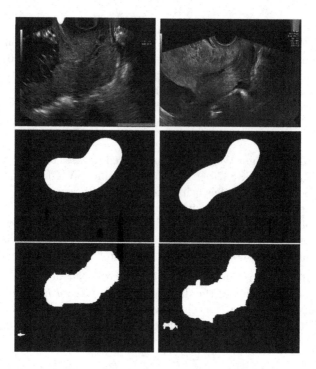

Fig. 5. Segmentation results on our dataset. We present from top to bottom: input image after removing the annotation from the original images, ground truth and prediction after applying the U-Net network. Our method allowed us to achieve an average Jaccard index of 0.91, a minimum of 0.89 and a maximum of 0.92, with a standard deviation of 0.1.

3.3   Preterm Birth Prediction

In this section we evaluate classification algorithm on cervical lengths and anterior cervical angles, to assign preterm *vs.* control label to the (CL, ACA) pair. For this purpose, we used four popular machine learning algorithms: Support Vector Machines (SVM), K-Nearest Neighbour, Naive Bayes and Decision Trees. We used the above algorithms for classification due to the fact that they perform well with this type of data.

The best results in terms of accuracy were obtained for classifiers, which were trained on data containing CL and ACA features of the first and second trimesters. This is due to the greater number of features in the set, thus increasing the diversity, which allows for better separation of classes in binary classification.

Despite the simplicity of the naive Bayes classifier, surprisingly high results were obtained, both by analyzing the measures of accuracy, precision and sensitivity for both classes. In addition we conducted a 5-fold cross validation and we obtained the result of accuracy 0.77, confirming the superiority of Bayes classifier. Using this classifier, the highest probability was also obtained that the

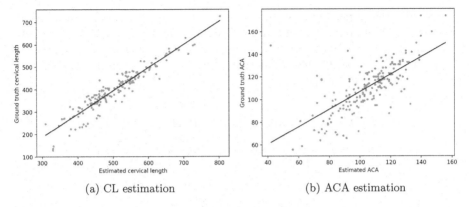

(a) CL estimation   (b) ACA estimation

Fig. 6. Evaluation of our estimation of: (a) cervical length (CL) and (b) anterior cervical angle (ACA). We obtain a RMSE of 110.88, correlation of 0.94 for cervical length and RMSE of 16.22 and correlation of 0.693 for the anterior cervical angle.

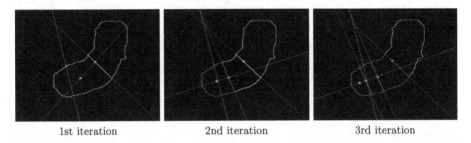

1st iteration   2nd iteration   3rd iteration

Fig. 7. Three first iterations of ACA estimation algorithm. On every iteration algorithm finds centroid point of a given shape, splits it into two shapes and proceeds further with the same steps. In the end, we measure ACA between the anterior wall (red line) and the line between the last two centroids. (Color figure online)

classifier would determine a randomly chosen positive example higher than the randomly selected negative example, based on the AUC score. Perhaps using the naive Bayes classifier the best results were obtained due to the small correlations between features.

The worst average results in terms of accuracy, precision, sensitivity and area under the ROC curve were obtained by using the algorithm K-nearest neighbors for classification. The probable reason is the small distance of the samples from each other, which significantly reduces the efficiency of the algorithm.

At this stage, to overcome fact that our ultrasound dataset, after balancing procedure, is very small and it could be a vital reason for poor performance of mentioned four algorithms, we decide to use a different dataset. It contains 380 balanced numerical samples with precomputed cervical length and anterior cervical angle for first and second trimester. It was obtained from King's College Hospital and Warsaw Medical University.

According to paper [12], we have got better results in the classification of spontaneous birth preterm than can be done manually by gynecologists. For the first trimester, we obtained 18% of false negatives, where manually it is 30%. This, in turn, can lead to significant time savings and increase the efficiency of prevention treatment (Table 1).

Table 1. Classification results for four different classifiers

Classifier	Trimester	Accuracy	Precision	Recall	AUC
SVM	I	69.56	77.0	65.0	70.19
	II	62.28	65.0	68.0	61.75
	I + II	72.5	71.0	75.0	72.5
KNN	I	71.74	78.0	73.0	72.1
	II	58.77	61.0	69.0	57.75
	I + II	72.5	75.0	78.0	71.43
Naive Bayes	I	73.91	82.0	69.0	74.62
	II	59.64	61.0	73.0	58.4
	I + II	**77.5**	85.0	74.0	**78.13**
Decision Trees	I	69.56	83.0	58.0	71.34
	II	59.65	61.0	69.0	58.72
	I + II	75.0	88.0	65.0	78.13

In Table 2, we presented the confusion matrix after classification on numerical data using the naive Bayesian classifier algorithm. We obtained 18% of false negatives and 14% false positives for the best classification results.

Table 2. Confusion matrix

		Predicted	
		Control	Preterm
Actual	Control	46	16
	Preterm	21	31

The false negative ratio in our study is higher than the one in [10], since we balanced our dataset (it was unbalanced in [10] which leads to the accuracy paradox and precision and recall bias.) Still, our reported detection rate is 74% - much higher than 54.8% reported in [10].

4   Conclusions

In this paper we propose a method to automatically extract and estimate two biophysical ultrasound markers: CL and ACA based on usage of convolutional neural network. In addition we show that those markers combined can be promising predictor of preterm birth. The results presented in this paper show that methods based on deep neural networks can provide automatic, quantitative analysis of ultrasound images. This, in turn, can lead to significant time savings and increase the efficiency of current diagnostic methods without losing its precision.

As future work, we plan to focus on predicting preterm birth with different biophysical markers like shape of cervix or cervix tissue density and on preparing end-to-end method for segmentation and classification task as well.

References

1. Howson, C., Kinney, M., Lawn, J.: March of Dimes, PMNCH, Save the Children, WHO. Born Too Soon: The Global Action Report on Preterm Birth. World Health Organization, Geneva (2012)
2. Barros, F., et al.: Epidemiology and causes of preterm birth. Lancet **371**, 75–84 (2008)
3. Celik, E., et al.: Cervical length and obstetric history predict spontaneous preterm birth: development and validation of a model to provide individualized risk assessment. Ultrasound Obstet. Gynecol. **31**, 549–554 (2008)
4. Arabin, B., et al.: Cervical pessaries for prevention of spontaneous preterm births: past, present and future. Ultrasound Obstet. Gynecol. **44**, 390–399 (2013)
5. Berghella, V., et al.: Cerclage for short cervix on ultrasonography: meta-analysis of trials using individual patient-level data. Ultrasound Obstet. Gynecol. **106**, 181–189 (2005)
6. Fonseca, E., et al.: Progesterone and the risk of preterm birth among women with a short cervix. N. Engl. J. Med. **357**, 462–469 (2007)
7. Goya, M., et al.: Cervical pessary in pregnant women with a short cervix (PECEP): an open-label randomised controlled trial. Lancet **379**, 1800–1806 (2012)
8. Myatt, L., et al.: A standardized template for clinical studies in preterm birth. Reprod. Sci. **19**, 474–482 (2012)
9. To, M., et al.: Cervical cerclage for prevention of preterm delivery in women with short cervix. Lancet **364**, 1849–1853 (2005)
10. Beta, J., et al.: Prediction of spontaneous preterm delivery from maternal factors, obstetric history and placental perfusion and function at 11–13 weeks. Prenat. Diagn. **31**, 75–83 (2011)
11. Ronneberger, O., Fischer, P., Brox, T.: U-Net: convolutional networks for biomedical image segmentation. In: Navab, N., Hornegger, J., Wells, W.M., Frangi, A.F. (eds.) MICCAI 2015. LNCS, vol. 9351, pp. 234–241. Springer, Cham (2015). https://doi.org/10.1007/978-3-319-24574-4_28
12. Sochacki-Wojcicka, N., et al.: Anterior cervical angle as a new biophysical ultrasound marker for prediction of spontaneous preterm birth. Ultrasound Obstet. Gynecol. **46**, 377–378 (2015)
13. https://github.com/ungarj/label_centerlines

Investigating Image Registration Impact on Preterm Birth Classification: An Interpretable Deep Learning Approach

Irina Grigorescu(✉)[iD], Lucilio Cordero-Grande[iD], A. David Edwards[iD],
Joseph V. Hajnal[iD], Marc Modat[iD], and Maria Deprez[iD]

School of Biomedical Engineering and Imaging Sciences, King's College London,
London SE1 7EH, UK
irina.grigorescu@kcl.ac.uk

Abstract. Deep learning algorithms have recently become the dominant trend in medical image classification. However, the decision-making rationale of convolutional neural network (CNN) classifiers can be obscure. Interpretable machine learning techniques, such as layer-wise relevance propagation (LRP), can provide a visual interpretation of these decisions. In this work, we build a 3D CNN model to classify neonatal T_2-weighted magnetic resonance (MR) scans into term or preterm. Additionally, we investigate the impact of different registration techniques applied to the image dataset on the classifier's predictions. Finally, we compute LRP 'relevance maps', which indicate each voxel's importance to the outcome of the decision. Our resulting LRP heatmaps show no visually striking differences between the different registration techniques, while also revealing anatomically plausible features for term and preterm birth.

Keywords: Preterm birth · Classification · Layer-wise relevance propagation

1 Introduction

In recent years, deep learning research has made incredible advances in solving a wide range of scientific problems. Despite their success, these models are often incapable of providing explanations for their predictions. As a result, it has become increasingly important for the machine learning research community to build explainable models that are able to provide insights into their behaviour and thought processes. This is particularly vital in medical imaging, where interpretable algorithms can provide a way of understanding if the model is taking decisions based on clinically plausible features, thus increasing the medical experts' trust.

Layer-wise relevance propagation [2] is one such technique which has been introduced as a way of illustrating network decisions. In LRP, a 'relevance' quantity is assigned to every voxel in the input image, where a high positive value

© Springer Nature Switzerland AG 2019
Q. Wang et al. (Eds.): PIPPI 2019/SUSI 2019, LNCS 11798, pp. 104–112, 2019.
https://doi.org/10.1007/978-3-030-32875-7_12

represents a strong influence of that particular voxel towards the network's decision. In this study, we aim to investigate the possibility of using the LRP method to uncover features of preterm birth by expanding on the work of [6]. Additionally, we assess our model's performance when different types of image registration have been applied to the input images prior to feeding them into the classifier. Finally, we apply the LRP method in order to identify regions of interest used by our classification models to distinguish between term and preterm birth.

2 Method

2.1 Data Acquisition

The image data used in this study was collected as part of the developing Human Connectome Project using a Philips 3T scanner and a 32-channels neonatal head coil [7]. A turbo spin echo (TSE) sequence was used to acquire the T2-weighted (T2w) images in two stacks of 2D slices (sagittal and axial planes), with parameters: $T_R = 12\,\mathrm{s}$, $T_E = 156\,\mathrm{ms}$, and SENSE factors of 2.11 for the axial plane and 2.58 for the sagittal plane. The data was subsequently corrected for motion [4] and resampled to an isotropic voxel size of 0.5 mm. The resulting images were checked for abnormalities by a paediatric neuroradiologist.

2.2 Image Selection

In this work we use a dataset of 157 MRI scans of infants born between $23-42$ weeks gestational age (GA) and scanned at term-equivalent age (after 37 weeks GA). Their age distribution is shown in Fig. 1.

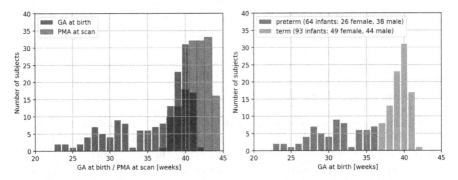

(a) Distribution of gestational age at birth and post-menstrual age (PMA) at scan

(b) Distribution of term (93 subjects) and preterm infants (64 subjects)

Fig. 1. Age distribution of subjects in our dataset

2.3   Image Preprocessing

In order to investigate the effect of registration on both the classification and interpretability of our study, we performed a series of pre-processing steps to our dataset. First, we registered all of our data to a common 40 weeks gestational age atlas space [11] using a rigid registration, an affine registration and a non-rigid B-spline registration (B-spline control point spacing 10 mm) available in the IRTK [10] software toolbox. Then, we downsampled the images to $1\,mm^3$ isotropic resolution. Finally, we performed skull-stripping and we cropped the volumes to a $112 \times 128 \times 112$ size in order to allow an entire 3D volume to be fed into the network at one particular time.

2.4   Data Preprocessing

Our dataset of 157 T2w 3D MRI scans was initially divided into 135 volumes for training and 17 volumes for holdout. When performing cross-validation, the 135 volumes were further divided into 90% training and 10% validation. In each division, the ratio between our two classes (term and preterm) was kept the same. The validation sets were used to inform us about our model's performance during training, while the holdout set was used to report our final model's results and showcase its capability to generalize. A full description of the dataset partition is shown in Table 1.

Table 1. Number of scans in different datasets used for the CNN model

Dataset	Total number of 3D volumes
Training	125 (74 term and 51 preterm)
Validation	15 (9 term and 6 preterm)
Holdout	17 (10 term and 7 preterm)

2.5   Network Architecture

The proposed 3D convolutional neural network (3D-CNN) architecture uses T_2w volumes of neonates at term equivalent age as inputs and classifies them into either *preterm* or *term*. A schematic illustration of the overall network is shown in Fig. 2. The network contains repeated blocks of $3 \times 3 \times 3$ convolutions (with a stride of 1), batch normalization [8], rectified linear unit (ReLU) activations and $2 \times 2 \times 2$ average pooling layers (with a stride of 1), followed by two fully connected layers. The network outputs the probabilities of an input image belonging to either of the two classes.

The network was trained by minimizing a categorical cross entropy loss function using the Adam optimizer with the default parameters ($\beta_1 = 0.9$ and $\beta_2 = 0.999$). The learning rate was varied in a decaying cyclical fashion [12] with

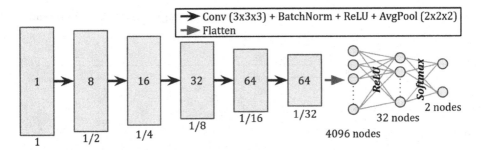

Fig. 2. The proposed network architecture for our classification task. Each rectangle represents a 3D volume, where the number of channels is shown inside the rectangle, while the spatial resolution with respect to the input volume is shown underneath.

a base learning rate of 10^{-5} and a maximum learning rate of 10^{-3}. To account for the class imbalance between the *preterm* and *term* classes, we introduced a stronger weight in the loss function for the under-represented class (*preterm*). Dropout layers, as well as image augmentation in the form of translations (of up to 3 voxels in x, y and z directions), rotations (of up to 30° in all three directions) and a combination of both were used during training in order to regularize the learning process.

2.6 Layer-Wise Relevance Propagation

Layer-wise relevance propagation [2] is a backward propagation technique that was found to be applicable in a variety of computer vision applications [1,3] and medical data [13]. This method assigns a 'relevance' score to each input voxel by iteratively propagating through the network each layer's output to its predecessors until the input layer is reached [9]. This redistribution rule is guided by a conservation principle, in which every neuron in the architecture receives a share of the network output [2]. For example, given two neurons from successive layers j and k, where layer k is closer to the output of the network than layer j, this rule can be written as:

$$R_j = \sum_k \frac{a_j w_{jk}^+}{\sum_j a_j w_{jk}^+} R_k^+ + \sum_k \frac{a_j w_{jk}^-}{\sum_j a_j w_{jk}^-} R_k^- \tag{1}$$

where: $R_k^+ = \alpha R_k$ and $R_k^- = -\beta R_k$, $\alpha - \beta = 1$ and $\beta \geq 0$ [3]. A graphic representation of the LRP method is shown in Fig. 3.

Setting $\alpha = 1$ and $\beta = 0$ discards the negative values and will produce relevance maps that only show regions in the input image which positively influence the network to classify into either *preterm* or *term*, while setting $\alpha = 2$ and $\beta = 1$ will propagate both positive and negative values, thus also showing the regions of the brain which negatively influenced the classifier. In this work we implemented the LRP rules, as described in [9], for our 3D classification network and applied them to compute relevance maps for both *preterm* and *term* neonates.

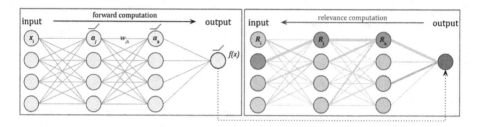

Fig. 3. Schematic representation of the LRP method. Figure adapted from [9].

3   Results

3.1   Cross-Validation Results

Figure 4 summarizes the results of our 10-fold cross-validation study for all three pre-processing steps (rigid, affine and non-rigid alignment). Having a small validation set (15 scans) in each of our 10 folds means that the accuracy metric can vary significantly between folds and between epochs, as a small change in the output probability can cause a sudden shift in the reported accuracy. However, based on the behaviour of the validation loss (categorical cross-entropy) and the validation accuracy across the 10 folds, we decided that the best performance of our model is achieved at 200 epochs of training. After 200 epochs, even if the loss function continues to decrease, the validation accuracy does not improve anymore, causing our model to overfit.

3.2   Final Model Results

Our final models were trained for 200 epochs for both affine, rigid and non-rigid datasets. Their performance on the holdout dataset is summarised in Table 2. In the rigid case, 1 subject was incorrectly classified as *preterm*, while another subject was incorrectly classified as *term*; in the affine case, 2 subjects were incorrectly classified as *preterm*, while 1 subject was incorrectly classified as *term*; and in the non-rigid case, 2 subjects were incorrectly classified as *preterm*, while all the remaining subjects were correctly classified.

3.3   Relevance Maps

We generate relevance maps using the $\text{LRP}_{\alpha=2,\beta=1}$ rules for all the correctly classified subjects in our datasets. Figure 5 shows the average relevance maps of both *term* and *preterm* classes, across different ages at scan. Our results

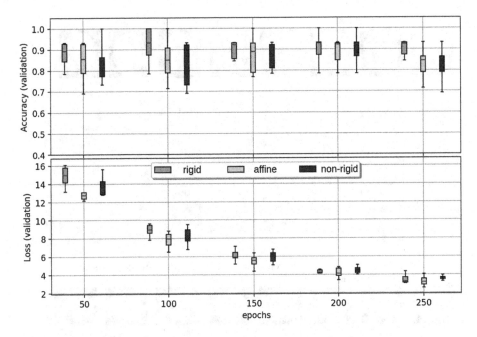

Fig. 4. The results of our 10-fold cross-validation for every 50 epochs during the training

show that in all of our three datasets, our trained models learnt to distinguish between *term* and *preterm* birth by looking at similar brain regions. In the case of the rigid and affine datasets, the resulting individual relevance maps were first propagated into a common space using the transformations generated through the creation of the non-rigid dataset, and then used to compute the average maps as shown in Fig. 5.

As a secondary analysis, we also investigated individual relevance maps. A few examples from the non-rigidly aligned dataset of both correctly classified and incorrectly classified cases are shown in Fig. 6, where the leftmost incorrectly classified subject was considered *preterm* by all three of our trained models. This

Table 2. Model performance on the holdout set, for all three types of data pre-processing, where: **rig** - rigid alignment, **aff** - affine alignment, **nrr** - non-rigid alignment, **TPR** - true positive rate (*term* class) and **TNR** - true negative rate (*preterm* class)

	Accuracy			TPR			TNR		
Dataset	**rig**	**aff**	**nrr**	**rig**	**aff**	**nrr**	**rig**	**aff**	**nrr**
Holdout	**0.88**	0.82	**0.88**	**0.9**	0.8	0.8	0.86	0.86	**1.0**

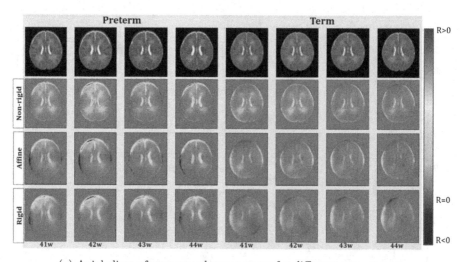

(a) Axial slices of average relevance maps for different ages at scan

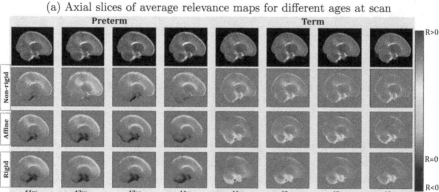

(b) Sagittal slices of average relevance maps for different ages at scan

Fig. 5. Average T2w images together with their average $\text{LRP}_{\alpha=2,\beta=1}$ relevance maps for both the *preterm* and *term* classes.

subject was born very close to the 37 weeks threshold (38 weeks gestational age and 42 weeks age at scan).

In both our individual and average relevance maps, our classifier learnt that the most prominent feature for *preterm* birth was the cerebrospinal fluid (CSF) found in the ventricles and surrounding the brain. This is in agreement with previous clinical literature where it was found that preterm babies have more CSF and less cortical folding due to impaired brain growth [5]. In fact, the subject that was incorrectly classified by our models as *preterm* appears to have a larger amount of CSF in its brain.

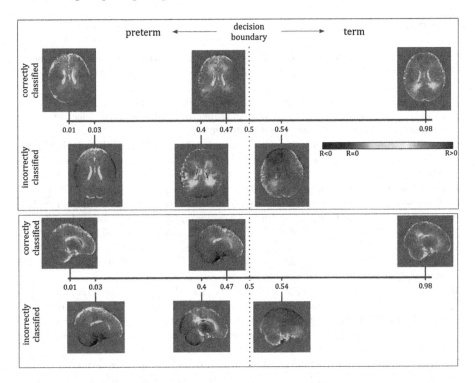

Fig. 6. $LRP_{\alpha=2,\beta=1}$ relevance maps for the non-rigid dataset of both axial and sagittal slices of individual subjects plotted against the decision boundary of our classifier.

4   Discussion and Future Work

In this study we showed the application of 3D convolutional neural networks with layer-wise relevance propagation for neonate T2w magnetic resonance imaging. Additionally, we investigated the impact of pre-registering our data to a common 40 weeks template on the classifier's performance. Our analysis showed that for our study the pre-alignment did not have a meaningful impact on the accuracy of our CNN model, and the generated relevance maps supported the same hypothesis.

Our study found that CSF is an important feature for distinguishing between *term* and *preterm* birth. For future work we plan to investigate the impact of registration errors in our proposed framework and to compare our results with voxel based statistical approaches, such as voxel-based morphometry. Moreover, we aim to include diffusion MRI data in our proposed framework in order to understand the different microstructural environments of term and preterm birth, and to explore and compare our current method with different interpretability techniques in order to evaluate the stability of our obtained results.

References

1. Arbabzadah, F., Montavon, G., Müller, K., Samek, W.: Identifying individual facial expressions by deconstructing a neural network. CoRR (2016). http://arxiv.org/abs/1606.07285

2. Bach, S., Binder, A., Montavon, G., Klauschen, F., Müller, K.R., Samek, W.: On pixel-wise explanations for non-linear classifier decisions by layer-wise relevance propagation. PLoS ONE **10**(7), e0130140 (2015)

3. Bach, S., Binder, A., Montavon, G., Müller, K., Samek, W.: Analyzing classifiers: Fisher vectors and deep neural networks. CoRR (2015). http://arxiv.org/abs/1512.00172

4. Cordero-Grande, L., Hughes, E.J., Hutter, J., Price, A.N., Hajnal, J.V.: Three-dimensional motion corrected sensitivity encoding reconstruction for multi-shot multi-slice MRI: application to neonatal brain imaging. Magn. Reson. Med. **79**(3), 1365–1376 (2018). https://onlinelibrary.wiley.com/doi/abs/10.1002/mrm.26796

5. Georgios, A., Hugo, L., Ulrika, A., Nelly, P., Mats, B.: Brain growth gains and losses in extremely preterm infants at term. Cereb. Cortex **25**(7), 1897–1905 (2014). https://doi.org/10.1093/cercor/bht431

6. Grigorescu, I., Cordero-Grande, L., Edwards, A.D., Hajnal, J., Modat, M., Deprez, M.: Interpretable convolutional neural networks for preterm birth classification. In: International Conference on Medical Imaging with Deep Learning - Extended Abstract Track, London, United Kingdom, 08–10 July 2019. https://openreview.net/pdf?id=SyevkEaEcE

7. Hughes, E.J., et al.: A dedicated neonatal brain imaging system. Magn. Reson. Med. **78**(2), 794–804 (2017). https://onlinelibrary.wiley.com/doi/abs/10.1002/mrm.26462

8. Ioffe, S., Szegedy, C.: Batch normalization: accelerating deep network training by reducing internal covariate shift. CoRR (2015). http://arxiv.org/abs/1502.03167

9. Montavon, G., Samek, W., Müller, K.R.: Methods for interpreting and understanding deep neural networks. Digit. Sig. Process. Rev. J. **73**, 1–15 (2018). https://doi.org/10.1016/j.dsp.2017.10.011

10. Rueckert, D., Sonoda, L.I., Hayes, C., Hill, D.L.G., Leach, M.O., Hawkes, D.J.: Nonrigid registration using free-form deformations: application to breast MR images. IEEE Trans. Med. Imaging **18**(8), 712–721 (1999). http://ieeexplore.ieee.org/stamp/stamp.jsp?tp=&arnumber=796284&isnumber=17288

11. Schuh, A., et al.: Unbiased construction of a temporally consistent morphological atlas of neonatal brain development. bioRxiv (2018). https://doi.org/10.1101/251512

12. Smith, L.N.: No more pesky learning rate guessing games. CoRR (2015). http://arxiv.org/abs/1506.01186

13. Sturm, I., Bach, S., Samek, W., Müller, K.: Interpretable deep neural networks for single-trial EEG classification. CoRR (2016). http://arxiv.org/abs/1604.08201

Dual Network Generative Adversarial Networks for Pediatric Echocardiography Segmentation

Libao Guo[1], Yujin Hu[1], Baiying Lei[1], Jie Du[1], Muyi Mao[2], Zelong Jin[2], Bei Xia[2(✉)], and Tianfu Wang[1(✉)]

[1] National-Regional Key Technology Engineering Laboratory for Medical Ultrasound, Guangdong Key Laboratory for Biomedical Measurements and Ultrasound Imaging, School of Biomedical Engineering, Health Science Center, Shenzhen University, Shenzhen 518060, China
tfwang@szu.edu.cn
[2] Ultrasound Department, Shenzhen Children Hospital, Hospital of Shantou University, Shantou, China
xiabeimd@qq.com

Abstract. Pediatric echocardiography is a commonly used medical imaging method for examining congenital heart disease (CHD). Accurate segmentation of pediatric echocardiography is usually used to derive quantitative measurements or biomarkers for subsequent CHD diagnosis and treatment planning. In order to achieve quality segmentation results, clinical pediatric echocardiography segmentation now is mainly performed by sonographers manually, which is time-consuming, labor-intensive, and highly dependent on the professional level of the sonographers. To address these issues, in this paper, we propose a novel convolutional neural network (CNN) architecture, called dual network generative adversarial networks (DNGAN). DNGAN consists of one generator and two discriminators, the generator uses parallel dual networks to extract more useful features to improve its performance. We use a dual discriminator to force the generator to learn more spatial features and segment the edges of the left heart more accurately. Experiments on the self-collected dataset shows that our proposed method achieves superior results over the state-of-the-art approaches and may help sonographers segment the left heart area faster and more accurately.

Keywords: Congenital heart disease · Pediatric echocardiography · Dual network generative adversarial networks · Dual discriminator · Image segmentation

This work was supported partly by National Natural Science Foundation of China (Nos. 61871274, 61801305 and 81571758), National Natural Science Foundation of Guangdong Province (No. 2017A030313377), Guangdong Pearl River Talents Plan (2016ZT06S220), Shenzhen Peacock Plan (Nos. KQTD2016053112051497 and KQTD2015033016 104926), and Shenzhen Key Basic Research Project (Nos. JCYJ20170413152804728, JCYJ20180507184647636, JCYJ201708181423 47251 and JCYJ20170818094109846).

© Springer Nature Switzerland AG 2019
Q. Wang et al. (Eds.): PIPPI 2019/SUSI 2019, LNCS 11798, pp. 113–122, 2019.
https://doi.org/10.1007/978-3-030-32875-7_13

1 Introduction

Congenital heart disease (CHD) refers to an abnormal anatomical structure of the heart or large blood vessels during the fetal period, or the automatically closed channel fails to close after birth. CHD has become China's most important birth defect, with an incidence rate about 1%, and the incidence in other parts of the world is similar [1, 2]. If the CHD is examined early and treated promptly, it can restore CHD back to normal [3]. The pediatric echocardiography is a commonly used medical imaging method for the CHD diagnosis. The physiological parameters by pediatric echocardiography can help diagnose and make treatment plans [4], while the accurate segmentation of cardiac anatomy is a key step for measuring physiological parameters. Currently, the CHD diagnosis is mainly based on the manual segmentation of sonographers, which has the low efficiency and the segmentation result is heavily dependent on the experience of the sonographers. The automated segmentation task of pediatric echocardiography has always been a hot topic for researchers.

For the cardiac segmentation, more and more researchers have focused on the convolutional neural network (CNN) and its variants since they have made remarkable achievements in the field of medical image analysis [5]. As one of the most segmentation structures, U-Net architecture has been widely used in medical image segmentation because of its flexible structure. For example, Zyuzin et al. [6] adopted U-Net architecture for echocardiographic left ventricle (LV) segmentation, and achieved good results of segmenting LV. Leclerc et al. [7] used U-Net and U-Net++ to segment LV of the echocardiogram, and measured the end-diastolic and end-systolic LV volumes, followed by the ejection fraction of the LV. Although the accuracy is lower than the ground truth, it opens the door to the field of automatic segmentation and echocardiography measurement. However, all these works are aimed at adult echocardiography. Unlike adult hearts, pediatric heart volume varies with age, and the heart is smaller than that of adult, which makes segmentation more difficult. Measuring the function of left heart clinically is very import for assessing the function of the heart. Hence, segmenting the LV and left atrium (LA) regions of the pediatric echocardiogram are quite important as well.

In Fig. 1, the first line indicates the pediatric echocardiogram four chamber (4CH) view and the second line shows the manual segmentation labels of LV and LA. The size of the LA changes more obviously during the cardiac cycle, and the boundary is more blurred. Hence, the accurate segmentation of LV and LA in 4CH echocardiography images has the following challenges: (1) Unclear boundaries due to noise and shadowing. (2) The size of the heart is different for everyone. (3) The size of the ventricles and atrium changes during each cycle of the heart. Based on the experience of our previous works, a wider network can learn more useful features and result in better segmentation results. Goodfellow et al. [8] proposed a generative adversarial net (GAN), which is a generative framework that uses generator and discriminator against each other to produce a better model. For the first time, Xue et al. [9] introduced adversarial neural network into medical image segmentation. By calculating multi-scale loss, the generator and discriminator are forced to learn more features of close and long distances, making the segmentation results better. In this paper, we propose a novel

CNN architecture using the FCN and U-Net networks to widen the network in parallel, which can extract more useful features. In order to achieve better segmentation performance of the network, the GANs framework is used to train the network. In order to extract both global and local features, we multiply the segmentation result by original image and label image, and calculate multi-scale l_1 loss. In order to learn more spatial features, the original image is connected with label image and segmentation result by width respectively, and the connection results are input to the discriminator. This will enable the model to segment the edges better. We test the proposed method on our own pediatric echocardiographic dataset, and find that the proposed method can reduce the influence of the changes of the left heart size and achieve better segmentation on the left heart region.

2 Method

2.1 Overview

Figure 2 demonstrates our proposed DNGAN architecture. DNGAN consists of one generator and two discriminators, the generator is composed of parallel fully convolutional network (FCN) and U-Net, FCN and U-Net extract features from image separately, multiply the extracted features elementally. This allows the generator to extract rich information and make the generator's segmentation results better. The structure of the two discriminators is the same. The segmentation result is multiplied by original image and label image respectively, and the results are input into the discriminator one to calculate multi-scale l_1 loss to force the generator and discriminator to learn both global and local features. The original image is connected with label image and segmentation result by width respectively, and the connection results are input to discriminator. Hence more spatial information can be learned.

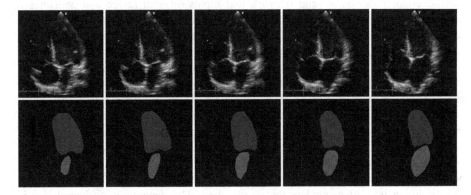

Fig. 1. The pediatric echocardiogram 4CH view is illustrated in the first line and the obvious noise is circled in red, the second line shows the manual segmentation labels of LV (in red) and LA (in green). (Color figure online)

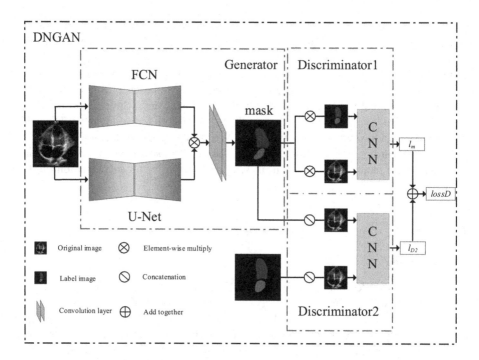

Fig. 2. Overview of the DNGAN, generator consists of two nets: FCN and U-Net. These two nets respectively extract features, and then fusion is adopted on these two nets. Discriminator has two identical CNN networks, each of them calculates the loss function, and then the loss is added and backward to generator.

2.2   Generator

The generator is an end-to-end network that inputs original image and generates a segmentation mask. Throughout the development of the entire neural network, the wider network makes it perform better by extracting more useful information. Therefore, we use the parallel dual networks as generators.

FCN [10] is a full convolutional network without a fully connected layer, which can adapt to any picture size input. FCN is an end-to-end network using original image as input and the segmentation result as output. By classifying the pixels of the image, semantic level image segmentation is achieved. In the feature extraction part, the original images are convolved by 3×3 kernel, convolution layer followed by batch normalization (BN) [11] and rectified linear unit (ReLU). BN layer is used to accelerate convergence and reduce over-fitting problems, and ReLU function can improve the nonlinearity of network. Down-sampling uses max pooling with size of (2, 2) and deconvolution is implemented in the up-sampling. The deconvolution kernel size is 3×3 and stride is 1.

The U-Net [12] network is similar to FCN, in which down-sampling first, and then up-sampling to the original size. In the feature extraction part, we use a 3×3 filter with stride = 1 like in FCN, convolution layer followed by BN and ReLU layers.

Down-sampling uses max pooling with size of (2, 2). In the up-sampling part, we use the method of bilinear interpolation. The method of skip connection is adopted between down-sampling and up-sampling. The feature map is cropped to ensure the same size before being concatenated to each other.

After the original image passes through FCN, the feature map f_1 is obtained. After the original image passes through U-Net, the feature map f_2 is obtained, and then f_1 and f_2 are multiplied. Hence, the final feature map F_G generated by the generator is:

$$F_G = f_1 \times f_2 \tag{1}$$

2.3   Discriminator

The discriminator is a six-layer convolutional neural networks and convolved by three kernels with size of 7×7, 5×5, and 3×3, respectively. Convolution layer is followed by batch normalization, and ReLU is replaced with LeakyReLU, which can effectively prevent the issue of gradient sparse. The feature maps of all layers are finally concatenated together, which can fuse features of different scales. By calculating multi-scale l_1 loss, it can capture long distance and short distance features, making segmentation results better. In order to study more spatial feature, the original image is connected with label image and segmentation result by width, respectively, and the connection results are input to the discriminator to calculate the loss. The two CNN networks have the same structure but the calculated loss functions are different. In details, the discriminator1 calculates the multi-scale loss, while the discriminator2 calculates the MESLoss and BCELoss.

2.4   Loss Function

The loss function of conventional GANs is defined as:

$$\frac{min}{G}\frac{max}{D} V(D, G) = E_{x \sim P_{data}(x)}[logD(x)] + E_{z \sim p_z(z)}log(1 - D(G(z)))] \tag{2}$$

In this function, x is the real image, and z is a random input for the generator, $G(z)$ is the generated mask, $D(x)$ indicates the probability that the discriminator discriminates whether the x is true, $D(G(z))$ indicates the probability that the discriminator discriminates whether the mask is true. The network achieves a balance by advertise learn. In our proposed DNGAN, the loss function is defined as:

$$\frac{min}{G}\frac{max}{D} L(D, G) = \frac{1}{N}\sum\nolimits_{n=1}^{N} l_m(f_{D1}(x_n \times G(x_n)), f_{D1}(x_n \times y_n)) + l_{cos}(G(x_n), y_n) + l_{D2}(G(x_n, y_n)) \tag{3}$$

In this function, given a dataset with N training images x_n and the corresponding ground truth label maps y_n, where l_m is the mean absolute error, l_m can be described as:

$$l_m(f_D(\mathbf{x}), f_D(\mathbf{x}')) = \frac{1}{L}\sum_{i=1}^{L} ||f_D^i(x) - f_D^i(x')||_1 \tag{4}$$

where $f_D(\mathbf{x})$ represents the feature extracted by the discriminator D, L represents the total number of layers of the discriminator, $f_D^i(x)$ represents the feature learned by the i-th layer, l_{cos} is a typical cross entropy loss, which can be described as:

$$l_{cos} = -\frac{1}{N}\sum_i log\frac{\exp(p_i)}{\sum_j \exp(p_j)} \tag{5}$$

where p_i is the probability distribution of prediction result, p_j is probability distribution of label maps. l_{D2} is the second loss function of the discriminator, and the discriminator discriminates whether the input image is a generated mask or a truth label. The loss function consists of two parts, the first part is to calculate the loss function of the input ground truth. We use *MESLoss* and the formula is:

$$lossd1 = \frac{\sum_{i=1}^{N}(x_i - y_i)^2}{N} \tag{6}$$

where x is the ground truth, y is the same as x, all tensors with a value of 1, i indicates the position of the element. The second part calculates the loss function of the generated mask input discriminator. We use *BCELoss* and the formula is:

$$lossd2 = -\frac{y_i log x_i + (1 - y_i)log(1 - x_i)}{w_i} \tag{7}$$

where x is generated mask, y is the same as x, all tensors with a value of 0, i indicates the position of the element. Finally, we define l_{D2} as:

$$l_{D2} = \frac{lossd1 + lossd2}{2} \tag{8}$$

3   Experiments and Results

3.1   Dataset and Implementation

The dataset we trained and tested includes a total of 87 pediatric echocardiographic videos, which are collected from the local hospital. The collected subjects are healthy child aged from 0 to 10 years. Each video has at least 24 frames and contains a complete cardiac cycle. We randomly select 67 videos to extract 1765 images as training set, and the rest of 20 videos are decompressed 451 images as test set. The resolution of the original image is 1016×708 and 636×432. Before training, all images are properly center cropped. The resolution of the cropped image is 704×704 and 448×448.

All experiments are conducted on a computer with Intel(R) Xeon(R) CPU E5-2620 v4 @ 2.10 GHz, GPU NVIDIA TITAN Xp, and 64G of RAM, using PyTorch deep learning framework. In the training phase, we set the initial learning rate of the generator to 1e-3, and gradually falling during training. The stochastic gradient descent (SGD) is utilized for optimization and updating weights. We set the momentum = 0.99. While training the discriminator, we initialize the learning rate to 1e-4. The adaptive moment estimation (Adam) is utilized for optimization and updating weights. To evaluate our approach, we use the Dice index, Jaccard similarity coefficient, Recall and Precision as evaluation indices.

In order to verify the effectiveness of our proposed approach, we design and complete the following experiments. The performances of FCN and U-Net networks are firstly evaluated. In order to verify that the wider network has better performance, we use two parallel FCN, two parallel U-Net, one FCN and one U-Net to expand the network and evaluate their performance separately. We train the network in adversarial framework to verify its effectiveness. The performance of different networks is shown in Table 1.

In this table, U_UNet means parallel U-Net, F_FNet means parallel FCN, UmulF means parallel FCN and U-Net and then the extracted features are fused by the multiply method, UmulF_G indicates that the UmulF network is trained with proposed GAN network framework. In order to find the best way to fuse network features, we perform the following experiments. We multiply the feature elements of FCN and U-Net networks, add the corresponding elements and concatenate them by channel, and then we use a 1 X 1 convolution with a stride = 1. The different fusion methods of the network are put into the proposed GAN framework for training, and the comparison results are shown in Table 2.

Table 1. Segmentation performance comparison of different networks.

Network	Dice			Jaccard			Recall			Precision		
	LV	LA	Mean	LV	LA	Mean	LV	LA	Mean	LV	LA	Mean
U-Net	0.918	0.846	0.882	0.853	0.748	0.800	**0.953**	0.899	0.926	0.894	0.831	0.863
U_UNet	0.923	0.868	0.896	0.860	0.778	0.818	0.918	0.898	0.908	0.932	0.862	0.897
FCN	0.927	0.847	0.887	0.867	0.751	0.809	0.942	0.892	0.917	0.918	0.840	0.879
F_FNet	**0.945**	0.893	0.919	**0.898**	0.813	0.855	0.937	**0.919**	**0.928**	0.956	0.883	0.920
UmulF	**0.945**	0.900	0.922	0.896	**0.824**	0.860	0.934	0.884	0.909	**0.959**	**0.930**	**0.945**
UmulF_G	**0.945**	**0.901**	**0.923**	0.897	**0.824**	**0.861**	0.938	0.898	0.918	0.955	0.918	0.936

Table 2. Network performance comparison with different fusion methods.

Network	Dice			Jaccard			Recall			Precision		
	LV	LA	Mean	LV	LA	Mean	LV	LA	Mean	LV	LA	Mean
UmulF	0.945	0.900	0.922	0.896	**0.824**	0.860	0.934	0.884	0.909	**0.959**	**0.930**	**0.945**
UmulF_G	0.945	**0.901**	**0.923**	0.897	**0.824**	**0.861**	0.938	0.898	0.918	0.955	0.918	0.936
UaddF	0.946	0.896	0.921	0.898	0.817	0.857	0.942	0.912	0.927	0.953	0.895	0.924
UaddF_G	**0.947**	0.889	0.917	**0.900**	0.806	0.854	**0.950**	**0.914**	**0.932**	0.947	0.884	0.916
UcatF	0.943	0.895	0.919	0.893	0.817	0.855	0.947	0.904	0.926	0.942	0.902	0.922
UcatF_G	0.944	0.897	0.921	0.896	0.820	0.857	0.947	0.910	0.928	0.945	0.901	0.923

In Table 2, UaddF indicates that the FCN and U-Net networks are fused by the addition method, UcatF indicates that the FCN and U-Net networks are fused by channel. The suffix _G indicates that the network is trained with the proposed GAN framework. The best results are bolded in Table 2. It can be observed that the performance of the wider network segmentation is better. By the additional GAN network framework, the performance is improved. The radar chart of the comparison results of different networks segmentation performance is shown in Fig. 3. We can see that different fusion methods have less impact on network performance, and network segmentation performance of different widths is quite different. The visual comparison of the segmentation results is shown in Fig. 4. On the other side, according to the results, we find that the segmentation result of the LA is worse than that of the LV.

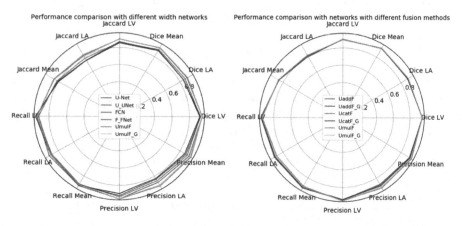

Fig. 3. Segmentation results of different networks in terms of a radar chart.

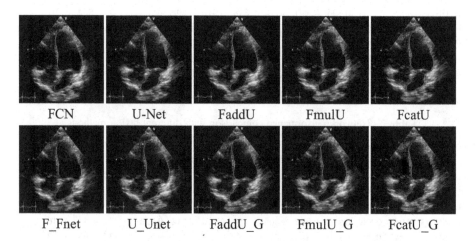

Fig. 4. Segmentation results of different networks, the red curve is the label marked by the expert manually, and the green curve is the prediction result of the network. (Color figure online)

That is because the size of LA changes more obviously than LA during the whole cardiac cycle, and the boundary is not clear enough.

4 Conclusion

In this paper, we propose a novel adversarial framework for pediatric echocardiographic segmentation. In this proposed framework, the structure of parallel FCN and U-Net is used to widen the network. Moreover, multi-scale l_1 loss is calculated so that generator and discriminator learn more features from long distance and short distance. Also, in this work, more spatial features are learned by concatenating the original image with segmentation result and the dimension image by width. The dual discriminator can boost the performance of the generator. Benefiting from the above contributions, our method has achieved better results in the pediatric echocardiography left heart segmentation task, compared to state-of-the-art methods. In the future, we plan to further measure the volumes of LV and LA. Moreover, our proposed method is memory consuming, we plan to use knowledge distillation to reduce memory consumption.

References

1. Linde, D.V.D., et al.: Birth prevalence of congenital heart disease worldwide: a systematic review and meta-analysis. J. Am. Coll. Cardiol. **58**, 2241–2247 (2011)
2. Ma, X.j., Huang, G.Y.: Current status of screening, diagnosis, and treatment of neonatal congenital heart disease in China. World J. Pediatr. **14**, 313–314 (2018)
3. Jone, P.N., Gould, R., Barrett, C., Younoszai, A.K., Fonseca, B.: Data-driven quality improvement project to increase the value of the congenital echocardiographic report. Pediatr. Cardiol. **39**, 726–730 (2018)
4. Lopez, L., et al.: Recommendations for quantification methods during the performance of a pediatric echocardiogram: a report from the pediatric measurements writing group of the american society of echocardiography pediatric and congenital heart disease council. J. Am. Soc. Echocardiogr. **23**, 465–495 (2010)
5. Greenspan, H., Ginneken, B.V., Summers, R.M.: Guest editorial deep learning in medical imaging: overview and future promise of an exciting new technique. IEEE Trans. Med. Imaging **35**(5), 1153–1159 (2016)
6. Zyuzin, V., et al.: Identification of the left ventricle endocardial border on two-dimensional ultrasound images using the convolutional neural network Unet. In: Ural Symposium on Biomedical Engineering Radioelectronics and Information Technology (2018)
7. Leclerc, S., et al.: Deep learning for segmentation using an open large-scale dataset in 2D echocardiography. IEEE Trans. Med. Imaging (2019)
8. Goodfellow, I.J., et al.: Generative adversarial nets. In: Advances in Neural Information Processing Systems, pp. 2672–2680 (2014)
9. Xue, Y., Xu, T., Zhang, H., Long, L.R., Huang, X.L.: SegAN: adversarial network with multi-scale L_1 loss for medical image segmentation. Comput. Vis. Pattern Recogn. **16**, 383–392 (2018)

10. Long, J., Shelhamer, E., Darrell, T.: Fully convolutional networks for semantic segmentation. In: Proceedings of the IEEE Conference on Computer Vision and Pattern Recognition, pp. 3431–3440 (2015)
11. Ioffe, S., Szegedy, C.: Batch normalization: accelerating deep network training by reducing internal covariate shift. arXiv:1502.03167 (2015)
12. Ronneberger, O., Fischer, P., Brox, T.: U-Net: convolutional networks for biomedical image segmentation. In: Navab, N., Hornegger, J., Wells, W.M., Frangi, A.F. (eds.) MICCAI 2015. LNCS, vol. 9351, pp. 234–241. Springer, Cham (2015). https://doi.org/10.1007/978-3-319-24574-4_28

Reproducibility of Functional Connectivity Estimates in Motion Corrected Fetal fMRI

Daniel Sobotka[1]([✉]), Roxane Licandro[1,3], Michael Ebner[4], Ernst Schwartz[1],
Tom Vercauteren[4], Sebastien Ourselin[4], Gregor Kasprian[2], Daniela Prayer[2],
and Georg Langs[1]

[1] Computational Imaging Research Lab, Department of Biomedical Imaging and
Image-Guided Therapy, Medical University of Vienna, Vienna, Austria
`daniel.sobotka@meduniwien.ac.at`
[2] Division of Neuroradiology and Musculoskeletal Radiology,
Department of Biomedical Imaging and Image-Guided Therapy,
Medical University of Vienna, Vienna, Austria
[3] Computer Vision Lab, Institute of Visual Computing and Human-Centered
Technology, TU Wien, Vienna, Austria
[4] School of Biomedical Engineering and Imaging Sciences, King's College London,
London, UK

Abstract. Preprocessing and motion correction are essential steps in
resting state functional Magnetic Resonance Imaging (rs-fMRI) of the
fetal brain. They aim to address the difficult task of removing artefacts caused by fetal movement or maternal breathing, and aim to suppress erroneous signal correlations caused by motion. While preprocessing standards have been established in the adult brain, motion correction of fetal rs-fMRI and subsequent interpretation of processed data is
still challenging. Here, we evaluate the effect of different preprocessing
methods and motion correction on rs-fMRI sequences by assessing reproducibility of functional connectivity estimates. For slice-based motion
correction of 4D fetal rs-fMRI, we extend a high-resolution reconstruction approach presented for structural fetal MRI. Correlation, standard
deviation and structural similarity index are evaluated on the whole cortex, on specific regions and at different gestational ages. Results show
improved reproducibility and signal interpretability after preprocessing
with motion correction enabling the quantification of long-range correlation patterns of the developing default mode network in the fetal brain.

1 Introduction

The analysis of spatial and temporal brain signal correlations forms a key component to understand the maturation processes of brain activity, their interaction and their link to cognition in the developing brain [4]. Preprocessing
methods used in functional Magnetic Resonance Imaging (fMRI) have been
developed for adult or infant brains and have recently been also applied on

© Springer Nature Switzerland AG 2019
Q. Wang et al. (Eds.): PIPPI 2019/SUSI 2019, LNCS 11798, pp. 123–132, 2019.
https://doi.org/10.1007/978-3-030-32875-7_14

fetal rs-fMRI [4,13]. Here, motion correction is particularly important and necessary, due to continuous movement of the fetus itself or causes such as maternal breathing. Subsequent analysis of Functional Connectivity (FC) relies on the assumption that measurements have neural origin, while signal disruption and motion artifacts can artificially increase the correlation between brain voxels even after re-alignment of image data and thus distort study results [10]. Existing fetal studies [3,14,15,17] used different processing combinations as normalization, smoothing, motion censoring, motion regression or motion correction. The specific effects of these methods on the reliability of the resulting fetal rs-fMRI signals and corresponding FC are poorly understood.

Contribution. Here, we assess the effect of state-of-the-art preprocessing techniques on the *reproducibility* of rs-fMRI signals and the computation of short- and long-range functional connectivity in the fetal brain, providing an evaluation scheme and corresponding metrics. Jakab et al. [5] used correlation, standard deviation and the structural similarity index as metrics for evaluating within-subject reproducibility in diffusion tensor imaging. Inspired by this approach, we applied these metrics on resting state fetal fMRI for the proposed preprocessing pipelines. To correct for motion, we extend the 3D Motion Correction (MC) and High-Resolution-Reconstruction (HRR) approach for fetal MRI proposed in [1] for 4D fetal rs-fMRI. Quality assessment of the signal is a necessary step, since there exists no standardized pipeline for fetal fMRI preprocessing. We present different quality assessment schemata to evaluate the signal before and after different preprocessing approaches on the cortex, on specific regions and age related dependencies. The proposed reproducibility evaluation scheme is introduced in Sect. 2. The evaluation results are presented in Sect. 3 and in Sect. 4 this work concludes with a discussion of optimal preprocessing of fetal rs-fMRI and discussion of possible future directions.

2   Methodology

In this section, the proposed evaluation framework and slice-based motion correction of 4D fetal rs-fMRI is summarized. Subsequently, the proposed signal quality assessment strategy is presented. The study population and imaging protocol used for evaluation is introduced in Sect. 3.

Structural Preprocessing: Fetal MRI preprocessing included atlas-based alignment, brain segmentation, generating of cortex meshes [11] and manual registration with functional data.

Preprocessing Pipelines: We incorporated 7 different fMRI preprocessing pipelines (cf. Table 1 for more detail) into the reproducibility test framework proposed. Inspired by [9] we used combinations of bias field correction [19], slice timing correction [6], high resolution 4D motion correction (see Sect. 2.1 for detailed information) and motion regression [9].

2.1   4D High Resolution Motion Correction (HRMC)

In this work, two different HRMC strategies are proposed: (1) Volume-to-Volume (V2V) and (2) Slice-to-Volume (S2V) HRMC for fetal brain rs-fMRI. *Volume-to-Volume HRMC* is performed by rigidly registering each stack (time point) individually to a target fMRI stack using symmetric block-matching based on normalized cross correlation [8]. For individual *Slice-to-Volume HRMC*, a higher-resolution reference volume is estimated by using the first 15 time points to create a 1 mm isotropic volume with the super-resolution reconstruction framework [1], whereby three two-step motion-correction/reconstruction cycles are performed. Subsequently, all slice stacks each acquired at the same time point are rigidly registered to this higher-resolution reference using normalized cross correlation as similarity measure. The final volumes are reconstructed on the original grid by solving the slice acquisition model [1,2] in a least-squares formulation using first-order Tikhonov regularization, i.e.

$$\min_{\mathbf{x} \geq 0} \left(\sum_{k=1}^{K} \frac{1}{2} \|\mathbf{y}_k - \mathbf{A}_k \mathbf{x}\|_{\ell^2}^2 + \frac{\alpha}{2} \|\boldsymbol{\nabla} \mathbf{x}\|_{\ell^2}^2 \right), \tag{1}$$

for all individual slices $\mathbf{x}_k$, $k = 1, \ldots, K$ associated with a single time point. This takes into account either the obtained Volume-to-Volume or Slice-to-Volume motion estimates for the linear blurring and downsampling operator $\mathbf{A}_k$ [1].

Table 1. Functional preprocessing pipelines incorporated into the framework proposed. Each pipeline has different combinations of bias field correction (BFC), slice timing correction (STC), Slice-to-Volume motion correction (S2V), Volume-to-Volume motion correction (V2V) and motion regression (MR)

	BFC	STC	BFC+STC	STC+BFC	S2V	V2V	MR
Pipeline 1 (P1)	✓						
Pipeline 2 (P2)		✓					
Pipeline 3 (P3)			✓				
Pipeline 4 (P4)				✓			
Pipeline 5 (P5)		✓			✓		
Pipeline 6 (P6)		✓				✓	
Pipeline 7 (P7)		✓			✓		✓

2.2   Short-Range and Long-Range Connectivity Computation

The Pearson correlation coefficient is computed between the time course t ($t = 1, \ldots, M$; M is the number of time frames) of each brain node $x_i(t)$ and $x_j(t)$ (i, j $= 1, \ldots, N$, where N is the number of nodes observed) [7,12]:

$$\mathbf{CM_t} = \frac{\sum[(x_i(t) - \bar{x}_i)(x_j(t) - \bar{x}_j)]}{\sqrt{\sum[(x_i(t) - \bar{x}_i)^2(x_j(t) - \bar{x}_j)^2]}} \tag{2}$$

As a result an $N \times N$ correlation matrix CM_t for every subject S was obtained, with $\bar{x}_i$, $\bar{x}_j$ the mean node intensity across all time points at position i and j. To define short- and long-range connectivity, we calculate the Euclidean distance (ED) between coordinates of nodes. For every cortical node, we count high correlating time courses (threshold ≥ 0.4), and assign them to short- and long-range splitting at a distance roughly equivalent to 15 mm in an adult brain [12]. This distance is changed from 4.4 mm (gestational age of 20 weeks) to 8.8 mm (gestational age of 40 weeks) in relation to the fetal brain size, since fetus' brains are resampled on a standard brain (fsaverage5)[1], which can introduce correlations from nearby brain nodes [7,12].

2.3   Assessment of Reproducibility

According to [10] signal disruption and motion artifacts increase the correlation between brain voxels and distort signals. We hypothesize that signals of two time ranges of a subject should be more similar after preprocessing, compared to the uncorrected signals, if artefacts are removed. Thus, we divided the rs-fMRI associated with each fetus in two time ranges u and v. We observed that there may be more fetal movement and maternal breathing at the beginning of the recording session, which led us to the following definition of the two time ranges: $u = [[1, \frac{M}{4}], [\frac{2M}{4}, \frac{3M}{4}]]$ and $v = [[\frac{M}{4}, \frac{2M}{4}], [\frac{3M}{4}, M]]$ where M is the number of time points in each dataset. For assessing the reproducibility of a subject's signal after preprocessing, the difference of correlations (ΔC) and standard deviations ($\Delta \sigma$) between a subject's S extracted time courses $x(u)$ and $x(v)$ are computed as well as the *SSIM* index [5].

Correlation Difference ΔC. In a first step for $x_S(u)$ and $x_S(v)$ correlation matrices CM_u^S and CM_v^S are computed following Eq. 2. Subsequently, the correlation difference is computed following Eq. 3

$$\Delta C_S = \frac{1}{N^2} \sum_{i=1}^{N} \sum_{j=1}^{N} |CM_u(i,j) - CM_v(i,j)| \tag{3}$$

Standard deviation Difference $\Delta \sigma$. The standard deviation σ of a time course t at node x of a subject is calculated using Eq. 4, where $\bar{x}$ is the mean of the time course $x(t)$ at node x:

$$\sigma_t = \sqrt{\frac{1}{M} \sum_{t=1}^{M} (x(t) - \bar{x})^2} \tag{4}$$

Subsequently, for every subject the standard deviation difference $\Delta \sigma$ is computed based on standard deviation estimates of time course u and v using Eq. 5.

$$\Delta \sigma = \frac{1}{N} \sum_{i=1}^{N} |\sigma_u - \sigma_v| \tag{5}$$

---

[1] https://surfer.nmr.mgh.harvard.edu/.

Structural Similarity (SSIM) Index. Is a quality assessment metric [5,16], which is calculated between $x(u)$ and $x(v)$ for all brain nodes of a subject.

$$SSIM(u,v) = [l(u,v)]^{\alpha}[c(u,v)]^{\beta}[s(u,v)]^{\gamma} \tag{6}$$

It consists of three terms, the luminance, contrast and structural term:

$$l(u,v) = \frac{2\mu_u\mu_v + c_1}{\mu_u^2 + \mu_v^2 + c_1} \tag{7}$$

$$c(u,v) = \frac{2\sigma_u\sigma_v + c_2}{\sigma_u^2 + \sigma_v^2 + c_2} \tag{8}$$

$$s(u,v) = \frac{\sigma_{uv} + c_3}{\sigma_u\sigma_v + c_3} \tag{9}$$

where μ_u, μ_v, σ_u, σ_v and σ_{uv} are the means, standard deviations and cross covariance. α, β and γ are used to adjust relative importance of the three terms, where the constants c_1, c_2 and c_3 are included to avoid term instabilities [16].

3   Results

We analysed the reproducibility of a subject's signal after the application of 7 different preprocessing pipelines using the difference of correlations (ΔC), standard deviations ($\Delta\sigma$) and the *SSIM* index [5] as evaluation metrics (introduced in Sect. 2.3).

Data. The study includes a total of 21 fMRI sequences from fetuses between the 20th and 40th gestational week (GW, mean: 28.43, standard deviation: 5.43) with normal brain development. Functional magnetic resonance imaging was performed on a 1.5 T clinical scanner (Philips Medical Systems, Best, The Netherlands) using a sensitivity encoding (SENSE) cardiac coil with five elements (three posterior, two anterior) wrapped around the mother's abdomen, utilizing single-shot gradient-recalled echo-planar imaging (EPI) and no cardiac gating with the following setup: 50 ms echo time, 1000 ms repetition time, 3 mm slice thickness, 18 slices and 96 volumes. The pregnant women were examined in the supine or left decubitus position (feet first), and no contrast agents or sedatives were administered. In order to receive the optimal MR signal, the coil was readjusted depending on the position of the fetal head during the imaging procedure.

3.1   Reproducibility of Functional Connectivity on the Cortex

In Fig. 1 (upper left plot) a boxplot of the ΔC metric estimated over all subjects, for the uncorrected signal and for the signal after every 7 preprocessing approaches is visualised. The $\Delta\sigma$ and *SSIM* metric are visualised in the same way in the upper right and lower right part of Fig. 1. In case of correlation and standard deviation a low value refers to better reproducibility, while for the similarity

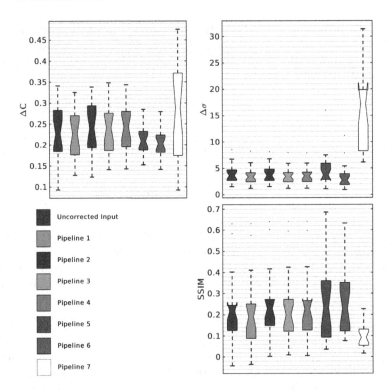

Fig. 1. Reproducibility metrics with correlation differences, standard deviation differences and structural similarity index comparison between the uncorrected input (UNC), bias field correction (BFC), slice timing correction (STC), Slice-to-Volume motion correction (S2V MC), volume to volume motion correction (V2V MC) and motion regression (MR).

index a higher value is interpreted as better reproducibility. First we evaluated if bias field correction and slice timing correction have a positive impact on the reproducibility. Therefore, the uncorrected signal (UNC) is preprocessed using Pipeline P1, P2, P3 and P4 introduced in Sect. 2.

Among P1–P4, P3 shows the best result, since the correlation differences (mean: 0.24, SD: 0.06) and standard deviation differences (mean: 3.53, SD: 1.65) are reduced and the SSIM score shows similar results (mean: 0.23, SD: 0.17) compared with the pipelines P1, P2 and P4. Thus, building on the P3, the Slice-to-Volume (S2V) and Volume-to-Volume (V2V) motion correction approaches are evaluated (P5 and P6) and visualised in Fig. 1. The correlation differences of S2V (P5, mean: 0.21) and V2V (P6, mean: 0.21) show similar results, while S2V leads to higher standard deviation differences (mean: 4.52), but a higher SSIM value (mean: 0.25, SD: 0.18, Q3: 0.36) compared to V2V (mean: 0.25, SD: 0.16, Q3: 0.35). Therefore, we chose P5 as the best preprocessing pipeline. An increase of the average SSIM mean value from 0.2 (UNC) to 0.25 is observable after motion correction, which can be refered to a positive effect from the motion correction technique. Motion regression (P7) relies on the precise estimate of motion parameters during the alignment, errors in the estimates can cause the regression to introduce or amplify artifacts in the data leading to comparably worse reproducibility (mean SSIM: 0.1, SD SSIM: 0.06, ΔC: 0.27, $\Delta \sigma$: 15.69). In that light, using other proxy measures of motion induced signal might be a better strategy. The three evaluation measures assess the reproducibility of signal correlation analysis, and the overall loss of structure in the data. The value of reproducibility as a quality measure relies on the assumption that motion is different across the entire scan.

3.2   Reproducibility of Functional Connectivity in 7 Yeo Networks

We used the Yeo parcellation [18] to subdivide the brain into seven networks (visual (Yeo 1), somatomotor (Yeo 2), dorsal attention (Yeo 3), ventral attention (Yeo 4), limbic (Yeo 5), frontoparietal (Yeo 6) and default mode network (Yeo 7)). Figure 2 shows boxplots of the correlation differences over all subjects for uncorrected (UNC, red) and Pipeline 5 (blue) for all Yeo networks. The results indicate that the signal after applying Pipeline 5 is more reproducible compared to the uncorrected input, since a reduced correlation difference and a higher SSIM values are observable. Furthermore it shows consistant differences across networks, with highest SSIM in ventral attention (mean: 0.27), limbic (mean: 0.36) and frontoparietal networks (mean: 0.3).

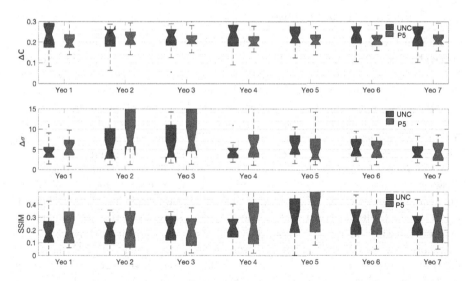

Fig. 2. Correlation differences (top), standard deviation differences (middle) and SSIM (bottom) between the uncorrected input (UNC) and after application of Pipeline 5 for each Yeo network. (Color figure online)

3.3 Age-Related Reproducibility

To test if age has an influence on reproducibility, we divided our dataset into two age ranges: GW 20–24 (6 subjects) and GW 25–40 (15 subjects), motivated by pronounced cortical folding process starting around the GW 24 [11]. In both ranges, motion correction improves reproducibility, and the resulting value ranges are largely comparable, but more data is needed to test for specific trends. Figure 3 shows values for the default mode network (Yeo 7).

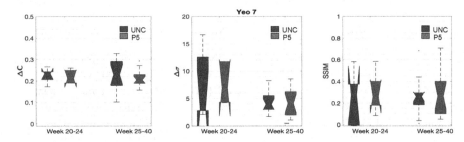

Fig. 3. Age related correlation differences (left), standard deviation differences (middle) and SSIM value (right) in the default mode network (Yeo 7) of the uncorrected input (UNC) and after application of Pipeline 5 (P5).

3.4 Connectivity Comparison

Finally, in the last experiment we compare the degree of short- and long-range connectivity before and after preprocessing on every cortical surface point. Figure 4 shows for the uncorrected input (top row) for each of the two parts of the time course the mean short- and long-range degree value visualized on the surface over all subjects. The bottom row shows the connectivity after the best reproducibility preprocessing pipeline P5 including bias field, slice timing and Slice-to-Volume motion correction. The short-range connectivity (left side) is less sensitive to motion compared to long-range connectivity (right side), and preprocessing shows a stronger effect. In particular long-range connectivity shows high values across the entire cortex, while after motion correction, a more nuanced image emerges. High long-range connection areas partly corresponding to the default mode network become visible, suggesting that these network develops already during gestation. The SSIM values between the two time windows on the cortex for the uncorrected input (short-range: 0.92, long-range: 0.36) and after preprocessing (short-range: 0.93, long-range: 0.26) indicate, that with preprocessing a higher short-range reproducibility is achieved. The limitations of the SSIM metric are visible in the long-range comparison, where the motion motivated uncorrected input obtained a higher SSIM value as after preprocessing.

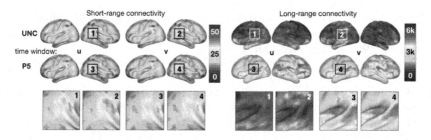

Fig. 4. Short- and long-range mean connectivity degree value visualized on the surface between the uncorrected input and after preprocessing with Pipeline 5. Long-range connections benefit substantially from preprocessing.

4   Conclusion

In this work, we introduced a *reproduciblity test framework*, for evaluating the effect of 7 different preprocessing and motion correction pipelines for fetal rs-fMRI sequences and corresponding functional connectivity estimates. The comparisons of the proposed pipelines were performed based on the reproduciblity of correlation, standard deviation and the structural similarity index for two parts of every time course from each subject. The combination of bias field, slice timing and slice-to-volume motion correction performed best. We showed that preprocessing with motion correction leads to better reproducibility results on the whole cortex and on the Yeo 7 networks. We show that preprocessing has a positive effect on reproducibility for in utero rs-fMRI acquisitions, and in particular that long-range connectivity is more sensitive to motion artefacts compared to short-range connectivity patterns. Reproducible long-range connectivity are located at the default mode network after applying preprocessing and motion correction. For future work, we will use a greater population to increase the generalisability and investigate how short-range an long-range patterns develop during gestation across the cortex. We did not study the link between motion and gestational age in this paper, but note that there might be a relationship. Another point of future work is to take motion estimates for assessing the impact of different levels of motion into account.

Acknowledgement. This work was supported by The Wellcome Trust [WT101957; 203148/Z/16/Z], the Engineering and Physical Sciences Research Council [NS/A000027/1; NS/A000049/1], Austrian Science Fund FWF (I2714-B31) and EU H2020 Marie Sklodowska-Curie No 765148.

References

1. Ebner, M., et al.: An automated localization, segmentation and reconstruction framework for fetal brain MRI. In: Frangi, A.F., Schnabel, J.A., Davatzikos, C., Alberola-López, C., Fichtinger, G. (eds.) MICCAI 2018. LNCS, vol. 11070, pp. 313–320. Springer, Cham (2018). https://doi.org/10.1007/978-3-030-00928-1_36

2. Gholipour, A., Estroff, J.A., Warfield, S.K.: Robust super-resolution volume reconstruction from slice acquisitions: application to fetal brain MRI. IEEE Trans. Med. Imaging **29**(10), 1739–1758 (2010)
3. van den Heuvel, M.I., et al.: Hubs in the human fetal brain network. Dev. Cogn. Neurosci. **30**, 108–115 (2018)
4. Jakab, A., et al.: Fetal functional imaging portrays heterogeneous development of emerging human brain networks. Front. Hum. Neurosci. **8**, 852 (2014)
5. Jakab, A., Tuura, R., Kellenberger, C., Scheer, I.: In utero diffusion tensor imaging of the fetal brain: a reproducibility study. NeuroImage Clin. **15**, 601–612 (2017)
6. Jenkinson, M., Beckmann, C.F., Behrens, T.E., Woolrich, M.W., Smith, S.M.: Fsl. Neuroimage **62**(2), 782–790 (2012)
7. Licandro, R., Nenning, K.H., Schwartz, E., Kollndorfer, K., Bartha-Doering, L., Langs, G.: Changing functional connectivity in the child's developing brain affected by ischaemic stroke. In: Proceedings MICCAI PIPPI (2016)
8. Modat, M., Cash, D.M., Daga, P., Winston, G.P., Duncan, J.S., Ourselin, S.: Global image registration using a symmetric block-matching approach. J. Med. Imaging **1**(2), 024003 (2014)
9. Poldrack, R.A., Mumford, J.A., Nichols, T.E.: Handbook of Functional MRI Data Analysis. Cambridge University Press, Cambridge (2011)
10. Power, J.D., Schlaggar, B.L., Petersen, S.E.: Recent progress and outstanding issues in motion correction in resting state fMRI. Neuroimage **105**, 536–551 (2015)
11. Schwartz, E., Kasprian, G., Jakab, A., Prayer, D., Schöpf, V., Langs, G.: Modeling fetal cortical expansion using graph-regularized Gompertz models. In: Ourselin, S., Joskowicz, L., Sabuncu, M.R., Unal, G., Wells, W. (eds.) MICCAI 2016. LNCS, vol. 9900, pp. 247–254. Springer, Cham (2016). https://doi.org/10.1007/978-3-319-46720-7_29
12. Sepulcre, J., Liu, H., Talukdar, T., Martincorena, I., Yeo, B.T., Buckner, R.L.: The organization of local and distant functional connectivity in the human brain. PLoS Comput. Biol. **6**(6), e1000808 (2010)
13. Thomason, M.E., et al.: Intrinsic functional brain architecture derived from graph theoretical analysis in the human fetus. PLoS ONE **9**(5), e94423 (2014)
14. Thomason, M.E., et al.: Prenatal lead exposure impacts cross-hemispheric and long-range connectivity in the human fetal brain. NeuroImage **191**, 186–192 (2019)
15. Thomason, M.E., et al.: Weak functional connectivity in the human fetal brain prior to preterm birth. Sci. Rep. **7**, 39286 (2017)
16. Wang, Z., Bovik, A.C., Sheikh, H.R., Simoncelli, E.P., et al.: Image quality assessment: from error visibility to structural similarity. IEEE Trans. Image Process. **13**(4), 600–612 (2004)
17. Wheelock, M., et al.: Sex differences in functional connectivity during fetal brain development. Dev. Cognitive Neurosci. **36**, 100632 (2019)
18. Yeo, B.T., et al.: The organization of the human cerebral cortex estimated by intrinsic functional connectivity. J. Neurophysiol. **106**(3), 1125–1165 (2011)
19. Zhang, Y., Brady, M., Smith, S.: Segmentation of brain MR images through a hidden Markov random field model and the expectation-maximization algorithm. IEEE Trans. Med. Imaging **20**(1), 45–57 (2001)

Plug-and-Play Priors for Reconstruction-Based Placental Image Registration

Jiarui Xing[1(✉)], Ulugbek Kamilov[2,3], Wenjie Wu[4,5], Yong Wang[5], and Miaomiao Zhang[1,6]

[1] Electrical and Computer Engineering, University of Virginia, Charlottesville, USA
jx8fh@virginia.edu
[2] Computer Science and Engineering, Washington University in St. Louis, St. Louis, USA
[3] Electrical and Systems Engineering, Washington University in St. Louis, St. Louis, USA
[4] Biomedical Engineering, Washington University in St. Louis, St. Louis, USA
[5] Obstetrics and Gynecology, Washington University in St. Louis, St. Louis, USA
[6] Computer Science, University of Virginia, Charlottesville, USA

Abstract. This paper presents a novel deformable registration framework, leveraging an image prior specified through a denoising function, for severely noise-corrupted placental images. Recent work on plug-and-play (PnP) priors has shown the state-of-the-art performance of reconstruction algorithms under such priors in a range of imaging applications. Integration of powerful image denoisers into advanced registration methods provides our model with a flexibility to accommodate datasets that have low signal-to-noise ratios (SNRs). We demonstrate the performance of our method under a wide variety of denoising models in the context of diffeomorphic image registration. Experimental results show that our model substantially improves the accuracy of spatial alignment in applications of 3D in-utero diffusion-weighted MR images (DW-MRI) that suffer from low SNR and large spatial transformations.

1 Introduction

Placental pathology, such as immune cell infiltration and inflammation [4], is a common reason for preterm labor. It occurs in around 11% of world pregnancies. *Diffusion-weighted magnetic resonance imaging (DW-MRI)* is a non-invasive technique that is extensively used to monitor placental health and to assess its function throughout the entire pregnancy. However, this method is quite susceptible to motion artifacts caused by maternal breathing and fetal movements [13]. Additionally, DW-MRI scans often suffer from noise and severe artifacts induced by low signal-to-noise ratios (SNRs) at high b-values [22,32]. To address these issues, a noise-robust registration algorithm is needed.

Many attempts have been made to develop registration methods that are robust to image noise [12,14,17,25]. A traditional approach integrates an image

© Springer Nature Switzerland AG 2019
Q. Wang et al. (Eds.): PIPPI 2019/SUSI 2019, LNCS 11798, pp. 133–142, 2019.
https://doi.org/10.1007/978-3-030-32875-7_15

reconstruction algorithm for removing noise and artifacts as a pre-processing step to the registration task [29]. Further improvements can be achieved by developing a joint framework that alternates between image reconstruction and registration [12,16,28,32]. The most widely used image reconstruction algorithms are based on optimization of an objective function that includes a regularization term for mitigating noise. Recently, however, the interest in the area has shifted towards a more flexible approach, known as *plug-and-play priors (PnP)* [30], that regularizes the problem using off-the-shelf image denoising algorithms. It has been shown that the combination of reconstruction algorithms with advanced denoisers, such as non-local means [7] or block matching and 3D filtering (BM3D) [11], leads to the state-of-the-art performance for various imaging problems [8,9,18,26].

In this paper, we extend the current family of joint reconstruction-registration algorithms by introducing a new method for deformable image registration called *PnP-RR* (where RR stands for *registration-reconstruction*). Our algorithm leverages PnP image priors, which makes it robust for registering severely noise-corrupted images. PnP-RR is very easy to implement by using a wide variety of existing algorithms with minimal effort to modify the infrastructure. We demonstrate how PnP priors can be used to mix and match a wide variety of existing reconstruction models with the state-of-the-art registration algorithm on both 2D synthetic data and real 3D images. To show the effectiveness of the algorithm in improving the performance of spatial alignment for severely noise-corrupted images, we test on 3D in-utero DW-MRI scans, affected by a low signal-to-noise (SNR) ratio and large motions.

2   Background: Deformable Image Registration

In this section, we briefly review the mathematical foundation of image registration. Consider a d-dimensional image I defined as a continuous mapping $I : \Omega \to \mathbb{R}^d$, where Ω is the image domain. The transformation $\phi : \Omega \to \Omega$ deforms a source image S by function composition $S \circ \phi^{-1}$, where $\circ$ denotes resampling. The goal of image registration is to find an optimal transformation ϕ, such that the deformed image $S \circ \phi^{-1}$ is similar to a target image T.

The desired transformation ϕ is typically computed by minimizing an energy function $E(\phi) = \text{dist}(S \circ \phi^{-1}, T) + \text{reg}(\phi)$. Here, the distance function $\text{dist}(\cdot, \cdot)$ measures the dissimilarity between two images, such as sum-of-squared differences of image intensities [3], mutual information [15], and normalized cross correlation [1]. The regularization term $\text{reg}(\cdot)$ guarantees the smoothness of the transformation. A very original function ϕ is defined as a linear function $\phi(x) = x + u(x)$, where $x \in \Omega$ and u is a displacement vector field. With the regularity being set to $\|Lu\|_{L^2}^2$ (L is a differential operator), the optimization of the energy function E over u arrives at a solution for elastic registration [6].

However, such algorithm is not able to avoid geometric artifacts (e.g., folding, tearing, or flipping) of the transformations, especially when large deformation occurs, and may destroy the topology of local structures [10]. Instead, an elegant algorithm called large deformation diffeomorphic metric mapping (LDDMM) was developed to ensure a smooth and invertible smooth mapping of ϕ between images [3]. The regularization term is defined as an integration over time-dependent velocity fields derived from the transformations. We have the objective function of LDDMM as

$$\arg \min_{v_t} \frac{1}{\sigma^2} \left\| S \circ \phi_1^{-1} - T \right\|_{L^2}^2 + \int_0^1 (Lv_t, v_t) \, \mathrm{d}t, \quad \text{s.t.} \quad \frac{\mathrm{d}\phi_t}{\mathrm{d}t} = v_t(\phi_t), \quad (1)$$

where σ^2 is a weighting parameter, and $(\cdot, \cdot)$ acts similar to an inner product.

The optimization of the original LDDMM is solved by gradient-based method over the entire time sequence of v_t, which is computationally expensive on high-dimensional images (e.g., a 3D placental MRI with the size of 128^3). Later, a geodesic shooting algorithm [19,31] shows that once given an initial velocity v_0, the shortest path of ϕ can be uniquely determined by integrating the geodesic evolution equation (also known as Euler-Poincare differential equation (EPDiff)) defined by

$$\frac{\mathrm{d}v_t}{\mathrm{d}t} = -K \left[(Dv_t)^T \cdot m_t + Dm_t \cdot v_t + m_t \cdot \operatorname{div} v_t \right], \quad (2)$$

where K is an inverse operator of the differential operator L, $m_t = Lv_t$ is a momentum vector living in the dual space of v_t, D denotes a Jacobian matrix, and div is a divergence operator.

The optimization of Eq. (1) can be equivalently reformulated as

$$\arg \min_{v_0} \frac{1}{\sigma^2} \| S \circ \phi_1^{-1} - T \|_{L^2}^2 + (Lv_0, v_0), \quad \text{s.t.} \quad \frac{\mathrm{d}\phi_t}{\mathrm{d}t} = v_t(\phi_t) \ \& \ \text{Eq. (2)}. \quad (3)$$

This effectively shrinks the searching space from a time collection of $\{v_t\}$ to a single initial point v_0, thus significantly reducing the computational complexity of the entire optimization.

It has been recently demonstrated that the initial velocity v_0 can be efficiently captured via a discrete low-dimensional bandlimited representation in the Fourier space [33]. We develop our model by employing this fast registration algorithm named FLASH, which is the start-of-the-art variant of LDDMM with geodesic shooting algorithm [34,35].

3 Our Method: Image Registration with PnP Priors

In this section, we introduce a novel noise-robust registration model that incorporates a PnP prior as an additional image regularizer. We show that the our model can be implemented using two independent software modules – one for image reconstruction and the other for image registration. Therefore, changing the prior model only involves the implementation of image reconstruction. That is to say, our framework can be used to match a wide variety of priors with a suitable registration model.

3.1 Formulation as a Proximal Algorithm

We first consider the following joint objective function that builds on Eq. (3) to combine image regularization with deformable registration

$$\mathcal{F}(v_0, \tilde{T}) = \frac{1}{\sigma^2}\|S \circ \phi_1^{-1} - \tilde{T}\|_{L^2}^2 + (Lv_0, v_0) + \lambda_1 \mathcal{R}(\tilde{T}) + \lambda_2\|T - \tilde{T}\|_{L^2}^2, \quad (4)$$

where T is the target image, $\tilde{T}$ is the reconstructed image, $\mathcal{R}(\cdot)$ is the regularization term characterizing the prior on the image, λ_1 is the parameter controlling the strength of regularization, and λ_2 controls the fidelity of the reconstructed and noisy images.

In order to solve the problem (4) efficiently, we adopt an *alternating minimization* approach [20], where v_0 is first minimized for a fixed $\tilde{T}$ under the constraints in Eq. (3) and vice versa, as follows

$$v_0^k = \arg\min_{v_0} \mathcal{F}(v_0, \tilde{T}^{k-1}), \text{ s.t. } \frac{d\phi_t}{dt} = v_t(\phi_t) \text{ and Eq. (2)}, \quad (5a)$$

$$\tilde{T}^k = \arg\min_{\tilde{T}} \mathcal{F}(v_0^k, \tilde{T}), \quad (5b)$$

where k denotes the k-th iteration.

By ignoring the terms independent of v_0, the step (5a) can be expressed as

$$v_0^k = \text{register}_\sigma(S, \tilde{T}^{k-1}) = \arg\min_{v_0} \frac{1}{\sigma^2}\|S \circ \phi_1^{-1} - \tilde{T}^{k-1}\|_{L^2}^2 + (Lv_0, v_0),$$

where we didn't explicitly write the constraints for better readability. Note that this step precisely matches the deformable image registration problem in Eq. (3). Similarly, the step (5b) can be simplified to the following form

$$\tilde{T}^k = \text{prox}_{\tau\mathcal{R}}(Z^k) = \arg\min_{\tilde{T}} \frac{1}{2}\|\tilde{T} - Z^k\|_{L_2}^2 + \tau\mathcal{R}(\tilde{T}), \quad (6)$$

where we define

$$Z^k = \frac{\lambda_2 T + (1/\sigma^2)(S \circ \phi^{-1})}{\lambda_2 + (1/\sigma^2)} \quad \text{and} \quad \tau = \frac{\lambda_1}{2(\lambda_2 + (1/\sigma^2))}.$$

The minimization problem (6) is widely known as the *proximal operator* [21] and corresponds to an image denoising formulates as $\mathcal{R}(\cdot)$ regularized optimization. For many popular regularizers, such as ℓ_1-norm or total variation penalty, the proximal operator either has a closed form solution or can be efficiently implemented [2], without differentiating $\mathcal{R}(\cdot)$.

3.2 Formulation as a PnP Algorithm

Our alternating minimization algorithm in Eq. 5 iteratively refines a denoised image $\tilde{T}^k$ by applying the proximal operator defined in Eq. (6). Recently, the mathematical equivalence of the proximal operator to image denoising has inspired Venkatakrishnan *et al.* [30] to introduce a powerful PnP framework for image reconstruction. The key idea of PnP is to replace the proximal operator in an iterative algorithm with a state-of-the-art image denoiser (e.g., BM3D), which does *not* necessarily have a corresponding regularization function $\mathcal{R}(\cdot)$. This implies that PnP methods generally lose interpretability as optimization problems. Nonetheless, the framework has gained in popularity due to its effectiveness in a range of applications. Additionally, several recent publications have theoretically characterized the convergence and fixed points of PnP algorithms [8, 9, 24, 26, 27].

Algorithm 1 summarizes our PnP-RR algorithm for joint image reconstruction and registration. The fixed point $(v_0^*, \tilde{T}^*)$ of PnP-RR is defined by a balance between denoising and registration operators, rather than the minimum of a cost function. This makes the algorithm easy to adapt to specific datasets by simply swapping denoisers or registration operators. We corroborate the performance of PnP-RR in the next section by applying it to the challenging problem of image registration under severe amounts of noise.

Algorithm 1. PnP-RR

1: **input:** Source image S, target image T, parameters λ_1, λ_2, and σ
2: **set:** $\tau = \lambda_1/(2(\lambda_2 + (1/\sigma^2)))$
3: **for** $k = 1, 2, \ldots$ **do**
4:      $v_0^k \leftarrow \text{register}_\sigma(S, \tilde{T}^{k-1})$ ▷ registration step
5:      $Z^k \leftarrow (\lambda_2 T + (1/\sigma^2)(S \circ \phi^{-1}))/(\lambda_2 + (1/\sigma^2))$
6:      $\tilde{T}^k \leftarrow \text{denoise}_\tau(Z^k)$ ▷ denoising step
7: **end for**

---

4 Experimental Evaluation

To evaluate our proposed method, we test its performance with three existing reconstruction algorithms - total variation (TV) [23], total generalized variation (TGV) [5], and BM3D [11] on both synthetic 2D images and real 3D placental DW-MRI scans with different b-values.

We compare our method with the state-of-the-art fast registration method FLASH [34] (downloaded from: https://bitbucket.org/FlashC/flashc). In all experiments, we set L as a Laplacian operator, e.g., $L = -(\alpha\Delta + I)^c$ with a positive weight parameter $\alpha = 1.5$ and a smoothness parameter $c = 3.0$. We set $\sigma = 0.015$ and the number of time integration steps $n = 10$ across all algorithms. We also perform registration-based segmentation and examine the resulting segmentation accuracy of the algorithm. To evaluate volume overlap between the propagated segmentation A and the manual segmentation B for placenta, we compute the Dice Similarity Coefficient $DSC(A, B) = 2(|A| \cap |B|)/(|A| + |B|)$, where $\cap$ denotes an intersection of two regions.

Data. For 2D synthetic images, we generate a collection of binary images with resolution 100^2. We then add white Gaussian noise with standard deviation $\sigma = 0.3$ to the target images.

For real 3D placental DW-MRIs, two healthy pregnant subjects (singleton pregnancies) with gestational age between 20 ± 1 weeks were recruited and consented. All subjects were scanned in left lateral position during free breathing. Echo-planar DW-MRIs were acquired on a 3T Siemens VIDA scanner with a 30 channel phase-array torso coil (FOV $= 386 \times 386 \times 300 - 330$ mm^3, 3 mm isotropic voxels, interleaved slice acquisition, TR $= 14600$ ms, TE $= 62$ ms, Flip Angle $= 90°$). Multiple scans with different b values ($b = 0, 75, 100, 150$ s/mm^2) were tested and the placenta were manually delineated for images with $b = 0$ by radiologists. All DW-MRIs are of dimension $128 \times 128 \times 50$ and underwent bias field correction, co-registration with affine transformations and intensity normalization.

Experiments. We first run an experiment on 2D synthetic data registering from a clean source image to a noisy target image, and compare the performance of our method with the baseline algorithm FLASH. For the denoisers, we cross-validate a variety of different parameters and set $\lambda_1 = 0.045, \lambda_2 = 0.067$ for TV. Similarly, we have $\lambda_1 = 0.045, \lambda_2 = 0.015$ for TGV, and $\lambda_1 = 0.045, \lambda_2 = 0.225$ for BM3D. We run each algorithm till convergence.

We run similar experiments on real 3D placental DW-MRIs. MR images with low b-value (e.g., $b = 0$) are considered as source images, while others with high b-values (typically noisy images) are target images. After testing a set of different parameters, we set $\lambda_1 = 0.0225, \lambda_2 = 0.000225$ for TV, $\lambda_1 = 0.0338, \lambda_2 = 0.1$ for TGV, and $\lambda_1 = 0.0225, \lambda_2 = 0.1$ for BM3D. To further evaluate the registration accuracy, we measure the Dice score by applying the estimated transformation on manually labeled segmentations of placenta.

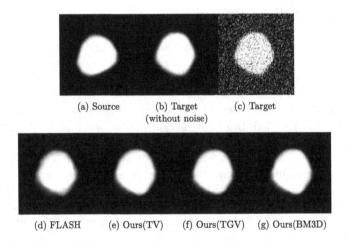

(a) Source   (b) Target   (c) Target
              (without noise)

(d) FLASH   (e) Ours(TV)   (f) Ours(TGV)   (g) Ours(BM3D)

Fig. 1. Top: source image, clean target image, and noisy target image; Bottom: registration results from the baseline method FLASH and our model with TV, TGV, and BM3D denoisers.

Results. Figure 1 displays the registration results of the baseline algorithm and our model with different denoisers. It shows that our method achieves better transformations that nicely deform the source image fairly close to the target image, without being affected by the noises.

Figure 2 demonstrates an example of the transformed segmentation of placenta (outlined in magenta) estimated by all algorithms. It clearly shows that the segmentations produced by our algorithm align better with the manual segmentation (outlined in blue) than the baseline algorithm. Our model provides much reliable segmentation than the baseline algorithm, especially on the left part of the placenta where relatively large deformation occurs.

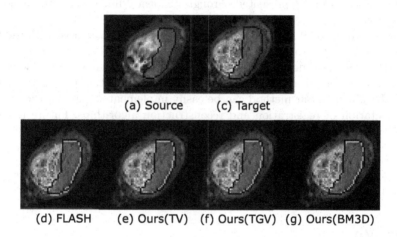

Fig. 2. Top: source and target images; Bottom: comparison of estimate segmentations of all algorithms overlapped with manually labeled delineation. (Color figure online)

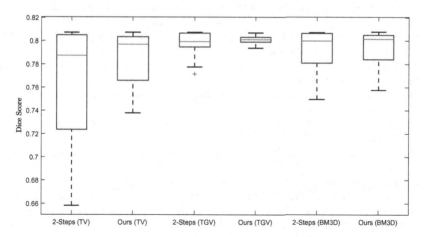

Fig. 3. Comparison of averaged Dice score estimated from two-step approaches and ours.

Figure 3 shows another advantage of our model compared to two-step approaches where image reconstruction is preformed before registration. We compute average dice scores with different parameter settings on both methods. Our higher average dice scores with smaller variations indicate that the proposed algorithm is more robust to parameter-tuning.

5   Conclusion

In this paper, we presented a novel reconstruction-based registration algorithm, named PnP-RR, for severely noise-corrupted images. Our method is the first to introduce PnP priors, represented through denoising functions, into the state-of-the-art registration framework. In contrast to previous approaches, our model has the flexibility to allow any reconstruction algorithm integrated with the registration task. This provides a much more robust way to register images with low SNRs and large motions. The theoretical tools developed in our work are broadly applicable to a wide variety of joint reconstruction-registration algorithms. In addition, our method can be easily implemented through the current implementation of registration and reconstruction algorithms. Future research will involve collecting more dataset on placental images and exploring other cutting-edge denoisers, such as deep learning based approaches.

Acknowledgement. This work was supported by NIH grant R01HD094381, NIH grant R01AG053548, and BrightFocus Foundation A2017330S.

References

1. Avants, B.B., Epstein, C.L., Grossman, M., Gee, J.C.: Symmetric diffeomorphic image registration with cross-correlation: evaluating automated labeling of elderly and neurodegenerative brain. Med. Image Anal. **12**(1), 26–41 (2008)
2. Beck, A., Teboulle, M.: Fast gradient-based algorithms for constrained total variation image denoising and deblurring problems. IEEE Trans. Image Process. **18**(11), 2419–2434 (2009)
3. Beg, M.F., Miller, M.I., Trouvé, A., Younes, L.: Computing large deformation metric mappings via geodesic flows of diffeomorphisms. Int. J. Comput. Vision **61**(2), 139–157 (2005)
4. Blencowe, H., et al.: Born too soon: the global epidemiology of 15 million preterm births. Reprod. Health **10**(1), S2 (2013)
5. Bredies, K., Kunisch, K., Pock, T.: Total generalized variation. SIAM J. Imaging Sci. **3**(3), 492–526 (2010)
6. Broit, C.: Optimal registration of deformed images (1981)
7. Buades, A., Coll, B., Morel, J.M.: A non-local algorithm for image denoising. In: IEEE Computer Society Conference on Computer Vision and Pattern Recognition (CVPR 2005), vol. 2, pp. 60–65. IEEE (2005)
8. Buzzard, G.T., Chan, S.H., Sreehari, S., Bouman, C.A.: Plug-and-play unplugged: optimization free reconstruction using consensus equilibrium. SIAM J. Imaging Sci. **11**(3), 2001–2020 (2018)

9. Chan, S.H., Wang, X., Elgendy, O.A.: Plug-and-play ADMM for image restoration: fixed-point convergence and applications. IEEE Trans. Comput. Imaging **3**(1), 84–98 (2017)
10. Christensen, G.E.: Deformable shape models for anatomy (1994)
11. Dabov, K., Foi, A., Egiazarian, K.: Video denoising by sparse 3D transform-domain collaborative filtering. In: 15th European Signal Processing Conference, pp. 145–149. IEEE (2007)
12. Han, J., et al.: A variational framework for joint image registration, denoising and edge detection. In: Handels, H., Ehrhardt, J., Horsch, A., Meinzer, H.P., Tolxdorff, T. (eds.) Bildverarbeitung für die Medizin 2006, pp. 246–250. Springer, Heidelberg (2006). https://doi.org/10.1007/3-540-32137-3_50
13. Le Bihan, D., Poupon, C., Amadon, A., Lethimonnier, F.: Artifacts and pitfalls in diffusion MRI. J. Magn. Reson. Imaging **24**(3), 478–488 (2006). An Official Journal of the International Society for Magnetic Resonance in Medicine
14. Lempitsky, V., Rother, C., Blake, A.: Logcut-efficient graph cut optimization for Markov random fields. In: IEEE 11th International Conference on Computer Vision, pp. 1–8. IEEE (2007)
15. Leventon, M., Wells III, W.M., Grimson, W.E.L.: Multiple view 2D-3D mutual information registration. In: Image Understanding Workshop, vol. 20, p. 21. Citeseer (1997)
16. Lombaert, H., Cheriet, F.: Simultaneous image de-noising and registration using graph cuts: application to corrupted medical images. In: 11th International Conference on Information Science, Signal Processing and their Applications (ISSPA), pp. 264–268. IEEE (2012)
17. Lombaert, H., Cheriet, F.: Simultaneous image denoising and registration using graph cuts, July 2012
18. Meinhardt, T., Moeller, M., Hazirbas, C., Cremers, D.: Learning proximal operators: using denoising networks for regularizing inverse imaging problems. In: Proceedings of IEEE International Conference on Computer Vision (ICCV), Venice, pp. 1799–1808, 22–29 October 2017
19. Miller, M.I., Trouvé, A., Younes, L.: Geodesic shooting for computational anatomy. J. Math. Imaging Vis. **24**(2), 209–228 (2006)
20. Nocedal, J., Wright, S.J.: Numerical Optimization, 2nd edn. Springer, New York (2006). https://doi.org/10.1007/978-0-387-40065-5
21. Parikh, N., Boyd, S.: Proximal algorithms. Found. Trends Optim. **1**(3), 123–231 (2014)
22. Partridge, S.C., McDonald, E.S.: Diffusion weighted MRI of the breast: protocol optimization, guidelines for interpretation, and potential clinical applications. Magn. Reson. Imaging Clin. N. Am. **21**(3), 601 (2013)
23. Rudin, L.I., Osher, S., Fatemi, E.: Nonlinear total variation based noise removal algorithms. Physica D **60**(1–4), 259–268 (1992)
24. Ryu, E.K., Liu, J., Wnag, S., Chen, X., Wang, Z., Yin, W.: Plug-and-play methods provably converge with properly trained denoisers. In: Proceedings of the 36th International Conference on Machine Learning (ICML), Long Beach, June 2019
25. Sanches, J.M., Marques, J.S.: Joint image registration and volume reconstruction for 3D ultrasound. Pattern Recogn. Lett. **24**(4–5), 791–800 (2003)
26. Sreehari, S., et al.: Plug-and-play priors for bright field electron tomography and sparse interpolation. IEEE Trans. Comput. Imaging **2**(4), 408–423 (2016)
27. Sun, Y., Wohlberg, B., Kamilov, U.S.: An online plug-and-play algorithm for regularized image reconstruction. IEEE Trans. Comput. Imaging (2019)

28. Telea, A., Preusser, T., Garbe, C., Droske, M., Rumpf, M.: A variational approach to joint denoising, edge detection and motion estimation. In: Franke, K., Müller, K.-R., Nickolay, B., Schäfer, R. (eds.) DAGM 2006. LNCS, vol. 4174, pp. 525–535. Springer, Heidelberg (2006). https://doi.org/10.1007/11861898_53

29. Tomaževič, D., Likar, B., Pernuš, F.: Reconstruction-based 3D/2D image registration. In: Duncan, J.S., Gerig, G. (eds.) MICCAI 2005. LNCS, vol. 3750, pp. 231–238. Springer, Heidelberg (2005). https://doi.org/10.1007/11566489_29

30. Venkatakrishnan, S.V., Bouman, C.A., Wohlberg, B.: Plug-and-play priors for model based reconstruction. In: IEEE Global Conference on Signal and Information Processing, pp. 945–948. IEEE (2013)

31. Vialard, F.X., Risser, L., Rueckert, D., Cotter, C.J.: Diffeomorphic 3D image registration via geodesic shooting using an efficient adjoint calculation. Int. J. Comput. Vision 97(2), 229–241 (2012)

32. Vishnevskiy, V., Stoeck, C., Székely, G., Tanner, C., Kozerke, S.: Simultaneous denoising and registration for accurate cardiac diffusion tensor reconstruction from MRI. In: Navab, N., Hornegger, J., Wells, W.M., Frangi, A.F. (eds.) MICCAI 2015. LNCS, vol. 9349, pp. 215–222. Springer, Cham (2015). https://doi.org/10.1007/978-3-319-24553-9_27

33. Zhang, M., Fletcher, P.T.: Finite-dimensional lie algebras for fast diffeomorphic image registration. In: Ourselin, S., Alexander, D.C., Westin, C.-F., Cardoso, M.J. (eds.) IPMI 2015. LNCS, vol. 9123, pp. 249–260. Springer, Cham (2015). https://doi.org/10.1007/978-3-319-19992-4_19

34. Zhang, M., Fletcher, P.T.: Fast diffeomorphic image registration via Fourier-approximated lie algebras. Int. J. Comput. Vision 127(1), 61–73 (2019)

35. Zhang, M., et al.: Frequency diffeomorphisms for efficient image registration. In: Niethammer, M., et al. (eds.) IPMI 2017. LNCS, vol. 10265, pp. 559–570. Springer, Cham (2017). https://doi.org/10.1007/978-3-319-59050-9_44

A Longitudinal Study of the Evolution of the Central Sulcus' Shape in Preterm Infants Using Manifold Learning

Héloïse de Vareilles[1]([✉])(iD), Zhongyi Sun[1], Manon Benders[2](iD), Clara Fischer[1], François Leroy[3](iD), Linda de Vries[2](iD), Floris Groenendaal[2](iD), Denis Rivière[1](iD), Jessica Dubois[4,5](iD), and Jean-François Mangin[1](iD)

[1] CEA, NeuroSpin, UNATI, Gif-sur-Yvette, France
heloise.devareilles@cea.fr
[2] Wilhelmina Children's Hospital and Brain Center Rudolf Magnus, University Medical Center, Utrecht, Netherlands
[3] Inserm, CEA, NeuroSpin, Paris-Saclay University, Cognitive Neuroimaging Unit U992, Gif-sur-Yvette, France
[4] Inserm, University of Paris, NeuroDiderot Unit U1141, Paris, France
[5] CEA, NeuroSpin, UNIACT, Gif-sur-Yvette, France

Abstract. Cortical folding in humans is different for every individual, and is associated with functional specificities. It forms mainly during the last trimester of pregnancy, hence its development lacks description, especially in a longitudinal way. To cope with this issue, this study focused on the evolution of the central sulcus' variability of 71 preterm infants studied longitudinally with MRI at 30 and 40 weeks (w) postmenstrual age (PMA). Our aim was to investigate the main shape characteristics and whether they are encoded early on or appear closer to term birth. We captured shape dissimilarity between the sulci using a distance matrix after pairwise co-registration using an Iterative Closest Point algorithm. We applied non-linear dimensionality reduction to this matrix using the Isomap algorithm in order to capture the most discriminative shape features among the central sulci. We characterized the three most discriminative features over the group, and found that the sulci evolved consistently from a given feature at 30w PMA to the 40w PMA equivalent feature. We incidentally captured a feature that could coincide with the most discriminative adult feature, both visually and by its asymmetry in left and right sulcal distribution. These results captured the main shape features of the central sulcus in preterm infants and suggest that they are already encoded at 30w PMA.

Keywords: Central sulcus · Preterm infants · Cortical development · Brain MRI

Supported by the Human Brain Project under the Specific Grant Agreements No. 785907 (SGA2), and by the FRM DIC20161236445.

© Springer Nature Switzerland AG 2019
Q. Wang et al. (Eds.): PIPPI 2019/SUSI 2019, LNCS 11798, pp. 143–152, 2019.
https://doi.org/10.1007/978-3-030-32875-7_16

1   Context and Purpose of the Study

In humans, the cortical folding pattern is unique among individuals. It is complex in shape but still presents a form of homogeneity within the species which allows us to label homologous sulci in individuals. Sulci are especially interesting as some have been observed to be proxies for localizing functional areas of the brain, specifically in primary regions. In particular, the link between their shape and the location of functional activations is being investigated [1]. Sulcal patterns have been used for brain cartography [2], and as neurosurgical landmarks [3]. These types of approach led to research efforts in pattern recognition, classification and automatic sulcal labelization [4], which in turn led to more recent findings about links between specific folding patterns and some clinical conditions (epilepsy [5], schizophrenia [6]).

These specific folding patterns are mostly already present at birth, since cortical folding mainly occurs during the third trimester of pregnancy. Therefore, following the development of sulcation longitudinally is a complex matter, as the transition between *in utero* and *ex utero* has an impact on cortical morphology [7]. Consequently, the choice is left between *in utero* longitudinal imaging, which is complex both because of fetal motion and the difficulty of acquisition just before birth, and *ex utero* longitudinal imaging on very preterm infants, which is the option chosen in this study.

The global complexity of the cortical gyrification and the ability to identify homologous sulci in a group of subjects makes it necessary to dissociate the problem in less complex sub-questions. Here we focused on a given sulcus, in order to restrict the question to a specific brain region and to enable a future extension of this study on topical functional aspects. In particular, we chose to focus on the central sulcus for three main reasons. First of all, it is the boundary between the primary motor and somatosensory areas (in the pre- and post-central gyri respectively), so it is rather easy to identify the potential functional implications linked to it. In particular, it benefits from classical somatotopic maps [8], in which the hand area is generally localized in a protrusion in the precentral gyrus inducing a hump on the upper part of the central sulcus referenced as the "hand knob" [9]. Secondly, it seems a good starting point for a sulcal-specific approach of cortical gyrification since it is one of the deepest and most stable sulci, as well as one of the first to appear [10]. Thirdly, shape variability of the central sulcus has already been studied on adults using a similar methodology, linking shape with handedness [11] and confirming the match between the anatomical "hand-knob" and the motor functional activation [1].

To investigate the shape development of the central sulcus, we observed it at 30 weeks (w) post-menstrual age (PMA) and 40w PMA. This allowed us to capture its shape at an early developmental stage – when the start of secondary folding is hardly observable – and at a developed stage – when this wave is mainly achieved while the tertiary folding is ongoing [12,13]–. As a result, in this study, we applied non-linear dimensionality reduction to a distance matrix capturing the intervariability of the central sulci of the preterm cohort in a descriptive aim.

2   Materials and Pre-processing of the Data

The cohort studied was the same as that presented in a previous study about cortical folding, risk factors and clinical outcome of very preterm children [14]. It was comprised of 71 infants with gestational age at birth between 24 and 28 weeks. Infants were scanned twice: once around 30w PMA (28.7–32.7w) and again around term equivalent age (TEA) (40.0–42.7w). MR imaging was performed on a 3-Tesla MR system (Achieva, Philips Medical Systems, Best, The Netherlands). The protocol included T2-weighted imaging with a turbo-spin echo sequence in the coronal plane (at early MRI: repetition time (TR) 10.085 ms; echo time (TE) 120 ms; slice thickness 2 mm, in-plane spatial resolution 0.35 × 0.35 mm; at TEA: TR 4847 ms; TE 150 ms; slice thickness 1.2 mm, in-plane spatial resolution 0.35 × 0.35 mm).

The images pre-processing is also described in the previous study [14]. After generating a brain mask, T2-weighted images were segmented using masks between grey matter, unmyelinated white matter and cerebrospinal fluid using supervised voxel classification. By adapting the anatomical pipelines of the BrainVISA software, the inner cortical surfaces of both hemispheres were reconstructed using these segmentations.

Using this preprocessed data, the brains were co-registered to the Talairach space [3] in order to dismiss brain shape and size variability. We then used the Morphologist toolbox of the BrainVISA software [15] for central sulci extraction, as shown on Fig. 1.

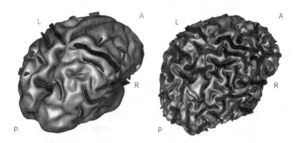

Fig. 1. Inner cortical surface and sulcus extraction for a given subject (L/R: left/right, A/P: anterior/posterior). Left: 30w PMA, right: 40w PMA. Red: central sulcus. (Color figure online)

The right central sulci were then mirrored in order for them to have the same spatial orientation as the left central sulci. 30w PMA and 40w PMA sulci were classified together on the same axes, in order to ensure that we could compare the relative positioning of the 30w PMA sulci and the 40w PMA sulci.

3   Methodology for Shape Characterization

The methodology applied in this study is inspired from a methodology assessed for sulcal shape characterization in the adult brain [11]. It had to be adjusted in order to fit the problematic of a longitudinal study and to allow comparisons to be made between sulci which presented different developmental stages. Let n_{sulci} be the number of sulci included for shape characterization.

3.1 Construction of a Distance Matrix for Shape Characterization

Each pair of sulci from the whole group (regardless of age and subject) was co-registered using the Iterative Closest Point (ICP) algorithm from the python Point Cloud Library [16] in order to capture its pairwise distance. For a given pair of sulci labeled i and j (with $(i, j) \in [1, n_{sulci}]$, $i \neq j$), the sulcus i was registered on the sulcus j using ICP, and the residual distance $d_{i \rightarrow j}$ was computed. The sulcus j was then registered on the sulcus i to obtain $d_{j \rightarrow i}$. We then defined the pairwise pseudo-distance $d_{i,j}$ between these sulci as the maximum of these two distances. This differs from the adult methodology which kept the minimal distance and not the maximum, but this would have resulted in smaller distances between registration of 30w PMA on 40w PMA sulci than between 40w PMA sulci pairs, independently from their shape similarity, just because of the smaller size of the 30w PMA sulci. Hence, we defined:

$$\forall (i, j) \in [1, n_{sulci}]^2, \ d_{i,j} = max(d_{i \rightarrow j}, d_{j \rightarrow i}) \tag{1}$$

$d_{i,j}$ is a pseudo-distance because it does not verify the triangle inequality: with registrations of uneven quality, it can verify $d_{i,j} > d_{i,k} + d_{k,j}$. A $n_{sulci} \times n_{sulci}$ symmetrical pseudo-distance matrix M_{dist} was then built, so that $M_{dist} = (d_{i,j})_{(i,j) \in [1, n_{sulci}]^2}$.

3.2 Dimensionality Reduction Using Isomap

The resulting pseudo-distance matrix captured the shape variability within the whole cohort but was of very high dimension (for the whole group, dimension = 284×284; for age subgroups, dimension = 142×142). In order to capture the main variability features, we had to operate a dimensionality reduction. Instead of applying a classical Multi-Dimensional Scaling (MDS) algorithm on the original pseudo-distance matrix, we preferred to use the Isomap algorithm [17], which takes a geodesic distance matrix as the input for the MDS. The geodesic distance matrix is built the following way: a graph is created using every sulcus' k nearest neighbours and weighted by their pairwise pseudo-distances $d_{i,j}$, with k as an adjustable parameter. The geodesic distance between any two sulci is then defined as the sum of the pseudo-distances traveled by following the shortest path in the graph between these two sulci. In our case, we computed a geodesic pseudo-distance matrix from the M_{dist} matrix, which allowed us to bypass links resulting from poor registration scores (in comparison to a classical MDS), and we used $k = n_{sulci} - 1$, which maximized the number of links in the weighted graph between the 30w and 40w PMA sulci (instead of using of a smaller value for k). This choice of k differs from the adult methodology which did not need to maximize interconnection between subgroups.

Here, we captured the first 4 axes obtained using this dimensionality reduction (the number of axes was chosen using shape considerations linked to the study on adults). In order to visualize the shape variability captured, we projected the sulci to their position on the axes studied, after aligning them on a template sulcus in order for their orientation to be consistent (the sulcus chosen for alignment was the one minimizing the distance to every other sulcus). Figure 2A shows an example of generated output for the first axis.

3.3   Genesis of Moving Averages for Interpretation

The visual result of the dimensionality reduction is hard to interpret because of the complexity of the shape of individual sulci, as can be seen on Fig. 2A. Moving averages were therefore computed in order to capture the average shape of sulci in different regions of the axis. Ten equidistant moving averages were computed for an axis. For each one of them, every sulcus from the graph was exponentially weighted depending on the distance to the location of the moving average; the closer a sulcus was to the position of a moving average, the more it affected its shape. The weighed sulci were then all summed. The resulting weighted point cloud was then convoluted with a 3D Gaussian in order to obtain an average volume, which was then thresholded for 3D rendering. The threshold was chosen at the lowest value preventing holes to appear in the moving averages. For visual interpretation, it was generally useful to dissociate 30w PMA sulci from 40w PMA sulci to generate the moving averages. Visual results of moving averages for the first axis can be seen on Fig. 2B.

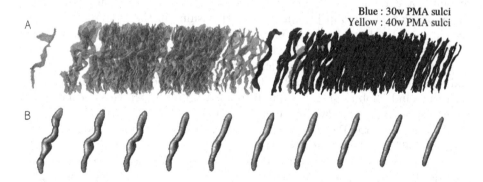

Fig. 2. A: projection of the sulci on the first axis of the Isomap. This axis specifically arranges the 40w PMA sulci (yellow) on the left and the 30w PMA sulci (blue) on the right, but it is generally not the case for other axes. B: Moving averages for the first axis of the Isomap. Here the moving averages make sense without differentiating the 30w and 40w PMA subgroups since they are already dissociated by their positioning on the Isomap axis. (Color figure online)

3.4 Statistical Analyses Led on Isomap Results

In addition to visual interpretation of the Isomap classification, statistical analyses were led to check for relationships between sulci subgroups and their relative
positioning on the Isomap axes. Three different tests were applied. The first one
was a Wilcoxon rank sum test comparing the median of the 30w PMA and 40w
PMA subgroups. This test allowed us to check for axes which would capture
inter-age shape differences. The second test applied was a Pearson correlation
between 30w PMA and 40w PMA sulci, to check if any axis captured shape features which were globally maintained along the time period observed. Thirdly,
we applied an age-subgroup-specific Wilcoxon sign-rank test to compare the relative positioning of left and right central sulci at a given age. This was applied
to check for hemispheric asymmetry regarding sulcal shape. For each statistical
test, p-values were corrected for multiple comparisons (4 axes) with the Bonfer-
roni method.

4 Results

The first Isomap axis was omitted because the 30w and 40w PMA subgroups
were too dissociated due to differences in size and other shape characteristics
not relevant for this study (see Fig. 2A, difference in median between subgroups:
Wilcoxon rank sum: $t = -15$, $p = 2.10^{-47}$).

Figure 3 displays the visual results of the second, third and fourth Isomap
axes and subsequent moving averages on the 30w and 40w subgroups after having been classified together. Reading from left to right, the second axis seems
to pinpoint a reduction of the amplitude of the hand knob, compensated by
the apparition of a hump just under it and pushing in the opposite direction,
accompanied by the widening of a second, lower knob on the bottom part of the
moving averages. On the third axis, we observe the amplification of both the
hand knob and the hump just under it, them being almost absent on the left
and very prominent on the right. The fourth axis varies from a configuration
with the hand knob as the only hump to a configuration where a second lower
hump appears, giving a "w" shape characteristic.

We calculated the Pearson correlation coefficients for the two age subgroups
and obtained the following results: axis 2: $r = 0.68$ ($p = 8.10^{-20}$), axis 3:
$r = 0.65$, ($p = 8.10^{-18}$), axis 4: $r = 0.70$, ($p = 8.10^{-22}$). These high correlations
suggest that the features captured by this method were evolving consistently
from a given shape at 30w PMA to its corresponding shape at 40w PMA.

In addition, we observed an asymmetry in positioning of the left and right
sulci on the fourth axis (Wilcoxon signed-rank test: stat $= 2904$, $p = 4.10^{-5}$),
as shown in Fig. 4A. This axis happened to be similar to the first axis captured
previously in adults [11] and which showed the same type of asymmetry, with
the right sulci tending towards a configuration referred as "single knob" and the
left ones tending towards a configuration referred as "double knob" (Fig. 4B).

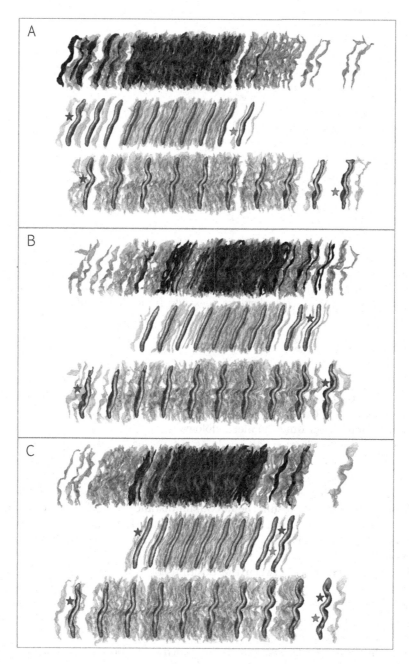

Fig. 3. Isomap results for the axes 2 (A), 3 (B), and 4 (C). Top: projection of the 30w PMA (blue) and 40w PMA (yellow) sulci on the axis. Middle and bottom: Moving averages (dark grey) superimposed with corresponding sulci (light grey) on the axis. Middle: 30w subjects, bottom: 40w subjects. The purple star indicates the hand knob, the orange star indicates the second lower hump. (Color figure online)

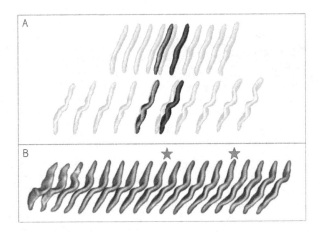

Fig. 4. A. Mean shape for right central sulci (pink) and left central sulci (green) shown over the moving averages for axis 4. Top/bottom: 30w/40w PMA moving averages. B. Moving averages captured for the first axis in adults (adapted from the paper on adults [11]). The pink (resp. green) star is added to indicate the location of average shape for right (resp. left) central sulci on dextrals. (Color figure online)

5   Discussion

In this study we have characterized the main shape variability of central sulci in a preterm cohort, and assessed that it is captured as soon as 30w PMA. We have also found the main variability trait reported by a previous study on adults in infants. Regarding the methodology, we believe it has been consistently adapted for a longitudinal study involving subgroups of sulci varying in length and depth, by choosing to use the maximum of the distances obtained after pairwise registration, and then by maximizing the number of nearest neighbours on the Isomap to encourage links in the neighbours graph between 30w and 40w PMA sulci. Nevertheless, using the maximum distance from the ICP calculation could impact the comparison of similar-sized sulci. It would be interesting to implement a different distance to characterize the registration by ICP (e.g. the Wasserstein distance).

The high correlation between the positions of 30w PMA sulci and that of 40w PMA sulci suggests a consistent evolution of the main shape of the central sulcus studied longitudinally. This gives insight about the fact that the wave of secondary folding does not seem to drastically alter the folding dynamic of a profound and early-developing fold such as the central sulcus. This infers that the growth of later folds, such as the precentral and post-central sulci, is not responsible for the main shape features of the central sulcus.

The finding of the main adult variability trait, but not encoded as the main trait in the preterm brain, raises questions about the shape features captured by the two prior axes: do they encode information about the developing brain? Or are these two axes also important in adult central sulci, but downgraded in importance relative to the main adult trait? An additional longitudinal study imaging subjects close to birth and at an older age (for example at adulthood) could enable us to answer these questions.

These first shape features could also be representative of abnormalities in sulcation linked to severe prematurity. Indeed, preterm infants have been reported to have an altered cortical gyrification compared to term-born infants [13], which would remain at the adult age [18]. To our knowledge, this deviation has not yet been quantified pattern-wise. Therefore, this study needs to be completed with a classification of the shape of central sulci in term-born infants, in order to assess whether the shape features captured here are representative of normal sulcation or are prematurity-induced. Furthermore, acquiring MRI data of the current cohort at an older age (late childhood, teenage or adulthood) could enable a quantitative comparison of shape variability between the 30w PMA, 40w PMA and more mature central sulci. This could both help investigate the question of prematurity-induced shape variability, and confirm quantitatively rather than visually the link between the fourth axis from this study and the main variability trait in the mature central sulcus.

It is common for studies to assess basic folding properties such as sulcal depth or length. In contrast, very few studies focus on characterizing the more complex shape of sulci. Studies have used voxel-wise approaches to quantify folding asymmetries in the fetus [10], in the preterm newborn [19] and in the infant [20], yet none have reported early asymmetries in the development of the central sulcus. Here, the left-right asymmetry captured on the fourth axis highlights the interest of studying the shape of sulci, especially since this asymmetry has been shown to be linked with hand-related features on adults [1,11].

Our approach can be applied to other sulci and help to assess the dynamics of cortical folding on a broader scale. Longitudinally evaluating the variability of the sulci in preterm infants is a milestone towards two important directions in the understanding of cortical development. On the one hand, it is an interesting way to assess the sulcal folding dynamics on a general point of view, since it is an efficient way to cope with the underlying problems of longitudinally comparing fetal and post-natal MRI. On the other hand, it could contribute to the understanding of developmental abnormalities induced by severe prematurity [18].

References

1. Sun, Z.Y., Pinel, P., Rivière, D., Moreno, A., Dehaene, S., Mangin, J.F.: Linking morphological and functional variability in hand movement and silent reading. Brain Struct. Funct. **221**(7), 3361–3371 (2016)
2. Ono, M., Kubik, S., Abernathey, C.D.: Atlas of the Cerebral Sulci. Thieme, Stuttgart (1990)
3. Talairach, J., Tournoux, P.: Co-planar Stereotaxic Atlas of the Human Brain: 3-D Dimensional Proportional System: An Approach to Cerebral Imaging. Thieme, Stuttgart (1988)
4. Rivière, D., Mangin, J.F., Papadopoulos-Orfanos, D., Martinez, J.M., Frouin, V., Régis, J.: Automatic recognition of cortical sulci of the human brain using a congregation of neural networks. Med. Image Anal. **6**(2), 77–92 (2002)

5. Mellerio, C., et al.: The power button sign: a newly described central sulcal pattern on surface rendering MR images of type 2 focal cortical dysplasia. Radiology **274**(2), 500–507 (2014)
6. Cachia, A., et al.: Cortical folding abnormalities in schizophrenia patients with resistant auditory hallucinations. NeuroImage **39**(3), 927–935 (2008)
7. Lefèvre, J., et al.: Are developmental trajectories of cortical folding comparable between cross-sectional datasets of fetuses and preterm newborns? Cereb. Cortex **26**(7), 3023–3035 (2016)
8. Penfield, W., Rasmussen, T.: The Cerebral Cortex of Man; A Clinical Study of Localization of Function. Macmillan, New York (1950)
9. Yousry, T.A., et al.: Localization of the motor hand area to a knob on the precentral gyrus. A new landmark. Brain J. Neurol. **120**(1), 141–157 (1997)
10. Habas, P.A., et al.: Early folding patterns and asymmetries of the normal human brain detected from in utero MRI. Cereb. Cortex **22**(1), 13–25 (2011)
11. Sun, Z.Y., et al.: The effect of handedness on the shape of the central sulcus. NeuroImage **60**(1), 332–339 (2012)
12. Chi, J.G., Dooling, E.C., Gilles, F.H.: Gyral development of the human brain. Ann. Neurol. **1**(1), 86–93 (1977)
13. Dubois, J., et al.: The dynamics of cortical folding waves and prematurity-related deviations revealed by spatial and spectral analysis of gyrification. NeuroImage **185**, 934–946 (2019)
14. Kersbergen, K.J., et al.: Relation between clinical risk factors, early cortical changes, and neurodevelopmental outcome in preterm infants. NeuroImage **142**, 301–310 (2016)
15. BrainVISA Suite. http://brainvisa.info. Accessed 30 July 2019
16. PointCloudLibrary, ICP algorithm. https://github.com/strawlab/python-pcl. Accessed 30 July 2019
17. Tenenbaum, J.B., De Silva, V., Langford, J.C.: A global geometric framework for nonlinear dimensionality reduction. Science **290**(5500), 2319–2323 (2000)
18. Hedderich, D.M., et al.: Aberrant gyrification contributes to the link between gestational age and adult IQ after premature birth. Brain J. Neurol. **142**(5), 1255–1269 (2019)
19. Dubois, J., et al.: Structural asymmetries of perisylvian regions in the preterm newborn. NeuroImage **52**(1), 32–42 (2010)
20. Li, G., et al.: Mapping longitudinal hemispheric structural asymmetries of the human cerebral cortex from birth to 2 years of age. Cereb. Cortex **24**(5), 1289–1300 (2013)

Prediction of Failure of Induction of Labor from Ultrasound Images Using Radiomic Features

María Inmaculada García Ocaña[1,2]([✉]), Karen López-Linares Román[1,2],
Jorge Burgos San Cristóbal[3], Ana del Campo Real[3], and Iván Macía Oliver[1,2]

[1] Vicomtech, San Sebastián, Spain
{igarcia,klopez,imacia}@vicomtech.org
[2] Biodonostia Health Research Institute, San Sebastián, Spain
[3] Obstetrics and Gynecology Service, Biocruces Bizkaia Health Research Institute,
Cruces University Hospital, Osakidetza, UPV/EHU, Baracaldo, Spain

Abstract. Induction of labor (IOL) is a very common procedure in current obstetrics; about 20% of women who undergo IOL at term pregnancy end up needing a cesarean section (C-section). The standard method to assess the risk of C-section, known as Bishop Score, is subjective and inconsistent. Thus, in this paper a novel method to predict the failure of IOL is presented, based on the analysis of B-mode transvaginal ultrasound (US) images. Advanced radiomic analyses from these images are combined with sonographic measurements (e.g. cervical length, cervical angle) and clinical data from a total of 182 patients to generate the predictive model. Different machine learning methods are compared, achieving a maximum AUC of 0.75, with 69% sensitivity and 71% specificity when using a Random Forest classifier. These preliminary results suggest that features obtained from US images can be used to estimate the risk of IOL failure, providing the practitioners with an objective method to choose the most personalized treatment for each patient.

Keywords: Radiomics · Ultrasound · Induction of labor · Machine learning

1 Introduction

Induction of labor (IOL) is a very common procedure in current obstetrics; according to the American College of Obstetricians and Gynecologists, between 20% and 40% of births are induced. IOL is the treatment that stimulates childbirth and delivery. About 20% of women who undergo IOL at term pregnancy end up needing a C-section, mainly due to the failure of induction, failure of progression of labor or fetal distress.

Bishop Score is the most widely used method for the assessment of cervical tissue properties and aims at determining the readiness of the cervix for IOL. However, it is a subjective measure and has been found to be inconsistent [9].

© Springer Nature Switzerland AG 2019
Q. Wang et al. (Eds.): PIPPI 2019/SUSI 2019, LNCS 11798, pp. 153–160, 2019.
https://doi.org/10.1007/978-3-030-32875-7_17

Thus, proposing a method for the proper selection of candidates for successful IOL is an open issue in obstetric practice.

During pregnancy and delivery, the cervix transforms from a stiff, long and closed structure to a soft, short and dilated structure that allows delivery. While collagen is aligned and organized in the cervix of non-pregnant women, it is more disorganized during the remodeling of the cervix during pregnancy. Water content of the cervical tissues is also increased in the process of preparation for delivery. All these changes are expected to be reflected in the image obtained from a transvaginal ultrasound (US), since the consistency of tissues affects their interaction with US waves.

Therefore, an analysis of image features extracted from US images could reveal the cervical tissue properties before IOL, even when they are not apparent to a human observer. This idea has been applied to study the neonatal respiratory morbidity from fetal lung US [5], to assess the cervical structure in spontaneous preterm births [2] or to predict the fetus gestational age [3]. In [10,11], US image analysis is also used to predict failure of induction of labor [10,11]. In [10], local binary patterns were used to extract texture features from the image, while in [11], symmetric local binary patterns and Gabor filterbanks were used.

The aim of this study is to analyze the predictive value of radiomic features extracted from transvaginal US images to predict IOL failure, and to compare their performance against other sonographical features studied in the literature, such as cervical length and cervical angle [1,4,8], and clinical data. To the best of our knowledge, this is the first study that uses radiomics, in the sense of a large amount of imaging features, to predict IOL failure, since previous works were limited to a reduced set of texture features [10,11]. Furthermore, clinical data is included as complementary information to the radiomics to build a predictive model. Different combinations of imaging and clinical data and different machine learning classifiers are explored, and an extensive comparison of the results is provided.

2   Materials and Methods

The following subsections describe the employed data, including the imaging and clinical data available for each patient, as well as the extracted radiomic features, the experiments and the proposed machine learning classifiers used to build the predictive models.

2.1   Dataset Annotation

The database used in this study consists of images and clinical data from patients admitted for IOL at Cruces University Hospital (Bilbao, Spain). The patients underwent a transvaginal US before IOL. Images were acquired with a Voluson ultrasound scanner from General Electric by an expert obstetrician following the same protocol for all patients. All images were provided in DICOM format. Image resolution is 720×960 pixels with a pixel spacing of 0.11. An expert

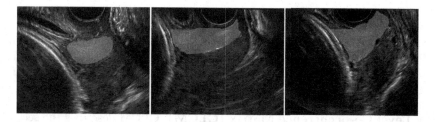

Fig. 1. Transvaginal ultrasound images of three patients and the selected region of interest for radiomic analysis.

obstetrician manually selected a region of interest (ROI) delimiting the upper part of the cervix, which is thought to have the most relevant information and less noise for the analysis. Figure 1 shows examples of the input images and ROIs.

Data from a total of 182 patients with US images, annotation of the ROI and clinical data was available, from which 130 had a vaginal delivery and 52 needed a C-section. Only in 30 cases the cause of the C-section was related to a cervical motive. Figure 2 summarizes the database composition.

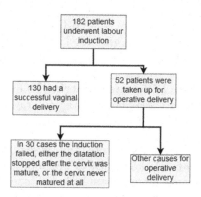

Fig. 2. Database composition.

Twenty relevant clinical attributes were selected from the database to be included in the study (such as age, weight, height, race, body mass index, number of abortions, weeks of gestation, information about previous pregnancies). Seven sonographic measurements, manually extracted from the transvaginal US, were also included. Sonographic features consist of different measures of the cervical anatomy: basal cervical length, compressed cervical length, basal anterior-posterior diameter, compressed anterior-posterior diameter, basal lateral diameter, compressed posterior diameter, compressed lateral diameter and segment.

2.2   Radiomic Feature Extraction

Radiomic features were extracted from the selected ROI using the PyRadiomics [7] Python software package. First order intensity-based features and texture-based features are included. To measure image texture, the following four matrices are calculated, from which descriptive values are computed:

Gray Level Co-occurrence Matrix (GLCM): GLCM describes the second-order joint probability function of an image region constrained by the mask. Each $(i, j)_{th}$ element of this matrix represents the number of times the combination of levels i and j occur in two pixels in the image that are separated by a given distance of pixels along a certain angle. We chose a distance of one pixel (angles are computed automatically).

Gray Level Run Length Matrix (GLRLM): GLRLM quantifies gray level runs, which are defined as the length in number of pixels of consecutive pixels that have the same gray value. In a GLRLM the $(i, j)_{th}$ element describes the number of runs with gray level i and length j that occur in the ROI along angle θ. The distance is 1 and angles are again computed automatically.

Gray Level Dependence Matrix (GLDM): GLDM quantifies gray level dependencies in an image. A gray level dependency is defined as a the number of connected voxels within a given distance that are dependent on the center voxel. A neighboring voxel with gray level j is considered dependent on center voxel with gray level i if $|i - j| \leq \alpha$. In a GLDM the $(i, j)_{th}$ element describes the number of times a voxel with gray level i with j dependent voxels in its neighborhood appears in image. The parameters used are distance $= 1$ and $\alpha = 0$.

Neighbouring Gray Tone Difference Matrix (NGTDM): it quantifies the difference between a gray value and the average gray value of its neighbours within a given distance (1 in this study).

By extracting mathematical descriptors from these matrices (mean, variance, entropy, uniformity ...), a total of 58 features were obtained. Moreover, 19 first-order features based on image intensity are included (energy, entropy, minimum, maximum, mean, median, interquartile range, skewness, kurtosis ...), resulting in a vector of 77 features.

2.3   Experimental Settings

Four experiments are proposed in order to find the best model for IOL failure prediction. In each experiment the following features are employed:

- **Experiment 1**: clinical data (20 features).
- **Experiment 2**: sonographic measurements (7 features).
- **Experiment 3**: sonographic measurements plus clinical data (27 features).
- **Experiment 4**: sonographic measurements, clinical data and radiomic features (104 features).

For some experiments, the feature vector is too long compared to the number of instances in the database, which can lead to poor performance of machine learning classifiers. Therefore, a filter method is applied to rank the features and select only the most relevant ones.

An additional problem when training machine learning classifiers for this task is class imbalance, which can lead the classifiers to have a bias towards the majority class. We used the *Synthetic Minority Over-sampling Technique-SMOTE* [6] to generate synthetic samples from the minority class (C-section deliveries), which are used to train the classifiers.

2.4   Machine Learning Classifiers

The following machine learning classifiers (from the Python *scikit learn* [12] library) are trained and validated to compare their performance: Gaussian Naive Bayes (GNB), Random Forest (RF), Multi Layer Perceptron (MLP), Support Vector Machine (SVM), Decision Tree (DT) and Extra Tree (ET). Table 1 summarizes the parameters used to train each classifier. Furthermore, to provide robustness to the results, we used a 10-fold cross-validation approach.

Table 1. Relevant meta-parameters for the classifiers used in the study. GNB: Gaussian Naive Bayes, RF: Random Forest, MLP: Multi Layer Perceptron, SVM: Support Vector Machine, DT: Decision Tree, ET: Extra Tree.

Classifier	Parameters
GNB	Variance smoothing: 1e–9
RF	Number of estimators: 150, impurity: Gini; minimum samples per split: 2
MLP	Maximum number of iterations: 1000; number of layers: 100
SVM	Kernel: radial basis function
DT	Impurity: Gini; minimum samples per split: 2
ET	Number of estimators: 150; minimum samples per split: 2; impurity: Gini

3   Results and Discussion

Table 2 summarizes the results obtained for each of the experiments described in Sect. 2.3. Clinical data alone (experiment 1) does not seem to have high predictive value, while the predictive value of the sonographical measurements alone (cervical length, cervical angle ...) is shown to be better, with a maximum AUC of 0.682 ± 0.009 when using a GNB classifier. This is consistent with previous studies in the literature which have shown a correlation between cervical length and other anatomical measurements and the outcome of IOL [8].

Regarding experiment 3, which combined clinical data and sonographic measurements, and experiment 4, including radiomic features, similar maximum AUC values are achieved. The RF and ET classifiers perform the best in both

Table 2. Mean AUC (area under the ROC, Receiver Operating Characteristic, curve) and standard deviation for the 10 k-fold cross validation for every classifier: GNB: Gaussian Naive Bayes, RF: Random Forest, MLP: Multi Layer Perceptron, SVM: Support Vector Machine, DT: Decision Tree, ET: Extra Tree. Results for all the experiments are shown.

Classifier	Experiment 1		Experiment 2		Experiment 3		Experiment 4	
	AUC	Std	AUC	Std	AUC	Std	AUC	Std
GNB	0.622	0.029	0.682	0.009	0.705	0.010	0.501	0.026
RF	0.621	0.014	0.652	0.012	0.763	0.011	0.750	0.017
MLP	0.512	0.058	0.678	0.012	0.582	0.040	0,505	0.051
SVM (RBF)	0.515	0.035	0.506	0.029	0.480	0.046	0.500	0
DT	0.572	0.030	0.525	0.037	0.637	0.018	0.62	0.031
ET	0.614	0.020	0.639	0.016	0.747	0.012	0.769	0.014

cases, yielding AUC values between 0.747 and 0.769. When comparing the highest AUC values from both experiments (experiment 3, random forest: 0.763 ± 0.011; experiment 4, extra trees: 0.769 ± 0.014) the obtained difference is not statistically significant (T-test, p value = 0.1934).

Nonetheless, differences in the performance of the classifiers can be seen by analyzing their behaviour with respect to false negatives and false positives. A more detailed analysis of the results is provided in Table 3, which shows the sensitivity, specificity, false positive rate and false negative rate for the classifiers that yielded the best AUCs for each experiment. Overall, false negative rate is higher than false positive rate. From a clinical point of view, this situation (sending a patient for IOL that ends up in C-section) is better than the opposite (performing a C-section when IOL would have succeeded).

Thus, comparing the models from experiment 4 with experiment 3, it can be observed that adding radiomic features increases the sensitivity and, consequently, reduces the false negative rate of the classifiers. We obtain useful information from the radiomic analysis that makes the model more balanced, with a sensitivity of 69% and a specificity of 71%, in contrast to the rest of models which achieve good specificity but have too low sensitivity. This means that radiomics contain relevant information and may help avoiding unnecessary C-sections.

It is worth noting that the same feature selection procedure was applied to experiment 3 and experiment 4, to make the results comparable. The feature selection process allows us to understand which features are more important. For experiment 3 many of the high-ranked features are sonographical (5 features), but a few clinical data are kept as well: weight, height, age, estimated fetal weight, number of previous pregnancies, previous vaginal births, weeks of pregnancy. While using only clinical data is not enough to predict IOL (experiment 1), adding this information to sonopraphical measurements helps improving the models, according to the results from experiments 2 and 3. In experiment 4, five

Table 3. Sensitivity, specificity, false positive rate (FPR) and false negative rate (FNR) for the best performing classifiers for every experiment

	Data	Classifier	Sensitivity	Specificity	FPR	FNR
Exp. 1	Clinical data	RF	0.808	0.338	0.662	0.192
		ET	0.423	0.885	0.223	0.635
Exp. 2	Sonographic measurements	GNB	0.632	0.682	0.318	0.368
		MLP	0.600	0.677	0.323	0.400
Exp. 3	Clinical data and sonographic measurements	RF	0.596	0.825	0.175	0.404
		ET	0.451	0.858	0.142	0.549
Exp. 4	Clinical data, sonographic measurements and radiomics	RF	0.692	0.715	0.285	0.308
		ET	0.481	0.846	0.154	0.519

sonographic measurements are again selected, as well as some clinical variables (height, estimated fetal weight, body mass index, number of vaginal births) and 4 radiomic values (energy, long run high gray level emphasis, run length non uniformity, run entropy). The fact that radiomic features are high-ranked in the feature selection process and that the results in experiment 4 are better than in experiment 3 suggests that radiomic features from transvaginal US can be useful for the prediction of IOL failure.

4   Conclusion

Correctly evaluating the probability of successful IOL is still an open issue in modern obstetrics, since 20% of the induced women have a C-section and the current evaluation method, Bishop Score, has been found to be subjective and inconsistent. Transvaginal US is cheap and widely available at hospitals, and it is performed routinely in other stages of pregnancy. The results presented in this paper agree with previously reported results [4,8] in that cervical length and cervical angle measured from the transvaginal US are useful for the prediction of IOL failure (0.682 AUC, 63% sensitivity, 68% specificity).

Furthermore, a novel methodology for IOL failure prediction based on radiomics has been applied to these images for the first time. We have shown how a combination of radiomic features with cervical measurements and clinical data can be used to build a predictive model that achieves an AUC of 0.75 with 69% sensitivity and 71% specificity. These preliminary results indicate that US can provide the clinicians with useful information prior to the IOL.

An important limitation of our study is the size of the patient cohort, with 182 patients from which only 52 had a C-section. Furthermore, only in 30 cases the IOL failure was related to a cervical motive. All the images come from the same hospital and have been acquired following the same protocol with US devices from the same vendor. Poor generalization is a common problem working with radiomics, as different protocols or vendors could result in different image properties, which implies that the selected features and models could be overfitted for the current available data. Further validation should be performed with a larger and more diverse database to assess the robustness of the proposed method. Future works should also develop a technique to obtain measurements as cervical length and cervical angle automatically from the US images.

References

1. Al-Adwy, A.M., et al.: Diagnostic accuracy of posterior cervical angle and cervical length in the prediction of successful induction of labor. Int. J. Gynecol. Obstet. **141**(1), 102–107 (2018)
2. Baños, N., Perez-Moreno, A., Julià, C., Murillo-Bravo, C., Coronado, D., Gratacós, E., Deprest, J., Palacio, M.: Quantitative analysis of cervical texture by ultrasound in mid-pregnancy and association with spontaneous preterm birth: cervical texture associated with spontaneous preterm birth. Ultrasound Obstet. Gynecol. **51**(5), 637–643 (2018)
3. Baños, N., et al.: Quantitative analysis of the cervical texture by ultrasound and correlation with gestational age. Fetal Diagn. Ther. **41**(4), 265–272 (2017)
4. Brik, M., Mateos, S., Fernandez-Buhigas, I., Garbayo, P., Costa, G., Santacruz, B.: Sonographical predictive markers of failure of induction of labour in term pregnancy. J. Obstet. Gynaecol. **37**(2), 179–184 (2017)
5. Burgos-Artizzu, X.P., Perez-Moreno, A., Coronado-Gutierrez, D., Gratacos, E., Palacio, M.: Evaluation of an improved tool for non-invasive prediction of neonatal respiratory morbidity based on fully automated fetal lung ultrasound analysis. Sci. Rep. **9**(1), 1950 (2019)
6. Chawla, N.V., Bowyer, K.W., Hall, L.O., Kegelmeyer, W.P.: SMOTE: synthetic minority over-sampling technique. J. Artif. Intell. Res. **16**, 321–357 (2002)
7. van Griethuysen, J.J., et al.: Computational radiomics system to decode the radiographic phenotype. Cancer Res. **77**(21), 104–107 (2017)
8. Kehila, M., Abouda, H., Sahbi, K., Cheour, H., Chanoufi, M.B.: Ultrasound cervical length measurement in prediction of labor induction outcome. NPM **9**(2), 127–131 (2016)
9. Kolkman, D., et al.: The bishop score as a predictor of labor induction success: a systematic review. Am. J. Perinatol. **30**(08), 625–630 (2013)
10. Obando, V.P., Arana, A.N., Izaguirre, A., Burgos, J.: Labor induction failure prediction based on B-mode ultrasound image processing using multiscale local binary patterns. In: International Conference on Optoelectronics and Image Processing, pp. 25–29 (2016)
11. Obando, V.P., Arana, A.N., Izaguirre, A., Burgos, J.: Labor induction failure prediction using Gabor filterbanks and center symmetric local binary patterns. In: IEEE 37th Central America and Panama Convention, pp. 1–5 (2017)
12. Pedregosa, F., et al.: Scikit-learn: machine learning in Python. J. Mach. Learn. Res. **12**, 2825–2830 (2011)

Longitudinal Analysis of Fetal MRI in Patients with Prenatal Spina Bifida Repair

Kelly Payette[1]([⊠]), Ueli Moehrlen[2], Luca Mazzone[2],
Nicole Ochsenbein-Kölble[2], Ruth Tuura[1], Raimund Kottke[3],
Martin Meuli[2], and Andras Jakab[1]

[1] Center for MR-Research, University Children's Hospital Zurich, Zurich,
Switzerland
kelly.payette@kispi.uzh.ch
[2] Fetal Surgery and Prenatal Consultation, University Children's Hospital
Zurich, Zurich, Switzerland
[3] Diagnostic Imaging and Intervention, University Children's Hospital Zurich,
Zurich, Switzerland

Abstract. Open spina bifida (SB) is one of the most common congenital defects and can lead to impaired brain development. Emerging fetal surgery methods have shown considerable success in the treatment of patients with this severe anomaly. Afterwards, alterations in the brain development of these fetuses have been observed. Currently no longitudinal studies exist to show the effect of fetal surgery on brain development. In this work, we present a fetal MRI neuroimaging analysis pipeline for fetuses with SB, including automated fetal ventricle segmentation and deformation-based morphometry, and demonstrate its applicability with an analysis of ventricle enlargement in fetuses with SB. Using a robust super-resolution algorithm, we reconstructed fetal brains at both pre-operative and post-operative time points and trained a U-Net CNN in order to automatically segment the ventricles. We investigated the change of ventricle shape post-operatively, and the impacts of lesion size, type, and GA at operation on the change in ventricle shape. No impact was found. Prenatal ventricle volume growth was also investigated. Our method allows for the quantification of longitudinal morphological changes to fully quantify the impact of prenatal SB repair and could be applied to predict postnatal outcomes.

1 Introduction

Neural tube defects are some of the most common types of congenital defects and can lead to long-term physical and cognitive disabilities as well as social and psychological issues [1]. Myelomeningocele (MMC) and myeloschisis (MS) are open dysraphic neural tube defects, more commonly referred to as spina bifida (SB). They occur when the neural tube does not neurulate properly during development. Subsequently, the exposed part of the spinal cord suffers progressive damage during gestation [26]. Advances in fetal magnetic resonance imaging (MRI) have better enabled identification and evaluation of SB at an early gestational age. The fetus can then undergo *in utero*

© Springer Nature Switzerland AG 2019
Q. Wang et al. (Eds.): PIPPI 2019/SUSI 2019, LNCS 11798, pp. 161–170, 2019.
https://doi.org/10.1007/978-3-030-32875-7_18

repair of the spinal lesion in which the anatomy is reconstructed, protecting the spinal cord from any further damage during gestation and birth [2, 3]. The procedure often leads to changes in brain structure, such as the reduction of the hindbrain herniation and the restoration of intracranial cerebrospinal fluid (CSF) space [4]. Reliability of the measurements of the posterior fossa and brain stem have been studied in SB using low resolution images, and while the posterior fossa measurements were reliable between observers, the brain stem measurements were not [5]. An early longitudinal MRI imaging analysis of the brain in SB fetuses would allow the visualization and objective quantification of changes occurring in the brain related to the pathology, and the impact of the surgical intervention on the developmental trajectory of the central nervous system.

Many advances have been made in the analysis of fetal MRI, especially in the creation of high resolution 3D volumes [6–10]. However, the analysis of these high-resolution volumes and their usage in longitudinal studies has not been explored in detail. In addition, the automatic segmentation of 3D volumes of pathological fetal brains and the usage of deformation-based morphometry (DBM) on fetal images to investigate brain growth of fetuses with SB have not been explored.

Automatic segmentation of fetal MRI has been explored in both pathological and healthy brains but has primarily focused on segmenting the fetal brain within the maternal tissue [10–14]. The segmentation of fetal brain tissues has been investigated to a lesser extent [12, 15–17]. However, many of these methods are atlas-based or rely on existing priors, which do not exist for fetal SB brains. Therefore, these methods are not yet applicable.

Another category of automatic segmentation methods that do not rely on atlases are convolutional neural networks (CNNs). One popular type of CNN for the automatic segmentation of medical images is the U-Net [18], which has been used for the localization and segmentation of the fetal brain within the overall fetal image [14] and has been tested on the segmentation of a normal fetal brain [19]. We propose to use the same network to segment brain tissues within a high-resolution 3D reconstructed volume of a fetal SB brain, both pre-operatively and post-operatively. These segmentations can then be used to perform a detailed longitudinal volumetric study of the brain growth and development of fetuses with SB.

In addition to a purely volumetric analysis, we propose the usage of DBM to explore changes in brain growth rates of the SB fetus through looking at deformation field for each subject between the pre-operative and post-operative period. This could potentially provide insight into regional changes in fetal brain shape, which isn't given just by looking at the volumes alone.

We propose a pipeline of fetal MRI image analysis, from fetal brain extraction and super-resolution reconstruction to automatic tissue segmentation of fetal SB brains and the quantification of structural brain growth in pathological brains using DBM. Due to its importance in SB and other congenital fetal pathologies, we demonstrate the applicability of a U-Net CNN to segment normal and dilated ventricles for longitudinal and volumetric analysis.

2   Methods

2.1   Dataset

Prenatal surgical repair of the MMC or MS lesion was carried out in 93 subjects at the Zurich Center for Fetal Diagnosis and Therapy between March 2012 and June 2019, with both pre- and post-operative MRIs available. Multiple MRI scans of the brain were acquired at each time point on 1.5T and 3T clinical GE whole-body scanners using a T2-weighted single-shot fast spin echo sequence (SSFSE), with an in-plane resolution of 0.5×0.5 mm and a slice thickness of 3–5 mm. The average gestational age in weeks (GA) of the subjects at the pre-operative scans, open fetal surgery, and post-operative scans were 23.2 ± 1.5 GA, 25.0 ± 0.8 GA, and 27.7 ± 1.2 GA, respectively. The length and width of the overall lesion size was measured and recorded intra-operatively for each patient. The MRI images of 15 non-pathological fetal brains were acquired in the same manner as the fetal SB brains. These fetuses were scanned to confirm or rule out suspected abnormalities and were determined to have unaffected brain development.

2.2   Brain Extraction and Super-Resolution Reconstruction

We reoriented and masked the fetal brains in each of the individual low-resolution (LR) scans for each subject using a semi-automated atlas-based custom MeVisLab module. A super-resolution (SR) algorithm was then applied to each stack of images (comprising of between 3 and 14 LR scans, with at least one scan in each orientation: axial, sagittal, coronal) for each subject at both the pre-operative and post-operative time points, creating a 3D SR volume of brain morphology [9]. See Fig. 1a for an overview of the processing steps for each subject. The quality of the SR reconstructions was then reviewed. Of the original 93 cases, 44 cases had both high quality pre- and post- operative images, while the remaining cases were excluded due to excess fetal movement present in the LR scans, causing movement artefact in the images. This results in a sub-optimal SR reconstruction in either the pre- or post-operative time point (see Fig. 2 for an example of SR reconstructions). The majority of poor-quality SR reconstructions were at the pre-operative time point (36 cases), due to the relatively small size of the fetus allowing for increased motion. SR reconstructions of the 15 fetuses with normal brain development were performed in the same manner.

2.3   Automatic Ventricle Segmentation Using U-Net

46 high quality SR volumes (15 normally developing fetal brains, 16 post-operative SB fetal brains, and 15 pre-operative SB fetal brains; the SB fetal brains were chosen from the larger 93 case sample set) were manually segmented into the following tissue classes: white matter, grey matter, ventricles, cerebellum, brain stem, CSF. More cases were not segmented due to the time-consuming nature of this task. Fetal brains from all three categories were chosen in order to create as general of a network as possible. The ventricle label was isolated from the overall segmentation in order to train the neural network. 43 ventricle cases were used as the training and testing data with an 80/20

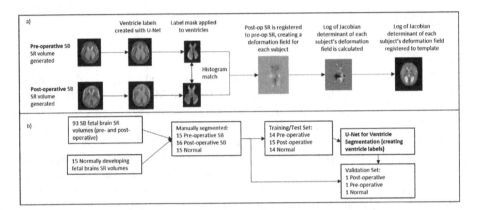

Fig. 1. (a) Flowchart of processing steps at a subject level. For each subject, the post-operative ventricles are registered to the pre-operative ventricles, creating a deformation field. The log of the determinant of the Jacobian is calculated for each deformation field, which is then registered to the custom template. (b) Flowchart of processing steps for training and validating the U-Net for ventricle segmentation. One case was kept out from each group (pre- and post-operative, and normally developing) for validation.

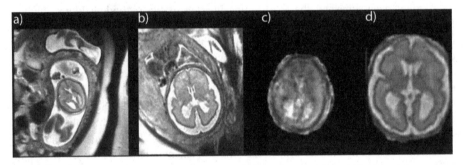

Fig. 2. Example SB SR reconstructions where the pre-operative reconstruction was poor (4 LR scans used, 21.6GA) and the post-operative reconstruction was successful (5 LR scans used, 27.0GA). (a) example pre-operative LR scan, (b) example post-operative LR scan, (c) pre-operative SR volume, (d) post-operative SR volume

split, with small amounts of data augmentation. The U-Net used in [14] was used and modified, adding batch normalization as well as changing the learning rate to 10E–5, and re-trained with the ventricle labels. The neural network was trained for 100 epochs. The additional 3 cases (one normally developing fetal brain, one pre-operative SB, and one post-operative SB) were preserved as an independent validation set (see Fig. 1b). A larger validation set would be desirable, however due to the relatively small training set we decided to maximize the cases used in the training in order to improve the performance of the network. Once the network was trained, the ventricles of the 46 post-operative and 46 pre-operative SR volumes were segmented using the network.

2.4   Deformation-Based Morphometry and Atlas Creation

The segmented ventricles of the pre-operative SR volume was resampled to 0.5 mm and histogram-matched to the respective resampled post-operative SR volume [20]. Ventricle enlargement between the two time points was determined for each subject using DBM. The post-operative image was registered to the pre-operative image using a series of rigid, affine, and SyN registrations, creating a deformation field representing the ventricle enlargement. This field was then transformed into the same space, using a custom-made atlas of the post-operative SB brain. The custom atlas was created using the ANTS template reconstruction software [21, 22]. The log of the Jacobian determinant map of the deformation between the two images was calculated, and then scaled to create a daily Jacobian, as the difference between the two imaging time points was variable. The registrations and Jacobian calculations were performed using ANTs [23]. The transformed ventricle enlargement maps were then combined into a single 4D volume. In addition, the volumes of the ventricles were determined using the label maps.

2.5   Statistical Analysis

FSL's randomise was used to perform a statistical analysis of the ventricle enlargement maps using a general linear model with threshold free cluster enhancement [24]. We looked at the effect on ventricle enlargement of the area of the lesion, lesion type (MMC or MS), lesion location, and gestational age at operation. Gestational age at both the pre-operative and post-operative time points were controlled for, as well as gestational age at time of surgery.

3   Results

3.1   Ventricle Segmentation

Ventricle segmentation was assessed using the Dice overlap coefficient, comparing the segmentation from the U-Net with the ground truth (Table 1). The segmentations created by the U-Net can be seen in Fig. 3.

Table 1. Dice coefficients of ventricle segmentation validation of the U-Net CNN.

Image	GA	Dice coefficient	Sensitivity	Specificity
Pre-operative MS	24.4	0.94	0.95	1.00
Post-operative MMC	30.1	0.91	0.91	1.00
Normal	23	0.91	0.90	1.00

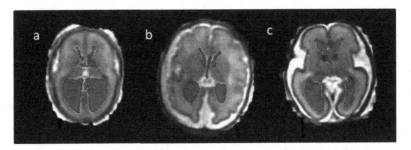

Fig. 3. Ventricle Segmentation with the U-Net of (a) pre-operative MS brain (24.4GA); (b) post-operative MMC brain (30.1GA); (c) normally developing fetal brain (23GA)

3.2   Longitudinal Analysis

Atlas Creation

A custom template was generated for both pre-operative and post-operative fetal brains with the average GA at each time point. The pre-operative custom template was generated using 10 pre-operative SR volumes with an average GA of 23.1 ± 0.3, and the post-operative template was generated using 20 post-operative SR volumes with an average GA of 27.3 ± 0.3. There were fewer good quality SR volumes available for the creation of the pre-operative template. However, there are fewer features and less variation at younger gestational ages, therefore fewer subjects are required [25]. The atlases created can be seen in Fig. 4.

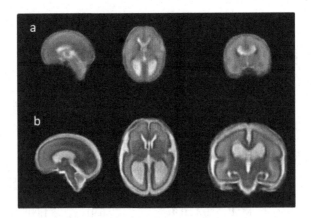

Fig. 4. Custom SB templates (a) pre-operative, 23 GA; (b) post-operative, 27 GA

Volumetry

From the segmented volumes, the volumes of each of the fetuses at both time points were determined and can be seen in Fig. 5 and Table 2. Two cases were excluded due to failure of the segmentation algorithm, mainly due to the quality of the SR reconstruction. The average daily volume growth within the ventricles was 449.8 ± 285.9 mm^3. All SB fetal ventricle volumes were determined based on segmentations created using the U-Net network and were reviewed for accuracy. In some cases where there were errors, minor adjustments were made to ensure that the wide range of ventricle volumes found reflected the pathology and not errors in segmentation. All normal fetal ventricle volumes were determined through manual segmentation and taken from the training set used for the U-Net.

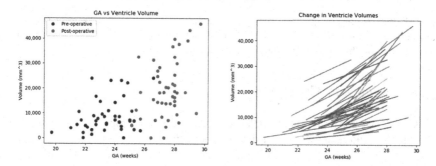

Fig. 5. Left: GA vs ventricle volume. Blue: pre-operative, Red: post-operative. Right: Change in ventricle volume for each fetus. (Color figure online)

Table 2. Ventricle volume overview for SB pre-operative, SB post-operative, and normal groups. The SB volumes were found using the U-Net, and the normal volumes from the manual segmentations performed for the U-Net training set.

Dataset	n	Average GA	Average volume (mm^3)
Pre-operative SB	44	23.5 ± 1.4	8953 ± 6345
Post-operative SB	44	27.5 ± 1	20480 ± 10922
Normal	15	27.9 ± 3.5	7139 ± 3063

DBM

Deformation based morphometry was performed on the segmented ventricles for each case and registered to the custom template. Mean ventricle enlargement can be seen in Fig. 6. As expected, ventricle enlargement occurs in all sections of the ventricles. However, some asymmetry in the ventricles is present, most likely due to the underlying pathology of the SB patients. The SR volumes used to create the atlas were a subset of the overall population, and there was potentially more asymmetry in the overall population than in the atlas subgroup.

In addition, a regression analysis using threshold free cluster enhancement was performed investigating the impact of lesion size, lesion type, and GA at operation on ventricular enlargement. Lesion size, lesion type. and GA at operation had no impact on the ventricular enlargement.

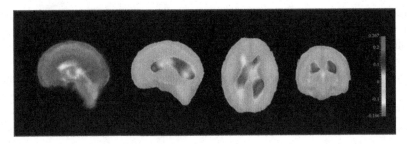

Fig. 6. Left: Custom pre-operative atlas; Right: Mean fetal ventricle enlargement (log of the Jacobian determinant of the deformation field) between the pre-operative and post-operative time points overlaid on the custom pre-operative atlas. (Color figure online)

4 Discussion and Conclusion

In this work, we have presented a fetal MRI image analysis pipeline for fetuses with SB, including automated fetal ventricle segmentation. We demonstrated its applicability with an analysis of ventricle enlargement in fetuses with SB. Using a robust super-resolution algorithm [9], we reconstructed fetal brains at both the pre-operative and post-operative time point, and then used 46 manual segmentations, applied data-augmentation, and trained a U-Net CNN in order to automatically segment the ventricles within the SB SR volume. We then used DBM to investigate the change in shape of ventricles of the SB fetuses post-operatively and the impact of lesion size, type, and GA at operation on the change in ventricle shape, all of which had no impact.

Overall, the quality of the automatic segmentation depended on the quality of the super-resolution reconstruction. As many subjects were excluded due to poor quality reconstructions, it would be beneficial to improve this step in order to reduce the number of subjects excluded.

The volumetric analysis of SR volumes using the U-Net is very promising and will be expanded to other brain tissues. Further data augmentation methods can potentially be applied in order to increase the training set without having to manually segment more volumes, as it is an incredibly time-consuming process prone to error.

The use of DBM as a method of quantifying brain growth is very dependent on the atlas creation and improved atlases would be beneficial. The pre-operative atlas is fuzzy when compared to standard atlases of healthy fetal brains. However, the quality of the atlas is directly related to the quality of the input volumes, which for the young pre-operative fetal brains are not as sharp as the post-operative brains. In addition, one cannot draw any results from only looking at the change in shape of the ventricles, as that does not consider all the other changes in the brain occurring. A more complete analysis would need to investigate all brain tissues.

In the future, we aim to expand the analysis of tissue brain growth of SB fetuses to other structures of the brain. In particular, we aim to explore the post-operative changes in the hindbrain herniation occurring in the context of Chiari II malformation. We aim to quantify the impact of fetal SB repair, and ideally to better predict the outcome of the surgery in order to aid prenatal parental guidance.

Acknowledgements. Financial support was provided by the OPO Foundation, Anna Müller Grocholski Foundation, the Foundation for Research in Science and the Humanities at the University of Zurich, EMDO Foundation, Hasler Foundation, and the Forschungszentrum für das Kind Grant (FZK).

References

1. Roach, J.W., Short, B.F., Saltzman, H.M.: Adult consequences of spina bifida: a cohort study. Clin. Orthop. **469**(5), 1246–1252 (2011)
2. Meuli, M., Moehrlen, U.: Fetal surgery for myelomeningocele is effective: a critical look at the whys. Pediatr. Surg. Int. **30**(7), 689–697 (2014)
3. Möhrlen, U., et al.: Benchmarking against the MOMS trial: Zurich results of open fetal surgery for spina bifida. Fetal Diagn. Ther. **5**, 1–7 (2019)
4. Adzick, N.S.: Fetal surgery for myelomeningocele: trials and tribulations. Isabella Forshall Lecture. J. Pediatr. Surg. **47**(2), 273–281 (2012)
5. Aertsen, M., et al.: Reliability of MR imaging-based posterior fossa and brain stem measurements in open spinal dysraphism in the era of fetal surgery. Am. J. Neuroradiol. **40**(1), 191–198 (2019)
6. Kim, K., Habas, P.A., Rousseau, F., Glenn, O.A., Barkovich, A.J., Studholme, C.: Intersection based motion correction of multislice MRI for 3-D in utero fetal brain image formation. IEEE Trans. Med. Imaging **29**(1), 146–158 (2010)
7. Kuklisova-Murgasova, M., Quaghebeur, G., Rutherford, M.A., Hajnal, J.V., Schnabel, J.A.: Reconstruction of fetal brain MRI with intensity matching and complete outlier removal. Med. Image Anal. **16**(8), 1550–1564 (2012)
8. Kainz, B., et al.: Fast volume reconstruction from motion corrupted stacks of 2D slices. IEEE Trans. Med. Imaging **34**(9), 1901–1913 (2015)
9. Tourbier, S., Bresson, X., Hagmann, P., Thiran, J.-P., Meuli, R., Cuadra, M.B.: An efficient total variation algorithm for super-resolution in fetal brain MRI with adaptive regularization. NeuroImage **118**, 584–597 (2015)
10. Ebner, M., et al.: An automated localization, segmentation and reconstruction framework for fetal brain MRI. In: Frangi, A.F., Schnabel, J.A., Davatzikos, C., Alberola-López, C., Fichtinger, G. (eds.) MICCAI 2018. LNCS, vol. 11070, pp. 313–320. Springer, Cham (2018). https://doi.org/10.1007/978-3-030-00928-1_36
11. Tourbier, S., et al.: Automated template-based brain localization and extraction for fetal brain MRI reconstruction. NeuroImage **155**, 460–472 (2017)
12. Wright, R., et al.: Automatic quantification of normal cortical folding patterns from fetal brain MRI. NeuroImage **91**, 21–32 (2014)
13. Keraudren, K., et al.: Automated fetal brain segmentation from 2D MRI slices for motion correction. NeuroImage **101**, 633–643 (2014)
14. Salehi, S.S.M., et al.: Real-time automatic fetal brain extraction in fetal MRI by deep learning. In: IEEE 15th International Symposium on Biomedical Imaging (ISBI 2018), pp. 720–724 (2018)
15. Habas, P.A., Kim, K., Rousseau, F., Glenn, O.A., Barkovich, A.J., Studholme, C.: Atlas-based segmentation of developing tissues in the human brain with quantitative validation in young fetuses. Hum. Brain Mapp. **31**(9), 1348–1358 (2010)
16. Moeskops, P., Viergever, M.A., Mendrik, A.M., de Vries, L.S., Benders, M.J.N.L., Išgum, I.: Automatic segmentation of MR brain images with a convolutional neural network. IEEE Trans. Med. Imaging **35**(5), 1252–1261 (2016)

17. Gholipour, A., Akhondi-Asl, A., Estroff, J.A., Warfield, S.K.: Multi-atlas multi-shape segmentation of fetal brain MRI for volumetric and morphometric analysis of ventriculomegaly. NeuroImage **60**(3), 1819–1831 (2012)

18. Ronneberger, O., Fischer, P., Brox, T.: U-Net: convolutional networks for biomedical image segmentation. In: Navab, N., Hornegger, J., Wells, W.M., Frangi, A.F. (eds.) MICCAI 2015. LNCS, vol. 9351, pp. 234–241. Springer, Cham (2015). https://doi.org/10.1007/978-3-319-24574-4_28

19. Li, W., Wang, G., Fidon, L., Ourselin, S., Cardoso, M.J., Vercauteren, T.: On the compactness, efficiency, and representation of 3D convolutional networks: brain parcellation as a pretext task. In: Niethammer, M., et al. (eds.) IPMI 2017. LNCS, vol. 10265, pp. 348–360. Springer, Cham (2017). https://doi.org/10.1007/978-3-319-59050-9_28

20. Fedorov, A., et al.: 3D slicer as an image computing platform for the quantitative imaging network. Magn. Reson. Imaging **30**(9), 1323–1341 (2012)

21. Avants, B.B., et al.: The optimal template effect in hippocampus studies of diseased populations. NeuroImage **49**(3), 2457–2466 (2010)

22. Avants, B.B., Tustison, N.J., Song, G., Cook, P.A., Klein, A., Gee, J.C.: A reproducible evaluation of ANTs similarity metric performance in brain image registration. NeuroImage **54**(3), 2033–2044 (2011)

23. Avants, B.B., Epstein, C.L., Grossman, M., Gee, J.C.: Symmetric diffeomorphic image registration with cross-correlation: evaluating automated labeling of elderly and neurodegenerative brain. Med. Image Anal. **12**(1), 26–41 (2008)

24. Winkler, A.M., Ridgway, G.R., Webster, M.A., Smith, S.M., Nichols, T.E.: Permutation inference for the general linear model. NeuroImage **92**, 381–397 (2014)

25. Gholipour, A., et al.: A normative spatiotemporal MRI atlas of the fetal brain for automatic segmentation and analysis of early brain growth. Sci. Rep. **7**, 476 (2017)

26. Meuli, M., Meuli-Simmen, C., Hutchins, G.M., Yingling, C.D., Hoffman, K.M., Harrison, M.R., Adzick, N.S.: In utero surgery rescues neurological function at birth in sheep with spina bifida. Nat. Med. **1**, 342–347 (1995)

Quantifying Residual Motion Artifacts in Fetal fMRI Data

Athena Taymourtash[1(✉)], Ernst Schwartz[1], Karl-Heinz Nenning[1],
Daniel Sobotka[1], Mariana Diogo[2], Gregor Kasprian[2], Daniela Prayer[2],
and Georg Langs[1]

[1] Computational Imaging Research Lab, Department of Biomedical Imaging and
Image-guided Therapy, Medical University of Vienna, Vienna, Austria
athena.taymourtash@meduniwien.ac.at
[2] Division for Neuroradiology and Musculoskeletal Radiology, Department of
Biomedical Imaging and Image-guided Therapy, Medical University of Vienna,
Vienna, Austria

Abstract. Fetal functional Magnetic Resonance Imaging (fMRI) has
emerged as a powerful tool for investigating brain development in utero,
holding promise for generating developmental disease biomarkers and
supporting prenatal diagnosis. However, to date its clinical applications
have been limited by unpredictable fetal and maternal motion during
image acquisition. Even after spatial realignment, these cause spurious
signal fluctuations confounding measures of functional connectivity and
biasing statistical inference of relationships between connectivity and
individual differences. As there is no ground truth for the brain's functional structure, especially before birth, quantifying the quality of motion
correction is challenging. In this paper, we propose evaluating the efficacy of different regression based methods for removing motion artifacts
after realignment by assessing the residual relationship of functional connectivity with estimated motion, and with the distance between areas.
Results demonstrate the sensitivity of our evaluation's criteria to reveal
the relative strengths and weaknesses among different artifact removal
methods, and underscore the need for greater care when dealing with
fetal motion.

Keywords: Fetal fMRI · Motion correction · Functional connectivity

1 Introduction

For over two decades, it has been known that motion artifacts cause serious dis-
ruptions to fMRI data such that even sub-millimeter head movement can add
spurious variance to true signal and bias inter-individual differences in fMRI
metrics [13,16]. The severity of this problem is especially pronounced in fetal
imaging due to unpredictable fetal movement, maternal respiration, and signal non-uniformities [10]. To date, advanced motion correction methods, often

© Springer Nature Switzerland AG 2019
Q. Wang et al. (Eds.): PIPPI 2019/SUSI 2019, LNCS 11798, pp. 171–180, 2019.
https://doi.org/10.1007/978-3-030-32875-7_19

relying on super resolution techniques, have been proposed to address motion artifact by reconstructing a high resolution motion-free volume from several clinical low resolution MR images of a moving fetus [3,7]. As methods to counteract motion artifacts are being developed, it is of critical importance to know if a technique has improved the quality of data or introduced additional artifacts. Among several quality-control benchmarks that have been recently employed in adult studies [2,9,12], Quality Control-Functional Connectivity (QC-FC) correlation was found to be the most useful metric of quality as it directly quantifies the relationship between motion and the primary outcome of interest over a population [13]. The QC-FC benchmark is based on the correlation between the FC of each pair of regions and the average motion of each subjects in the dataset to determine how that connectivity is modulated by subject motion. Since both FC and motion are calculated as a mean value over the entire scan, for the rest of paper we call it *static FC-FD*. For the purpose of assessing residual artifacts in fetuses, the average motion is insufficient, due to excessive fetal motion, exhibiting large movement spikes and overall more continuous motion during acquisition [10]. Furthermore, using the average motion as a means to quantify spurious connectivity allows for no subject-specific evaluation as it provides only group specific motion dependencies. It therefore is not able to decide whether a specific acquisition should be removed from analysis entirely, or could be salvaged by excluding specific contaminated time-points using methods such as scrubbing [14].

In this paper, we developed a *dynamic FC-FD* benchmark for systematic evaluation of subject-specific fMRI data quality, comparing the efficacy of existing regression strategies for mitigating motion-induced artefacts. We evaluated our benchmark on fetal fMRI as an application with irregular motion. However, the proposed methodology is general and can be applied to any fMRI study.

2   Data, Preprocessing and Motion Correction

Experiments in this study were performed on 24 in-utero BOLD MRI sequences obtained from fetuses between 19 and 39 weeks of gestation. None of the cases showed any neurological pathologies. Pregnant women were scanned on a 1.5T clinical scanner (Philips Medical Systems, Best, Netherlands) using single-shot echo-planar imaging (EPI), and a sensitivity encoding (SENSE) cardiac coil with five elements. Image matrix size was 144×144, with $3 \times 3\,mm^2$ in-plane resolution, 3 mm slice thickness, a TR/TE of 1000/50 ms, and a flip angle of 90. Each scan contains 96 volumetric images obtained in an interleaved slice order to minimize cross-talk between adjacent slices. Preprocessing of the resting-state data included correction for distortions induced by magnetic field inhomogeneity, slice timing correction, motion correction, de-meaning and removal of any linear or quadratic trends. Motion correction comprised iterative rigid-body registration of all slice stacks to a resulting mean volume so that the objective function of normalized correlation ratio was optimized. After 25 iterations, a realigned version of each volume was created using trilinear interpolation, and two slices were

Table 1. Eight nuisance regression strategies evaluated.

Strategy	Summary of regressors	#R
1: GSR	Mean time-series averaged across the entire brain	1
2: 2Phys	Two physiological time-series computed across white matter (WM) and cerebrospinal fluid (CSF)	2
3: 6HMP	6 motion parameter estimates derived from realignment	6
4: 6HMP + 2Phys + GSR	6 motion parameter estimates, 2 physiological compartments and GSR	9
5: 24HMP	6 motion parameters, their temporal derivatives, together with quadratic expansions of parameters and derivatives	24
6: 24HMP + 8Phys + 4GSR	Quadratic expansion of model 4: 9 regressors, their derivatives, quadratic terms, and squares of derivatives	36
7: aCompCor	5 principal components each from the WM and CSF [1]	10
8: tCompCor	6 principal components from high-variance voxels [1]	6

interpolated between every two slices to eliminate the effect of slice interleaving in different stacks, tripling the slice number after motion correction.

3   Functional Connectivity After Nuisance Regression

Individual functional connectivity analysis was performed in the native functional space. For this, cortical regions of interest (ROIs) were first obtained using an automatic atlas-based segmentation of $T2$ scans of the same subject acquired during the same scan session as the fMRI volumes, using a publicly available atlas of fetal brain anatomy [4]. The resulting parcellation consists of 98 ROIs and was mapped to the motion corrected fMRI space using a rigid transformation computed between each individual structural T2 scan and the first volume of fMRI data. For each parcel, we calculated the mean time course of all voxels, and applied one of eight different common nuisance regression strategies (Table 1). The resulting time course served as basis for calculating functional connectivity in the form of a correlation matrix estimated using Pearson's correlation.

4   Assessing Spurious Motion Artifacts in fMRI Data

Motion correction first aims to re-align individual slices of the fMRI volume sequence such that the anatomical position of a voxel is consistent for the whole time-series. Then, information such as spatial displacement and other surrogate measurements of non-neural signal are used as nuisance regressors to remove non-physiological residual signal components. We propose a dynamic FC-FD method based on the fact that the sources of motion in fMRI time series are non-stationary and can potentially induce changes in FC over time [5,8]. It expands on subject level *static FC-FD* [13] by taking variation of motion and FC over time into account. We use the association between FC variation and motion before and after the application of each nuisance regression strategy to evaluate its effectiveness in fMRI data of a subject. FC varies over time due to noise and actual non-stationary neural behavior with the magnitude of variation not differing from simulated stochastic time-series [5]. Nevertheless, we can exploit the relationship between FC fluctuation, estimated motion, and the distance between areas to quantify possible residual non-neural confounds in the signal after motion correction and nuisance regression. Here we focus on comparing different variants of the latter based on several measures. It includes three steps: quantifying FC variation, measuring a subject-specific motion time-course, and evaluating the association between these two together with the distance between regions.

4.1   Capturing Fluctuations of Connectivity with a Sliding Window

We estimate fluctuating connectivity over time using a sliding window approach, resulting in a vector of FC values for every pair of regions. Ideally, the window should be large enough to permit robust estimation of FC, yet small enough to detect transient effects properly. We extracted 50 overlapping windows for each time series, corresponding to a duration of 46 s and 1 s step-size of the sliding window. This is consistent with the majority of previously published values ranging from 30- to 60-s [15]. Finally, a Fisher z-transformation was applied to all correlations, resulting in a three-dimensional ($98 \times 98 \times 50$) tensor of FC values for each subject.

4.2   Capturing Head Motion as Framewise Displacement Vector

For measuring subject-specific motion, we used rigid body realignment estimates obtained from motion correction step. These six realignment parameters (translation: x, y, z; rotation: α, β, γ) describe the relative displacement of every volume from a fixed reference volume in the scan. Based on these parameters we calculated framewise displacement (FD) as proposed in [6]. For each sliding window, we then computed the average FD to quantify a dynamic subject-specific vector of head motion.

4.3   Evaluating the Association Between FC and Motion

Static association is measured across the study population using the correlation of mean functional connectivity and framewise displacement averaged over the whole fMRI scan [13]. For example, 24 fetuses in our study would yield 24 mean FD and 24 FC values for a specific edge in their FC map. The correlation between these two is used as surrogate for the modulated of this edge by subject motion. [14] provides an extended rationale. To take the dynamicity of motion within each fMRI sequence into account, we can calculate FC-FD association analogously on measurements in sliding windows. For each pair of regions, we calculated correlation between FC and FD across the sequence of sliding windows, resulting in a *dynamic FC-FD association*. This captures the subject-specific residual effect of motion for each pair of regions. To assess the efficacy of nuisance regression strategy, we compared the proportion of edges with significant correlations of FC and FD as well as the median absolute value of their distribution. Fewer significant correlations or lower absolute median of correlations are indicative of better performance.

4.4   Evaluating the Association Between Distance and FC-FD Correlations

Previous studies have shown that in-scanner movement primarily inflates short-range FC while decreases long-range connectivity [13,16]. Motion thus affects more severely the FC of short range connections, and the correlation between FC-FD association and distance of region is a possible marker of residual motion artifacts. To determine the residual distance-dependence effects of motion on FC variation, We calculated the distance D_{ij} between regions based on the center of

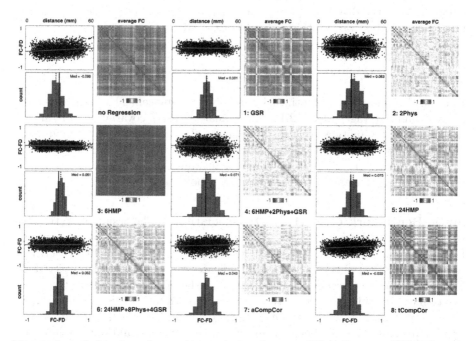

Fig. 1. A static benchmark reveals associations between FC and motion (FC-FD), and the association between distance and FC-FD (FC-FD-D) on a population level. Note that every point in the FC-FD-D plots shows the correlation between the FC of one specific edge and the average FD over the whole sample. Quantitative values can be found in Table 2. According to this benchmark, 6HMP outperforms other strategies, as no significant FC-FD association remained. However, the average FC map after 6HMP exhibits dramatically increased FC values across the cortex.

Table 2. The summary metrics of the static FC-FD/-D association benchmark for each nuisance regression method.

Pipeline	#Edges related to motion (%)	Absolute median FC-FD assoc.	FC-FD-D assoc.
No Regression	242 (5.09)	−0.099	0.007
1: GSR	8 (0.17)	0.001	−0.03
2: 2Phys	361 (7.60)	0.083	−0.01
3: 6HMP	0 (0.00)	0.061	−0.03
4: 6HMP + 2Phys + GSR	283 (5.95)	0.071	−0.04
5: 24HMP	40 (0.84)	0.075	0.029
6: 24HMP + 8Phys + 4GSR	15 (0.31)	0.052	0.02
7: aCompCor	95 (2.00)	0.043	0.08
8: tCompCor	103 (2.16)	0.029	0.14

mass of each parcel resulting in distance matrix D. We then calculated the correlation between the distance between each pair of parcels and the corresponding FC-FD correlation, we call this *FC-FD-D association*.

5   Results

Fetal head motion were quantified by framewise displacement ranged from $\sim$0 to 43.06 [mm, average: 1.84 ± 2.12]. To evaluate possible covariation of fetal age and the estimated motion, we measured the correlation between gestational week of subjects and both mean and maximum FD. Although in our study cohort, neither mean FD ($r = 0.16$, $p = 0.43$) nor maximum FD ($r = 0.33$, $p = 0.12$) doesn't show significant correlation with gestational age.

Static Benchmark of FC-FD/-D Associations. The result of static FC-FD analysis is illustrated in Fig. 1, where for each method, in the top panel FC-FD correlations for all possible pairs of parcels are plotted against their Euclidean distance. The bottom panel indicates the distribution of static FC-FD correlations across the study cohort, and the right panel shows the average connectivity matrix of the study cohort. According to this benchmark, all regression techniques were very effective in removing the effects of head motion on FC, reducing the number of connections that were significantly related to motion to less than 8% with the corresponding absolute median ranging from 0.01 to 0.001. In addition, very small correlation values of the static FC-FD-D association suggest that the relationship between motion, FC, and distance has become negligible after applying regression techniques (see Table 2). However, the average connectivity matrices are different, and suggest that the resulting FC still carries motion effects, or that these artifacts have even be increased.

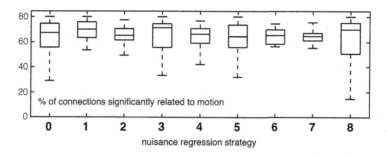

Fig. 2. Dynamic FC-FD association: the proportion of functional connectivity variations that showed significant associations ($p \leq .05$, uncorrected) with subject-motion
after nuisance regression. Fewer significant correlations is indicative of better performance.

Notably, the regression with realignment parameters (3:6HMP) yielded all FC-
FD correlations near zero and removed the distance dependent slope and positive
offset in the FC-FD measure, whereas it is obvious from the resulting average
FC matrix that FC values are entirely dominated by motion-induced variance,
resulting in a strong increase in connectivity among brain regions, regardless of
their distance. This suggests that motion parameter estimates were not accurate,
or linear regression is not a suitable strategy to remove associated signal components, and in both cases *static FC-FD* couldn't correctly reveal the residual
effects of motion on data.

Therefore, although this benchmark has been successfully used in adult studies, it doesn't establish reliable results for fetal studies. The most likely expla-
nation is that in contrast to adult studies where subjects span a wide range
of mean FD values, all fetuses show similarly high levels of motion. Hence, the
resulting FD vector for adult studies covers a large range of variability, allowing
FC-FD correlations to reveal distance-dependence, however, the narrow-ranged
FD vector over the fetal sample cannot adequately account for subject's motion
and so the reliability of FC-FD correlations would be questionable.

Dynamic FC-FD Association. The correlation between head motion and FC
variation was measured for each subject independently across the sliding windows to see if performing a certain regression strategy has decreased the effect of
motion on the data or induced additional artificial variance. Figure 2 shows the
percentage of network connections where a significant relationship (correlations
with p-value $\leq .05$, uncorrected) with motion was present. The benchmark suggests no regression strategy was effective, leaving the majority of network edges
with a residual relation with motion. However, aCompCor showed more homo-
geneous performance over subjects and the commonly used regression strategy
relying only on the six motion parameters fared the worst.

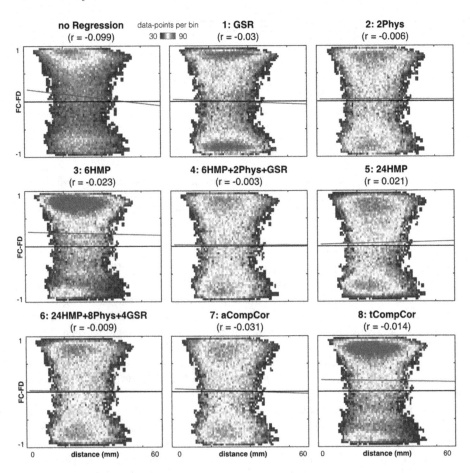

Fig. 3. A density plot of FC-FD association over distance between regions. Trendlines are shown in red. A successful strategy should remove the distance dependent slope and positive offset in of FC-FD vs. distance. Besides, there should be a more density of datapoints around zero axis for an effective strategy. Consistent with previous measure, aCompCor performed better than other strategies, however, this dynamic FC-FD/-D benchmark reveals that clear remaining signs of motion artifacts are still present in datasets.

Dynamic FC-FD-D Association. The benchmark yields an assessment for each subject, with 4753 FC-FD associations per subject. To provide an interpretable visualization of the relationship between edge-wise FC-FD association and region distance, we use a binned scatter plot indicating the density of points with color (Fig. 3).

Using no regression model shows that motion influenced BOLD signal in proximal regions homogeneously, resulting in spuriously inflated correlations among those regions. The least effective methods in mitigating such effect were tCompCor and 6HMP. As expected, global signal regression introduced negative

correlations due to spurious anti-correlations [11]. aCompCor and the
24HMP + 8Phys + 4GSR model showed overall better performance relative to
other regression strategies. However, the latter is the costliest strategy in terms
of the loss of temporal degrees of freedom leading to less statistical confidence
in the analysis of fMRI data.

6   Discussion

Quality control of fetal fMRI is of utmost importance since its susceptibility to
motion artifacts can result in false observations. A variety of regression strategies provides a choice for removal of non-neural fMRI signal components. As it
increasingly becomes more common to use hundreds or even thousands of scans
for a single study, it is not practical to manually assess data quality, and in
addition, manual assessments are biased and suffer from lack of reproducibility.
Group-wise assessment of motion artifacts, such as *static FC-FD*, can be decep-
tive when there are excessive motion spikes, or generally high motion across the
entire population, leading to a ceiling-like effect of motion on correlation values
[14]. Here, we present a dynamic FC-FD/-D benchmark for single-subject fMRI
acquisitions that at the same time enables the comparison of nuisance regression
approaches. The proposed method was applied to fetal fMRI scans as an application of particularly pronounced and irregular motion. Results suggest that a
static FC-FD benchmark is not suitable for fetal fMRI studies, as it is not able to
capture the relationship between fetal motion and FC, leading to false negative
results.

A general limitation of benchmarks evaluating the association with motion
is their dependency on realignment based estimates of movement. This is particularly challenging for irregular and substantial motion of fetuses moving inside
the uterus and exhibiting spurious large motion spikes. We used one motion
correction algorithm to re-align the image data and obtain movement parameter estimates, and better results might be obtained by a different approach.
The scope of the paper is the comparison of nuisance regression approaches
given likely imperfect movement parameter estimates, and not the comparison
of the motion correction approaches themselves. A limiting factor of fetal fMRI
is the typically shorter acquisition time, resulting in limitations of FC reliability
regardless of motion. Never-the-less quantitative assessment of motion related
artifacts is feasible, and dynamic measures as those evaluated in this paper do
offer a means to compare methods. In summary, we presented a benchmark for
the efficacy of nuisance regression. Results suggest that while they improve the
signal, they are not yet adequately effective in removing motion-related variance,
given the used motion correction approach.

Acknowledgement. This project has received funding from the European Union's
Horizon 2020 research and innovation programme under the Marie Skłodowska-Curie
grant agreement No. 765148.

References

1. Behzadi, Y., Restom, K., Liau, J., Liu, T.T.: A component based noise correction method (CompCor) for BOLD and perfusion based fMRI. NeuroImage **37**(1), 90–101 (2007)
2. Ciric, R., et al.: Benchmarking of participant-level confound regression strategies for the control of motion artifact in studies of functional connectivity. NeuroImage **154**, 174–187 (2017)
3. Ebner, M., et al.: An automated localization, segmentation and reconstruction framework for fetal brain MRI. In: Frangi, A.F., Schnabel, J.A., Davatzikos, C., Alberola-López, C., Fichtinger, G. (eds.) MICCAI 2018. LNCS, vol. 11070, pp. 313–320. Springer, Cham (2018). https://doi.org/10.1007/978-3-030-00928-1_36
4. Gholipour, A., et al.: A normative spatiotemporal MRI atlas of the fetal brain for automatic segmentation and analysis of early brain growth. Sci. Rep. **7**(1), 476 (2017)
5. Hindriks, R., et al.: Can sliding-window correlations reveal dynamic functional connectivity in resting-state fMRI? NeuroImage **127**, 242–256 (2016)
6. Jenkinson, M., Bannister, P., Brady, M., Smith, S.: Improved optimization for the robust and accurate linear registration and motion correction of brain images. NeuroImage **17**(2), 825–841 (2002)
7. Kuklisova-Murgasova, M., Quaghebeur, G., Rutherford, M.A., Hajnal, J.V., Schnabel, J.A.: Reconstruction of fetal brain MRI with intensity matching and complete outlier removal. Med. Image Anal. **16**(8), 1550–1564 (2012)
8. Lurie, D., et al.: On the nature of resting fMRI and time-varying functional connectivity. PsyArXiv Preprints (2018)
9. Lydon-Staley, D.M., Ciric, R., Satterthwaite, T.D., Bassett, D.S.: Evaluation of confound regression strategies for the mitigation of micromovement artifact in studies of dynamic resting-state functional connectivity and multilayer network modularity. Netw. Neurosci. **3**(2), 427–454 (2019)
10. Malamateniou, C., et al.: Motion-compensation techniques in neonatal and fetal MR imaging. Am. J. Neuroradiol. **34**(6), 1124–1136 (2013)
11. Murphy, K., Birn, R.M., Handwerker, D.A., Jones, T.B., Bandettini, P.A.: The impact of global signal regression on resting state correlations: are anti-correlated networks introduced? NeuroImage **44**(3), 893–905 (2009)
12. Parkes, L., Fulcher, B., Yücel, M., Fornito, A.: An evaluation of the efficacy, reliability, and sensitivity of motion correction strategies for resting-state functional MRI. NeuroImage **171**, 415–436 (2018)
13. Power, J.D., Barnes, K.A., Snyder, A.Z., Schlaggar, B.L., Petersen, S.E.: Spurious but systematic correlations in functional connectivity MRI networks arise from subject motion. NeuroImage **59**(3), 2142–2154 (2012)
14. Power, J.D., Mitra, A., Laumann, T.O., Snyder, A.Z., Schlaggar, B.L., Petersen, S.E.: Methods to detect, characterize, and remove motion artifact in resting state fMRI. NeuroImage **84**, 320–341 (2014)
15. Preti, M.G., Bolton, T.A., Van De Ville, D.: The dynamic functional connectome: state-of-the-art and perspectives. NeuroImage **160**, 41–54 (2017)
16. Van Dijk, K.R., Sabuncu, M.R., Buckner, R.L.: The influence of head motion on intrinsic functional connectivity MRI. NeuroImage **59**(1), 431–438 (2012)

Topology-Preserving Augmentation for CNN-Based Segmentation of Congenital Heart Defects from 3D Paediatric CMR

Nick Byrne[1,2]($\boxtimes$), James R. Clough[2], Isra Valverde[2,3], Giovanni Montana[4], and Andrew P. King[2]

[1] Medical Physics, Guy's and St. Thomas' NHS Foundation Trust, London, UK
[2] School of Biomedical Engineering & Imaging Sciences, King's College London, London, UK
nicholas.byrne@kcl.ac.uk
[3] Paediatric Cardiology, Guy's and St. Thomas' NHS Foundation Trust, London, UK
[4] Warwick Manufacturing Group, University of Warwick, Coventry, UK

Abstract. Patient-specific 3D printing of congenital heart anatomy demands an accurate segmentation of the thin tissue interfaces which characterise these diagnoses. Even when a label set has a high spatial overlap with the ground truth, inaccurate delineation of these interfaces can result in topological errors. These compromise the clinical utility of such models due to the anomalous appearance of defects. CNNs have achieved state-of-the-art performance in segmentation tasks. Whilst data augmentation has often played an important role, we show that conventional image resampling schemes used therein can introduce topological changes in the ground truth labelling of augmented samples. We present a novel pipeline to correct for these changes, using a fast-marching algorithm to enforce the topology of the ground truth labels within their augmented representations. In so doing, we invoke the idea of cardiac contiguous topology to describe an arbitrary combination of congenital heart defects and develop an associated, clinically meaningful metric to measure the topological correctness of segmentations. In a series of five-fold cross-validations, we demonstrate the performance gain produced by this pipeline and the relevance of topological considerations to the segmentation of congenital heart defects. We speculate as to the applicability of this approach to any segmentation task involving morphologically complex targets.

Keywords: Image segmentation · Data augmentation · Topology

Nick Byrne is funded by a National Institute for Health Research (NIHR), Doctoral Research Fellowship for this research project. This report presents independent research funded by the NIHR. The views expressed are those of the author(s) and not necessarily those of the NHS, the NIHR or the Department of Health and Social Care. The authors have no conflicts of interest to disclose.

G. Montana and A. P. King—*Joint last authors.*

© Springer Nature Switzerland AG 2019
Q. Wang et al. (Eds.): PIPPI 2019/SUSI 2019, LNCS 11798, pp. 181–188, 2019.
https://doi.org/10.1007/978-3-030-32875-7_20

1   Introduction

Medical image segmentation is an integral part of many pipelines for the analysis of clinical data. For many applications, such as the calculation of ventricular volumes, algorithmic approaches need only achieve a segmentation that shares a sufficient overlap with an expert defined reference standard. This can be assessed using the Dice Similarity Coefficient (DSC). However, in other cases the topology of the segmentation is also important. For example, topologically correct segmentation is a prerequisite for the detailed visualisation of paediatric congenital heart disease (CHD) anatomy using patient-specific 3D printed models.

Segmentation of the congenitally malformed heart from CMR images is a challenging task due to inhomogeneity in signal intensity, limited contrast-to-noise ratio and the presence of image artefacts [5]. Furthermore, significant variation in the structural presentation of disease limits the success of conventional methods such as atlas-based strategies [9]. Finally, patient-specific 3D printing demands a high fidelity representation of disease, demonstrating anatomy at the limit of spatial resolution. Segmentation results should accurately represent clinically meaningful thin tissue interfaces such as the atrial septum (see Fig. 1). Inaccurate interface segmentation introduces anomalous topological features that may falsely indicate the presence of congenital heart defects. Consequently, exponents of patient-specific 3D printed heart models have hitherto relied on manual and semi-automated segmentation methods, typically requiring at least an hour of manual interaction per patient [5].

Convolutional neural networks (CNNs) have been successfully applied to a multitude of image segmentation tasks, including the delineation of congenital heart defects from CMR data. Wolterink et al. [6] trained a slice-wise, 2D CNN using dilated convolutions. Meanwhile, Yu et al. [7] explored deep supervision [8] and dense connectivity within 3D CNNs. Considering a limited training set of just ten cases, these approaches achieved impressive results in terms of spatial overlap. However, automated approaches cannot yet match the overlap performance of the leading semi-automated procedures [3,5], and have largely paid little attention to topological correctness.

Especially in the paediatric setting, developers of medical image segmentation algorithms cannot generally assume a database of thousands or millions of training cases. Instead, state-of-the-art CNNs have relied on data augmentation schemes. Augmentation acts as a source of regularisation and generalisation, capturing modes of variation likely to exist in the underlying population but which are absent from the training data. Spatial scaling, small angle rotation and non-rigid deformation are attractive transformations for augmentation, accounting for variation in patient size, orientation and posture. However, under such schemes, and when subsequently resampled by nearest neighbour interpolation, each of these can cause violations of ground truth topology near thin tissue interfaces (see Fig. 2(b)).

Knowingly or otherwise, the best-performing previous work [6–8] has limited spatial augmentation to a subset of transformations that are topology-preserving: orthogonal rotation and lateral inversion only. However, given that

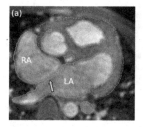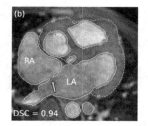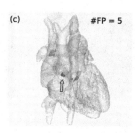

Fig. 1. An error in the segmentation of thin tissue interfaces such as the septum between left and right atria (LA, RA) can give rise to topological changes and the anomalous appearance of a congenital heart defect (yellow arrow). Whilst the DSC between ground truth (orange) and inferred (green) blood pool is high, (c) demonstrates the presence of five topologically and clinically relevant segmentation errors. (Color figure online)

orthogonal rotation has no clinical rationale, this is unlikely to aid the generalisation of CNNs, providing a source of regularisation alone.

We hypothesise that topology-preserving label map augmentation is a prerequisite to any advanced provision for topologically-informed deep learning. To investigate this hypothesis we make the following contributions in the context of CHD segmentation from 3D CMR:

- We present a novel pipeline for the augmentation of label map data in a topology-preserving manner.
- We present a novel metric for assessing the topological correctness of segmentation results, using it to demonstrate improved performance compared with previous work and with conventional image resampling schemes.

2   Methods

2.1   Topology-Preserving Augmentation Pipeline

The notion of *simple points*[1] is central to the fast-marching topology correction tool developed by Bazin et al. [1]. Starting from a scalar representation of the naively transformed object, this algorithm removes non-simple points from all isosurfaces, correcting the topology to match a known template. Whilst correcting object topology to match that of a ball is straightforward, defining the template for morphologically complex congenital anatomy presents a greater algorithmic challenge.

Our solution (see Fig. 2) is predicated on the idea that the whole heart blood pool has an uncomplicated topological representation. In reality, the topology of the blood pool label can be highly complex, demonstrating numerous fine-scale

---

[1] Those whose binary label value can be flipped without changing the topology of the overall label map.

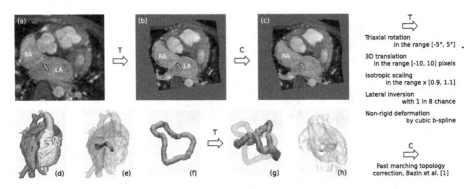

Fig. 2. Spatial transformation and nearest neighbour resampling of a ground truth label set (a), can result in anomalous topological changes such as defects within the atrial septum (b). Such changes can be corrected by consideration of a CCT template (f). Having two shunts between the respectively topologically spherical left and right heart (ventricular and atrial septal defect), this patient exhibits toroidal CCT. The template is derived by topological erosion of a multi-class representation of the blood pool (d, e) and subsequently transformed to the space of the augmented image (g, h).

features associated with the trabeculated, endocardial surfaces. To avoid this complexity, we invoke a property that we refer to as cardiac contiguous topology (CCT). This describes the structural relationships between sub-classes of the cardiac blood pool and their communication. Importantly, the CCT captures the appearance of thin tissue interfaces and defects by defining how and where the heart's chambers and vessels are contiguous.

To remove topological features associated with trabeculation, each sub-class is corrected (via the approach in [1]) to have topology equivalent to a ball at the outset. Once recombined, the topology of the blood pool is defined only by the connections of each cardiac sub-class. Furthermore, we require that the blood pool class constitutes a well-composed set[2]. Such label maps have the advantageous property that repeated topological erosion is guaranteed to result in a one voxel wide CCT template. This captures the topology of the ground truth blood pool in a morphologically simple object free from thin interfaces (see Fig. 2(f)).

Having established a CCT template for each ground truth label map, the two can be spatially transformed in tandem. Whilst nearest neighbour resampling is likely to cause topological errors in the label map, the morphologically simpler CCT template can be resampled without incurring such changes.

We resample the transformed blood pool label using trilinear interpolation, realising an image bounded in the range $[0, 1]$. Akin to a probability map, this is corrected to share the topology of the transformed CCT template, ensuring that the arbitrary CCT of the ground truth labels is maintained (see Fig. 2(c)).

Most often, the sub-valvular apparatus and its association with the papillary muscles are only partially visualised in CMR: the true-to-life topological

---

[2] The topology of a well-composed set is independent of neighbourhood connectivity.

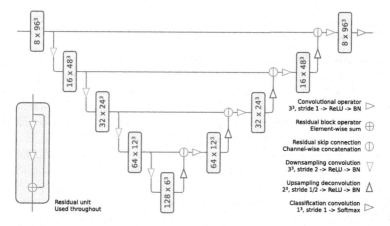

Fig. 3. The V-net architecture used. Output feature map sizes at training are indicated.

properties of the myocardium are rarely apparent. Hence, we resample the spatially transformed myocardium label by naive nearest neighbour interpolation.

2.2 Study Design

Data—We employ the ten cases provided during the training phase of the HVSMR Challenge 2016 (see [5] for acquisition and clinical details). Each case includes an isotropic, high-resolution, axially-reformatted, 3D CMR volume acquired at Boston Children's Hospital and demonstrating CHD anatomy. This is tightly cropped around a provided set of manually segmented labels, delineating the whole heart blood pool and myocardium as two separate classes.

Prior to experimentation, an expert in paediatric, CHD segmentation corrected small topological errors that were present in the provided blood pool label maps. The vast majority of corrections removed false positive voxels from within thin interfaces. Totally, 0.098% and 0.0059% of the blood pool and myocardium classes were changed respectively. In a series of five-fold cross-validations (train on eight, test on two), we address a three-class segmentation problem, separating the blood pool, myocardium and background classes. In the context of a deep CNN, the performance of the topology-preserving augmentation pipeline is compared with a naive, nearest neighbour resampling of label data and with augmentation by orthogonal rotation and lateral flipping only (as in [6–8]).

Architecture—We adopt the V-net architecture (see Fig. 3) in all experiments [4], using 3D convolution to learn residual features across spatial scales.

Metrics—Overlap performance was assessed using the DSC. However, such global metrics are largely insensitive to errors in thin interface regions. To characterise the topology of the inferred blood pool, we introduce a novel, interpretable metric. This extends the notion of simple points to connected components, algorithmically counting the number of topologically relevant clusters of voxels where inferred and ground truth segmentations disagree (see Fig. 1(c)). This approach is clinically meaningful as clusters of topologically relevant errors indicate the anomalous appearance of congenital defects.

Implementation—Prior to augmentation, all CMR data were normalised to have zero mean and unit variance. The topology-preserving augmentation pipeline used the SimpleITK package for spatial transformation and resampling; fast-marching topology correction [1] and associated topological operations used relevant plugins for the Medical Image Processing And Visualisation (MIPAV) platform. From the ten cases provided by the HVSMR Challenge, a total of 10,000 training examples were pre-computed by data augmentation according to Fig. 2. For comparison we pre-computed a further 10,000 training examples by augmentation using orthogonal rotation and lateral inversion alone. In both cases we also made small perturbations to the voxel intensity of the image data.

All models were trained for 8,000 iterations using the Adam optimiser (Pytorch default settings for learning rate and beta parameters) and the categorical cross entropy loss. Each batch contained eight image patches of $96 \times 96 \times 96$ voxels, randomly cropped from the augmented data. With respect to the submission of batches and weight initialisation, models were trained identically.

3   Results and Discussion

Our results assess the impact of two characteristics of data augmentation: (i) whether spatial transformation is clinically informed; and (ii) whether label map topology is preserved after transformation and resampling.

Perhaps for their ease of implementation, previous work has employed orthogonal rotations [6–8] and lateral inversion [7,8] only. Whilst these transformations are guaranteed to preserve label map topology, they are not representative of the distribution of CMR data seen in the clinic. For example, since patient position is invariably head first-supine, orthogonal rotations are unrealistic. Though small variations in patient orientation are observed, these are best captured by small angle rotations. We seek to describe this distribution through the use of the clinically justified transformations shown in Fig. 2.

With respect to spatial overlap, Fig. 4 suggests a benefit to this approach. The DSC improves from 0.918 $(0.891, 0.934)^3$ to 0.925 (0.918, 0.938) and from 0.839 (0.808, 0.854) to 0.868 (0.828, 0.888), for the blood pool and myocardium classes respectively. These results suggest that unlike orthogonal rotation, clinically justified transformations act not only as a source of regularisation but are also beneficial to the generalisability of the network. Overall, these results are consistent with, or in the case of the myocardium class, exceed those achieved by previous work [2,6–8].

As well as spatial overlap, we are also concerned with the topology of the inferred blood pool label map. Of particular interest are the false positive clusters which characterise defective interface segmentations and the anomalous presence of defects. Figure 4 demonstrates that compared to previous work, the naive

---

^{3} All results reported as median (interquartile range).

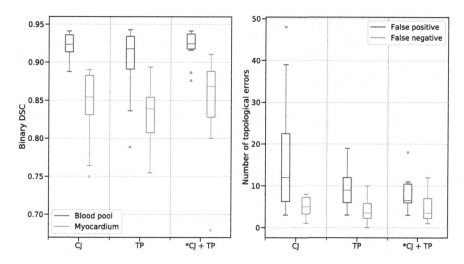

Fig. 4. CNN segmentation performance in terms of spatial overlap (left) and topological accuracy (right), where training data are augmented by spatial transformation which is: CJ - clinically justified; TP - topology-preserving; CJ + TP - clinically justified and topology-preserving *using our novel augmentation pipeline.

introduction of clinically justified transformations has a detrimental effect on inferred blood pool topology. The median number of topologically relevant false positive clusters increases from 9.0 (6.0, 12.0) to 12.0 (6.3, 22.5). However, when coupled with our topology-preserving augmentation pipeline and its consideration of CCT, this number falls dramatically to 6.5 (6.0, 10.5): a statistically significant improvement according to Wilcoxon Signed Rank test ($p = 0.022$). This also represents improved performance compared with the clinically unrealistic though topology-preserving augmentation schemes used in previous work.

These observations suggest that the topological features of inferred cardiac segmentations are strongly dependent on the training data. Though perhaps predictable, it must be remembered that in the context of complex morphology, topological features can be encapsulated by relatively few voxels. In fact, across the ten thousand augmented representations of the ten ground truth label sets we produced, less than 0.5% of blood pool voxels were changed by our topology-preserving pipeline.

Figure 4 shows that best performance can be attributed to augmentation pipelines which are both clinically justified and which preserve ground truth label topology. Our topology-preserving augmentation pipeline provides a means of simultaneously achieving both qualities.

4   Conclusion

Our work demonstrates for the first time the importance of label map topology to the task of CNN-based CHD segmentation from 3D CMR images of paediatric patients. We have presented a novel pipeline for the augmentation of training data for CNN optimisation. Invoking the concept of CCT and developing an associated, clinically meaningful metric, we show that the properties of this pipeline - allowing for clinically justified data augmentation whilst preserving arbitrary label map topology - are beneficial to the topological properties of inferred segmentations. We speculate that these findings may be applicable to any medical image segmentation task for which morphologically complex foreground objects can be represented as a number of contiguous sub-classes.

References

1. Bazin, P.L., Pham, D.L.: Topology correction of segmented medical images using a fast marching algorithm. Comput. Methods Programs Biomed. **88**(2), 182–190 (2007)
2. Li, J., Zhang, R., Shi, L., Wang, D.: Automatic whole-heart segmentation in congenital heart disease using deeply-supervised 3D FCN. In: Zuluaga, M.A., Bhatia, K., Kainz, B., Moghari, M.H., Pace, D.F. (eds.) RAMBO/HVSMR – 2016. LNCS, vol. 10129, pp. 111–118. Springer, Cham (2017). https://doi.org/10.1007/978-3-319-52280-7_11
3. Lösel, P., Heuveline, V.: A GPU based diffusion method for whole-heart and great vessel segmentation. In: Zuluaga, M.A., Bhatia, K., Kainz, B., Moghari, M.H., Pace, D.F. (eds.) RAMBO/HVSMR – 2016. LNCS, vol. 10129, pp. 121–128. Springer, Cham (2017). https://doi.org/10.1007/978-3-319-52280-7_12
4. Milletari, F., Navab, N., Ahmadi, S.A.: V-Net: fully convolutional neural networks for volumetric medical image segmentation. In: 2016 Fourth International Conference on 3D Vision (3DV), pp. 565–571. IEEE (2016)
5. Pace, D.F., Dalca, A.V., Geva, T., Powell, A.J., Moghari, M.H., Golland, P.: Interactive whole-heart segmentation in congenital heart disease. Med. Image Comput. Comput. Assist. Interv. **9351**, 80–88 (2015). https://doi.org/10.1007/978-3-319-24574-4_10
6. Wolterink, J.M., Leiner, T., Viergever, M.A., Išgum, I.: Dilated convolutional neural networks for cardiovascular MR segmentation in congenital heart disease. In: Zuluaga, M.A., Bhatia, K., Kainz, B., Moghari, M.H., Pace, D.F. (eds.) RAMBO/HVSMR – 2016. LNCS, vol. 10129, pp. 95–102. Springer, Cham (2017). https://doi.org/10.1007/978-3-319-52280-7_9
7. Yu, L., et al.: Automatic 3D cardiovascular MR segmentation with densely-connected volumetric ConvNets. In: Descoteaux, M., Maier-Hein, L., Franz, A., Jannin, P., Collins, D.L., Duchesne, S. (eds.) MICCAI 2017. LNCS, vol. 10434, pp. 287–295. Springer, Cham (2017). https://doi.org/10.1007/978-3-319-66185-8_33
8. Yu, L., Yang, X., Qin, J., Heng, P.-A.: 3D FractalNet: dense volumetric segmentation for cardiovascular MRI volumes. In: Zuluaga, M.A., Bhatia, K., Kainz, B., Moghari, M.H., Pace, D.F. (eds.) RAMBO/HVSMR – 2016. LNCS, vol. 10129, pp. 103–110. Springer, Cham (2017). https://doi.org/10.1007/978-3-319-52280-7_10
9. Zuluaga, M.A., Biffi, B., Taylor, A.M., Schievano, S., Vercauteren, T., Ourselin, S.: Strengths and pitfalls of whole-heart atlas-based segmentation in congenital heart disease patients. In: Zuluaga, M.A., Bhatia, K., Kainz, B., Moghari, M.H., Pace, D.F. (eds.) RAMBO/HVSMR – 2016. LNCS, vol. 10129, pp. 139–146. Springer, Cham (2017). https://doi.org/10.1007/978-3-319-52280-7_14

Author Index